Tales of Banks Peninsula

Howard Charles Jacobson

BIBLIOLIFE

TALES

OF

BANKS PENINSULA

Second Edition.

AKAROA :
PRINTED BY H. C. JACOBSON, "MAIL" OFFICE.
1893.

PREFACE TO FIRST EDITION.

When I began to compile the following collection of Peninsula narratives, I never for a moment thought that they would assume such dimensions as to warrant their being published in book form, and I merely wished to collect some information that might be interesting to the readers of the "Akaroa Mail," and also be of use to some future historian of New Zealand.

Banks Peninsula is one of the few places in this Island that has a history, and many of the original settlers are passing away, so that it was desirable to procure their records without loss of time.

It has been a most pleasing task, and the universal kindness and sympathy shown to me by all to whom I have gone for aid has been deeply felt by me.

The Rev. J. W. Stack's Maori History is a most important part of the book, and no other European could possibly have collected so full and accurate an account. It was from papers in the possession of Mr. J. Aylmer and Mr A. L. McGregor that the story of Hempleman and his claims and diary was written. The description of the French Settlement was principally furnished by Mr Waeckerlie, one of the original settlers ; and Mr. S. C. Farr wrote the Voyage of the Monarch. To Mrs. Brown I was indebted for much of the narrative of the Early Days, and Billy Simpson's tale was told by himself. Mr. G. J. Black gave most of the information regarding Robinson and Walker, but " Chips " was the narrator of his own autobiography. Mr. J. D. Gar-

wood assisted in many of the articles, and wrote the
Loss of the Crest ; and the Rev. R. R. Bradley, Mr.
F. Moore, Mr. T. Adams, Mr W. Masefield, and
others, gave the information from which the other
·articles were prepared.

It will thus be seen that my task has been comparatively an easy one, aided as I have been by so
many kind friends ; and I can truly say, in conclusion—" Here is only a nosegay of cut flowers, and
nothing is my own but the string that binds
them."

H. C. JACOBSON.

PREFACE TO MAORI HISTORY.

I am indebted to Mr. and Mrs Tikao, Wiremu,
Karaurko, Hakopa te ata o Tu, Te Aika, and
many other well-informed Natives, for the materials
to compose this history of the Maori occupation of
Banks Peninsula ; and having written down the
narrative from their verbal statements, I have often
followed the Maori rather than the English idiom
in my translation, which, however distasteful it may
prove to the reader, will afford satisfactory evidence
in future of the source from which my information
was derived.

J.W.S.

Duvauchelle's Bay,
     July 28th, 1883.

PREFACE TO SECOND EDITION

It is now nearly ten years ago since I published the first edition of the Stories of Banks Peninsula. They were so well received that in a few weeks all had gone ; and from that time to this I have been collecting fresh matter with a view to the publication of the second enlarged edition that is now before you. There is a sort of mournful congratulation in looking over the preface of 1883—congratulation in having secured the information before those who gave it had passed away—sorrow that so many who were then in strength and health have since ceased to live. Mr. Justin Aylmer, Mr. Garwood, Mr. Moore, the Rev. R. R. Bradley, Billy Simpson, and a host of others who aided me in my first pleasant task have since joined the majority, and had I waited a year or two longer it would have been impossible to procure the records which are now before you for the second time. Greatly enlarged as the edition is, I have not had room for all the matter at my command, and live in the hope of yet publishing a third and larger issue in the years to come. Need I record my thanks to the public for their kind reception of my former effort, and my hope that a similar fate may be accorded to the second.

H. C. JACOBSON.

Akaroa, June 4th, 1893.

CONTENTS.

PART THE SECOND.

STORIES

OF

BANKS PENINSULA.

No. 1.—MAORI HISTORY OF BANKS PENINSULA.

(Contributed by the Rev. J. W. Stack)

To all who know how attentively the Maoris noted the physical features of the country, and the prolific character of their geographical nomenclature, it is somewhat perplexing to find that an isolated region, with a conformation so marked as Banks Peninsula, does not possess a distinctive Maori name : unless, indeed, the present inhabitants have lost the knowledge of it, and confined to a part a name which originally embraced the whole. I am inclined to think that this is the case. In ancient times the whole island was spoken of as " The fish," and even now the northern part of it is called " Mua upoko " (the front-head), while the southern part is called " Muri-hiku " (rear-tail). I think it is highly probable that when the first explorers, looking southwards from the neighborhood of Kaikoura, saw the Peninsula looming up against the sky, they took it to be the limit of the land's extent, and called it accordingly the Hiku, or tail-end of the fish. But the combination of Rangi (sky) with Hiku may point to another derivation, since Hikurangi is the name of a mountain at the head of the Waiapu Valley, near East Cape. The name may possibly

B

have been applied to this peninsula from some fancied resemblance in its appearance, when first sighted
from the north, to the well-known mountain near the
ancient home of the Ngatikahunu tribes.

Whether the Peninsula was ever inhabited by
people of another race it is impossible to say, owing
to the absence of conclusive evidence either one way
or the other. My friend Dr. Von Haast rather
inclines to the opinion that it was, being led to the
conclusion by some discoveries he made in the moa
bone cave near Sumner. But there is nothing to be
found in the existing traditions relating to the
locality, which can be relied upon as affording any
evidence that the Maoris knew that the country was
occupied before they came here. The demigods of
whom they speak as having been the first discoverers
and explorers of these islands, cannot be regarded as
the representatives of an aboriginal people, because
the stories relating to them are common to all sections of the Polynesian race, and *evidently belong to
persons and events connected with Maori history in
distant ages, long before the migration from Hawaiki.*

There is reason to believe that Banks Peninsula
has been occupied by the Maori for a period of four
hundred years, though the existing historical traditions of the people only reach back for half that
period. The absence of the earlier traditions is,
however, easily accounted for by the fact that two
successive waves of conquest swept over the entire
South Island after it was first peopled, the conquering tribe in each case being careful to obliterate as
far as possible all traces of the former inhabitants,
in order to render its own title to possession more
secure.

The Waitaha, who came originally from Hawaiki
to Maketu, in the canoe Arawa, were the first Maori
inhabitants of these parts. They gradually made
their way from the Bay of Plenty to the South Island

(then known as Tumuki), where they multiplied so
rapidly that they are said " to have covered the face
of the land like myriads of ants."

The Waitaha were conquered and destroyed, somewhere about the year 1577, by the Ngatimamoe, a
tribe from the East Coast of the North Island,
whose ancestors came to Poverty Bay from Hawaiki
in the canoe Tokomaru. The Ngatimamoe did not
long enjoy the fruits of their triumph.   In little more
than a hundred years they were despoiled by Ngai
Tahu, also an East Coast tribe, descendants of the
crew of the canoes Taki timu, Kura haupo, and Mata
horua, and were by them subjected to the same cruel
process of extermination by which they had secured
their own conquest of Waitaha.

Before entering on the narrative of Ngai Tahu's
doings on Banks Peninsula, it may be interesting to
relate what the Maoris say about one monument of
the former inhabitants that still remains, known
as the

PA OF NGA-TOKO-ONO
(THE PA OF THE SIX).

Between Fisherman's and Paua Bay, on the edge
of a bold cliff, may still be seen the remains of the
most ancient Maori pa in this locality.   The date
of its occupation can only be a matter of conjecture,
but if it belonged to the Ngatimamoe, as generally
reported, it must be from three to four hundred years
old.   When Ngai Tahu first arrived, the pa was in
much the same condition that it is now : nothing
but the earthworks remained to mark where it once
stood.   In answer to their inquiries respecting its
origin, they were told that it was the pa of Nga-
toko-ono, and that the tradition about it was, that
six chiefs once dwelt there, who went out one day in
their canoes to fish, about a mile from the coast, when
they were caught by a violent north-west wind, and
were blown out to sea and never heard of again.

Some light has lately been thrown upon the fate
of these men by the Chatham Islanders, who say that
their ancestors arrived at Wharekauri after being
blown off the coast of their own land.   They also
speak of some of their ancestors coming from the
foot of Te-ahu-patiki (Mount Herbert), and that the
reason for their leaving was owing to the defeat and
death of their chief Tira, who was killed while endeavouring to punish his daughter's husband, who had
been guilty of adultery.   On reaching Wharekauri,
they were kindly received by Marupo, the chief of a
Maori-speaking race.   By the advice of their hosts,
the new arrivals resolved to give up fighting and
cannibalism.   The Maori refugees carried kumara
seeds with them, but on planting them they died, so
they returned to New Zealand for a further supply.
The question naturally arises, How did Tira's people
know of the existence of Wharekauri?   It seems
highly probable that, after discovering the islands,
Nga-toko-ono or some of them returned to inform
their friends, who gladly availed themselves of a safe
refuge from the relentless Ngai Tahu, whose suc-
cesses in the northern parts of the island were beginning to cause them anxiety regarding their future
safety.

PARAKAKARIKI.

Not far from the pa of Nga-toko-ono may be seen
the outlines of the protective works of another ancient
pa, known as Parakakariki.   It was situated at the
end of one of the spurs on the south side of Long
Bay, and was an important stronghold of the Ngatimamoe.   It was captured and destroyed by Moki,
who, in the celebrated war canoe Makawhiu, coasted
round the Peninsula, and completely subdued all the
Ngatimamoe inhabitants.

This chief, who resided, after the Ngai Tahu
migration, at Ote Kaue, near the mouth of the

Wairau River, was induced to undertake the expedition against the Peninsula by the report brought to him by his wife's two brothers, Kaiapu and Te Makino, who had accompanied Waitai on his voyage from Wairau to Otago, when that chief, offended by Maru's determination to spare the Ngatimamoe, seceded from the Ngai Tahu confederacy.   These two men had noticed, while coasting southwards, the vast extent of the plains stretching from the sea shore to the snowy ranges, and had also been particular to mark the position of the numerous Ngatimamoe pas passed during the voyage.   When their canoe touched at Hikurangi, they had learnt that their old tribal enemy Tu te kawa was living not far off at Waikakahi, a piece of information which afterwards led to important results.

After accompanying Waitai to Murihiku, and taking part in various encounters between his forces and the hostile tribes by which he was surrounded, Kaiapu and Te Makino were seized with a longing desire to avenge the death of a near female relative, and, in order to accomplish their purpose, they resolved to risk the journey overland to Wairau. As they travelled over the plains between the Waitangi and Waipara Rivers, they remarked with covetous eyes the luxuriant growth of the cabbage palms, so highly valued for the favorite kauru food prepared from the stems.   They were astonished at the immense numbers of wekas and rats which they came across in the long tussock grass, and were equally astonished to find all the streams and lakes throughout the country swarming with eels and lampreys and silveries, and the great Waihora Lake full of flat-fish.

They passed safely through the hostile country, and reached the outskirts of Ote Kaue, when they made enquiries for Moki's house. They were told that they could not mistake it, as it was the loftiest

building in the pa, with the widest barge boards to
the porch. They did not enter the pa until every
one had retired to rest, when they made their way to
the house indicated, and sat down close to the breakwind near the porch, where they waited till some one
appeared to whom they could make themselves
known. About midnight their sister came out, and
after sitting a few minutes in the yard, rose to return
to the house. Hoping to attract her notice without
making any noise, one of them opened a parcel of
tara mea scent, which he had concealed about him.
She no sooner perceived the delicious fragrance than
she approached the spot where her brothers were
crouching, feeling her way towards them along the
breakwind. As soon as she reached them they
caught hold of her, when she gave a sharp cry, but
they at once silenced her fears by telling her who
they were. She was overjoyed by the discovery, and
quickly re-entered the house to inform her husband.
" Rise up, rise up, O Moki !" she cried, " here are
your brothers-in-law, the sons of Pokai whao ; they
have returned, and are awaiting your pleasure outside." Moki told her to bring the travellers in, and
to prepare some food at once for them, but not to
make their arrival known to the pa till the morning.
Marewa knew how important it was for her brothers'
safety that they should take food under Moki's roof,
because it would ensure his protection in the event
of their meeting with persons inclined to kill them ;
for in these stormy times it was the common practice
for individuals to avenge their private wrongs, and
in doing so it was quite immaterial whether they
killed the person who had done them the injury, so
long as they killed some one connected with him ;
unprotected people were therefore always in great
danger of losing their lives. It was not surprising,
therefore, that under the circumstances Moki's wife
displayed the greatest alacrity in providing refresh-

ments for her husband's guests, selecting the materials from her choicest stores. She listened till dawn
to the story of their adventures by sea and land, and
then she went to carry the news of their arrival to
the other great chiefs of the place.

Te Rangi Whakaputa was the first to come and
welcome them. He asked whether they had seen
any good country towards the south. They replied
that they had. " What food," he asked, "is pro-
curable there ?" " Fern root," they replied, " is one
food, kauru is another, and there are wekas and rats
and eels in abundance." He then retired, and
Mango took his place and asked, " Did you see any
good country in your travels ?" " Yes," they replied,
" Ohiriri (Little River), that is, a stream, we saw,
and Wairewa is the lake." " And what food can be
got there ?" he asked. " Fern root," they said, "is
one food, but there are many kinds ; there are wekas
and kaka and kereru and eels." Mango replied,
" Inland is a pillow for my head, on the coast a rest
for my feet." Te Rua hiki hiki, son of Manawa,
was the next to enter and interrogate them. He,
too, asked, " Have you seen any land ?" They replied, " We saw Kaitorete, a plain, and Waihora, a
lake." " What food can be got there?" " Eels,"
they said, " abound there, and patiki and ducks and
putangitangi are food to be got there." " That
shall be my possession," said Te Rua hiki hiki.

But there was another and still more powerful
incentive than the acquisition of a rich food-produc-
ing district to induce Ngai Tahu to undertake an
expedition to the south, and that was the desire to
vindicate the tribal honour. No sooner did Moki
and the rest of the leading chiefs learn from the two
travellers that Tu te kawa was still living at Waikakahi, than orders were immediately issued to prepare
the great war canoe, Te Maka whiu, for sea. This
canoe was made out of an enormous totara tree

which grew in the Wairarapa Valley, the stump of which was shown until quite lately by the old Maoris there. On the completion of the conquest of Ngati-mamoe, the canoe was drawn up at Omihi, where it was subsequently buried by a landslip, the projecting bow only being left exposed. It was regarded as a sacred treasure under the immediate guardianship of atuas, and one man, who presumed to chip a piece off as a memento, paid the penalty of his sacreligious rashness by dying immediately afterwards.

TU TE KAWA.

The feud between the chief Tu te kawa and the ruling family of Ngai Tahu was caused by his having put Tuahuriri's wives to death at Te-mata-ki-kai-poika, a pa on the south-east coast of the North Island. Tuahuriri had from some cause incurred the ill-will of a powerful member of his own tribe, the renowned warrior Hika-oro-roa. That chief assembled his relations and dependents, amongst whom was Tu te kawa, and led them to attack Tuahuriri's pa. When they were approaching the place at dawn of day, and just as the leader was preparing to take the foremost post in the assault, a youth named Turuki, eager to distinguish himself, rushed past Hika-ora-roa, who uttered an exclamation of surprise and indignation at his presumption, asking in sneering tones " how a nameless warrior could dare to try and snatch the credit of a victory he had done nothing to win." Turuki, burning with shame at the taunt, rushed back to the rear, and addressed himself to Tu te kawa, who was the head of his family, and besought him to withdraw his contingent, and proceed at once to attack the pa from the opposite side, and thus secure the victory for himself, and for ever prevent such a reproach from again being uttered against any one of his family. Tu te kawa, who resented keenly the insult

offered to his young relative, instantly adopted his
suggestion, and so rapidly did he effect the movement, that his absence was not discovered till he had
successfully assaulted the pa, and his name was
being shouted forth as victor.   A few moments
before the assault took place, Tu te kawa said to his
nephew, " Go quickly and rouse Tuahuriri."   The
young warrior ran forward, and on reaching the pa
called out, " O Tu."   " What is it?" he asked.
" Come forth."   " Wait till I fasten on my waist-
belt."   " Wait for nothing ; escape, they are close
here !"   " Where?"   " Just behind my back."
Without stopping to put on a garment or to pick
up his weapons, Tuahuriri rushed out of his house,
climbed over the wall, and ran for his life to the
shelter of a neighbouring wood.   Tu te kawa was the
first to enter the pa, and at once made his way to
Tuahuriri's house, where he found his two wives,
Hina kai taki and Tuara whati.   These women were
persons of great distinction, being related to all the
principal families in that part of the country, and
their lives ought to have been quite safe in the hands
of their husband's relatives.   But Tu te kawa turned
a deaf ear to their appeal for protection, and killed
them both.   Though accused of killing these women
unnecessarily, it is very probable that he may have
put them to death to save the family honour, as it
was no disgrace to die by the hands of a near kinsman,
and he had good reason to suspect that Hika-oro-roa,
having lost the credit of the victory, and having failed
to secure the husband, would take his revenge on the
wives.   Tu te kawa might have argued, if they must
die, it was better he should kill them.

When the war party were re-embarking in their
canoes, a few hours after, Tuahuriri came out to the
edge of the forest, and called to Tu te kawa, and
asked him whether he had got his waist-cloth, belt,
and weapons.   On being answered in the affirmative,

he begged that they might be returned to him. Tu
te kawa stood up in his canoe and flung them towards
him, telling him at the same time what had happened to his wives. After picking up his weapons,
Tuahuriri turned towards his cousin, whom he wished
to reward for having saved his life, and called out,
" O Tu, keep out to sea, or keep in shore, rather
keep in shore." This was a friendly intimation
intended to save Tu te kawa from the destruction
about to fall upon his companions in arms ; for no
sooner were the canoes under weigh than Tuahuriri
retired into the depths of the forest, and there invoked
the help of his atuas to enable him to take vengeance
on his enemies, and by their agency he raised the
furious wind known as Te-hau-o-rongo mai. This
tempest dispersed Hika-oro-roa's fleet, and most of
his canoes were upset, and the crews drowned, in the
stormy waters of Raukawa (Cook Straits). Tu te
kawa, forewarned, had hugged the coast, and so
escaped destruction. After crossing the straits, he
landed on the South Island, where he decided to
remain, and so escape the inevitable consequences of
the attack on Tuahuriri's pa. He had nothing to
fear from the Ngatimamoe, to whom he was related
on the mother's side ; and further, he knew that his
presence amongst them would be welcomed, because
he was willing to employ the armed force that accompanied him against the remnant of Waitahi who
continued to maintain their independence. Passing
down the coast, Tu te kawa took up his residence at
Okohana (Church Bush), near Kaiapoi, where eels
were plentiful. He employed the few Waitahi whom
he spared from destruction to work the eel fishery
there for him. Hearing after a time that the eels of
Waihora (Lake Ellesmere) were of a better quality,
he removed to the shores of that lake, and built a
pa at Waikakahi (Wascoe's), while his son Te Rangi
tamau built another at Taumutu. Surrounded by his

allies, and at such a distance from his enemies, Tu te kawa felt quite secure But after the lapse of many years, and when he had grown old and feeble, his followers grew alarmed for his safety, owing to the rapid advance southwards of the Ngai Tahu. They urged the old chief to escape while the opportunity of doing so remained, but all their entreaties were in vain ; his only reply was, " What will then become of the basket of flat-fish spread open here ?" (in allusion to the lake).

They soon had ample evidence that their fears were well grounded, for the war canoe Te Maka whiu, manned by the choicest warriors of Ngai Tahu, and commanded by the experienced leader Moki, was rapidly approaching his retreat, with the avowed intention of avenging Tuahuriri wives. When the expedition arrived at Koukourarata, a Council of war was held, to decide whether to approach Waikakahi by sea or by land. Some advised an immediate advance on the place overland. This was opposed by Moki, who said he had been warned that Tu te kawa was sitting like a wood pigeon on a bough, facing his foes, and that if they approached him from the direction he faced, he would take flight before they could catch him. After much discussion, it was decided to go by sea. The warriors accordingly re-embarked, and pulled southwards. As they approached Okain's Bay, Moki observed the groves of karaka trees growing near the shore, and wishing to become the possessor of them, he whispered the following directions in his attendant slave's ear :—
" When I order the canoe to be beached, take care to be the first to reach the shore, and at once cry out aloud, ' My land, O Karaka !' " The slave prepared to carry out his master's instructions, and, as the canoe neared shallow water, he jumped overboard, and tried to wade ashore in advance of anyone else. But he was forestalled by Mahi ao tea, one of the

crew, who, suspecting Moki's design. sprang from
the bows of the canoe on to the beach, shouting aloud,
" My pa, Karaka ! my bay, Kawatea !" Encouraged
by the success of the attempt to secure an estate for
himself, this young man, who was only a chief of
secondary rank, resolved to proceed overland to the
destination of Te Maka whiu   Accompanied by a
few followers, he made his way from Okain's to
Gough's Bay.   In the forests he encountered Te
aitanga a Hine mate roa, a wild race (thought to be
enchanted black pine trees), whom he overcame and
destroyed ; and between Poutakaro and Otu tahu ao
he fell in with Te ti a Tau whete ku, enchanted
cabbage trees, that moved about and embraced each
other like human beings.   He also came across Te
papa tu a Mauheke, an enchanted broadleaf tree.
After a very adventurous march, Mahi ao tea
rejoined the expedition at Karuru (Gough's Bay),
where he found the canoe already drawn up on the
land, and preparations being made for the advance
on Parakakariki.   He learnt that after his departure
from Okain's the expedition had moved on to Otu-
tahuao (Hickory), where they encamped.   There an
incident occurred which had caused considerable
amusement.   One of the leading chiefs had presented a basket of dried barracouta for distribution
among the crew.   Those whose place was nearest
the stern got the first helping, and by the time the
basket reached those who occupied the bows, only a
few fine fragments remained.   These were handed to
a conceited chief named Whakuku, a sort of captain
of the forecastle, who, on seeing what had fallen to
his share, said to his companions, "Hold tight, hold
tight to the fish dust!" (meaning that when his
men fell in with Ngatimamoe, they should take care
to secure for themselves something better than the
leavings of the persons of higher rank).   He dubbed
the cave where they took their meal " The cave of

fish dust eating," to commemorate his having been
fed with the dust of Hikatutu's fish basket.

While the plan of attack was under discussion,
Moki, the commander-in-chief, suddenly called out to
Turangipo, a noted veteran, famed for deeds of valour
performed on many a battle-field in the North Island.
Turangipo asked what Moki wanted.   " You may
eat," he replied, " the head of your Lady Paramount."
Turangipo remained silent for some time, pondering
over what was meant by this strange speech.   He
felt convinced that Moki was employing some spell
to paralyse his energies, and rob him of any chance
of gaining distinction in the coming encounter with
Ngatimamoe.   He conjectured that Moki, annoyed
at the failure of his attempt to secure for himself the
karaka groves at Okain's Bay, was now bent on
making sure of better success at Parakakariki, and
that, in order to gain his end, he was endeavoring to
cast a spell over the man most likely to defeat his
purpose.   Turangipo was, however, equal to the
occasion, and, having exhausted every means he
could think of to break the spell and neutralise its ill
effects, he resolved to try its potency on Moki himself.   "Moki," he cried.   "What?" replied he.
" You may eat the head of your Lady Paramount."
Moki made no reply, and, from the course of subsequent events, it became evident that he neglected to
employ any precautions to neutralise the spell.
While these two chiefs were exchanging these ques-
tionable civilities, the bulk of the warriors were
wondering what their object could be in bandying
such shocking expressions, for such allusions to the
sacred head of a person of rank were regarded as
blasphemous.   Their speculations were interrupted
by Moki suddenly calling out, " Who is for us?"
(meaning who will act as scout). Whakuku instantly
replied, " I am ; I will act as scout."   " How will
you proceed ?"   " I will get above the pa, and, if you

hear my voice sounding from high up the hill, then
you will know that the pa is guarded ; if my voice
sounds low down, the pa is not guarded." Whakuku
then proceeded at once to reconnoitre. He was followed by the main body, who, as they approached the
cliffs to the north of Fisherman's Bay, saw several
canoes anchored off the coast opposite the mouth of
Long Bay. Moki, wishing to know whether the
presence of his force on the coast had been observed
by Ngatimamoe, fastened his white whalebone weapon
to his foot, and dangled it over the brink of the
cliff ; but the fishers failed to take any notice of it,
and Moki accordingly concluded that they were unconscious of the approach of enemies, and resolved to
continue his march without waiting to conceal his
movements under the cover of darkness. He proceeded till he reached the woods on the south side of
Long Bay. There the final disposition of the force
for the meditated attack on the pa was completed ;
and, having found a suitable place of concealment,
the men waited impatiently for the promised signals
of their scout. Whakuku did not keep them long
in suspense, for he soon succeeded in reaching a
position overlooking the pa, where he at once commenced to imitate the cry of a wood-hen, ko-ee, ko-
ee, ko-ee. The women of the pa listened, and said
one to another, " Hark ! what bird is that ? Surely
it is a female weka that is crying in the wood above
us." He then climbed to a point still higher above
the pa, where he commenced to cry tee-wake, tee-
wake, tee-wake. The women said again, " Hark !
Surely that is the cry of a male weka." He then
descended, and concealed himself in a shallow cave
close to the pa. His companions, on hearing his
signals, interpreted them to mean that although
there were many women in the pa, they were not
altogether unprotected. So the order was passed
along the line to delay the assault till dawn. The

warriors with difficulty restrained their impatience,
and as soon as the first rosy tints appeared in the
eastern sky, they rushed out from their place of concealment, and took the pa by storm. Moki, who
wished to secure the coveted distinction awarded to
the warrior who killed the first foeman in battle,
took care to occupy the foremost place. As he
rushed forward, he encountered what he imagined, in
the dim light, to be two of the enemy. He struck
a furious blow with his taiaha, first at one and then
at the other, shouting out at the same time, " By my
hand has fallen the first foeman." But, to his
extreme mortification, he discovered that, instead of
men, he had only aimed mortal blows at two upright
blocks of stone that came in his way, and which were
ever afterwards known as " Moki's pair." His
failure on this occasion was attributed to his having
omitted to remove the spell which he provoked
Turangipo to cast upon him. That warrior having
discovered the mistake Moki had made, rushed past
him, and, having entered the pa, secured two women,
Te maeke and Ta whera, as his prisoners. Te ao tu
tahi, the principal chief of the pa, was killed by Mahi
ao tea. His son Uruhanga made an attempt to
escape by a path along the cliffs, but, being observed,
was pursued. His superior knowledge of the dangerous footway might have enabled him to get off
safely, but for Whakuku, who, concealed in a cave
above him, was intently watching his approach ;
and, the moment he came within reach, Whakuku
plunged his spear into his shoulder, and hurled him
down the cliff in the direction of his pursuer, calling
out at the same time, " Your man." " No," replied
the other, " yours." " No," said Whakuku, " you
may have him, but do not conceal my name." After
the fall of Parakakariki, Moki returned to Koukourarata, carrying his prisoners with him. Having
drawn up his canoe, and placed a guard over the

prisoners, he advanced by a forced march over the hills to Waikakahi.

WAIKAKAHI (WASCOE'S).

The shadow of Moki's form across his threshold was the first intimation Tu te kawa had of the arrival of the Ngai Tahu. The old chief, infirm and helpless, was found coiled up in his mats in a corner of his house, and Tuahuriri's sons, mindful of their father's last words, "If you ever meet that old man, spare him," were prompted at the last moment to shield their kinsman, but the avenger of blood thrust his spear between them, and plunged it into the old man's body. It may be necessary to explain here why the Ngai Tahu chiefs hesitated at the last moment to carry out the avowed purpose of the expedition. Tuahuriri's injunction, and their desire to carry it out, were quite consistent with the Maori customs relating to feuds of this nature. Tu te kawa had spared Tuahuriri's life, and therefore merited like protection at his hands. But Tu te kawa had killed Tuahuriri's wives, and their death required to be avenged, but not necessarily by the death of the person who killed them ; it would be sufficient atonement if one of his nearest blood relations suffered for the crime. This practice will be fully illustrated in subsequent pages containing the account of the Kai Huanga feud.

Having ascertained that Te Rangi tamau was away at Taumutu, and not knowing what course he might take to avenge his father's death, Moki gave orders that a watch should be kept at night round the camp, to guard against surprise, but his orders were disregarded. Te Rangi tamau, whose suspicions were aroused by observing a more than ordinary quantity of smoke arising from the neighborhood of his father's pa, set off at once for Waikakahi, and arrived there after dark. Waiting till the camp

was quiet, he passed through the sleeping warriors
and reached his father's house. The door was open,
and, looking in, he saw a fire burning on the hearth,
and his wife, Puna hikoia, sitting beside it with
her back towards him. Stepping in, he touched
her gently on the shoulder, and placing his finger on
his lips as a signal to keep silence, he beckoned her
to come outside. Then he questioned her about
what had happened, and finding that she and his
children had been kindly treated, he told his wife to
wake Moki after he was gone, and give him this
message : " Your life was in my hands, but I gave
it back to you." Then, taking off his dogskin mat,
he re entered the house, and placed it gently across
Moki's knees, and then hurried away to the citadel
of Waikakahi, which stood on the hill between Birdling's and Price's Valley, a few chains from the
point where the coach road passes. The spot is still
marked by the ditch and bank of the old fortress.
When Puna hikoia thought her husband was safe
from pursuit, she woke Moki and gave him Te Rangi
tamau's message. Moki felt the mat, and was then
convinced the woman spoke the truth. He was
greatly mortified at having been caught asleep, as it
was always injurious to a warrior's reputation to be
caught off his guard Issuing from the house, he
roused his sleeping warriors with a mighty shout,
and the expression used upon the occasion has since
become proverbial—" Ngai tu whaitara mata hori,"
O unbelieving Tu whaitara ! The next day negotiations were entered into with Te Rangi tamau, and
peace restored between him and his Ngai Tahu
relations.

NGAI TAHU TAKING POSSESSION.

After the destruction of Parakakariki and the
death of In te kawa, the various chiefs of Ngai Tahu
engaged in Moki's expedition, who had not already

secured a landed estate elsewhere for themselves, took immediate steps to acquire some part of the Peninsula. The rule they adopted was, that whoever claimed any place first, should have the right to it, provided he went at once and performed some act of ownership there ; and also that he should be entitled to as much land around it as he could traverse before encountering another selector. Te Rangi Whakaputa hastened to secure Te Whakaraupo (Port Cooper) ; Huikai hurried off to Koukourarata ; Mango to Wairewa ; Te Rua hikihiki landed at Wainui, and commenced at once to dig fern root, and prepare it for food ; he then passed round the coast, leaving Manaia at Whaka Moana, and others of his party at Waikakahi, taking up his own permanent residence at Taumutu. Tutakakahikura, one of Mrs Tikao's ancestors, leaving his sisters and his family at Pohatupa, walked quickly round the coast by the North Head of Akaroa Harbor, and up the shore as far as Taka Matua, and thence round by Parakakariki to starting point. While crossing one of the streams that flow through the present township of Akaroa, he encountered O-i-nako, a Ngatimamoe chief, and a fugitive from Parakakariki. They engaged in mortal combat, and O-i naka was killed, and the stream was ever after known by his name. Te Ake, the ancestor of Big William, landed at the Head of the Bay, and after trying in vain to reach Wainui, owing to the rough nature of the coast, he retraced his steps, and tried to get round the other side of the harbor, but on reaching the grassy slopes between Duvauchelle and Robinson's Bay, he felt too tired to go any further, and took possession of the point and its surroundings by planting his walking stick in the ground ; hence the place obtained the name of Otokotoko (walking stick). Fearing that his boundary towards the south might be disputed, Te Ake begged Te Rangi Taurewa to

cross over in his canoe to a headland he pointed out,
and there to hold up his white whalebone weapon,
while he himself stood at Otokotoko and watched
him.   His friend did as he was requested, and the
headland has ever since been known as the " Peg on
which Te Rangi Taurewa's patu parao hung "—
south side of French Farm.   The beach below the
point was called " The shell of Hine Pani," after
some Maori lady who found a shell there, which she
greatly prized.

Some years after these events took place, another
section of Ngai Tahu, under the command of Te
Wera, a fiery warrior, destined to play an important
part in the history of his tribe in the South, came in
search of a new home   They landed at Hikurangi,
but finding that the place was already occupied, they
sent to Whaka Moana for Manaia, a chief of very
high distirction, the Upoka ariki, or heir to all the
family honors of more than one hapu in the tribe.
On his arrival, a war dance was held in his honor,
and there was much friendly speechifying.   Te Wera,
after indulging in some rude witticisms on the personal appearance of their " squint-eyed lord," extended his right arm, and called upon Manaia to
enter.   Manaia rose up and passed under his arm,
and so peace was confirmed between them ; but, to
cement their friendship still more firmly, Te Wera
gave Irakehu, grand-daughter of Te Rangi Whakaputa, to Manaia in marriage, and she became the an-
cestress of Mr. and Mrs. Tikao, Paurini, and the other
chief persons in the Maori community here.   Te Wera
and his party then sailed away to the South, and
established themselves for a time near Waikouaiti,
where they were as much dreaded for their ferocity
by other sections of their own tribe as by the Ngatimamoe, whom they were trying to exterminate.

For many generations the Maoris on the Peninsula remained in peaceful occupation of their new

homes, undisturbed by foreign attacks or internal
strife. Occasionally the bolder spirits amongst them
would go away to take part in the wars against
Ngatimamoe, which were carried on for many years
in districts further to the South, or else to take part
in some quarrel between different sections of the
Ngai Tahu tribe located elsewhere. Among those
who went off in search of military honors was a certain heretical teacher named Kiri mahi nahina, who
left Akaroa for the seat of war near Moeraki, and
fell at the battle of Tara ka hina a tea. This
tohunga had told Turakautahi the younger that Tiki
made man, whilst the fathers had always maintained
that it was Io. Te Wera adopted a novel method
to prevent the survival of this man's false teaching,
through his spirit escaping and getting into some
other tohunga. When the battle was over, he made
an oven capable of containing the entire body, and
then he carefully plugged the mouth, ears, nose, and
every other aperture, and having cooked the heretical
teacher, he managed, with the assistance of some of
his warriors, to eat up every portion of him, and so
successfully extinguished the incipient heresy.

The condition of those who remained quietly at
home was enjoyable enough, for it is a great mistake
to suppose that the old Maori life in peaceful times
was one of privation and suffering ; on the contrary,
it was a very pleasant state of existence ; there was
a variety and abundance of food, and agreeable and
healthy occupation for mind and body. Each season
of the year, and each part of the day, had its specially
alloted work, both for men and women. The women,
besides such household duties as cooking and cleaning
their houses, made the clothing and bedding required
for their families. They gathered the flax and ti
palm fibres used, and prepared and worked them up
into a great variety of garments, many of which took
several months to complete, and which, when finished,

were very beautiful specimens of workmanship. The
men gathered the food and stored it in whatas or
storerooms, which were attached to every dwelling,
and built on tall posts to protect the contents from
damp and rats.   Besides such natural products of
the soil as fern root, ti palm stems, and convolvulus
roots, they cultivated the kumera, hue, taro, and
karaka.   Fish of various kinds were caught during
the proper season, and cured by drying in the sun.
Wild pigeons, kakas, paradise ducks, and mutton
birds were cooked and preserved in their fat in vessels made out of large kelp leaves, and bound round
with totara bark to strengthen them.   Netting,
carving, and the grinding and fitting of stone implements and weapons, occupied the old men, and much
of the leisure time of the young.   They beguiled the
long winter evenings by reciting historical traditions
and tribal genealogies, by repeating poetry and fairy
tales, and by songs, dances and round games.   It
was only when they fell ill, or were harrassed by their
enemies, that the Maoris of olden time can with any
truth be represented as having been miserable and
unhappy.

TE MAI HARA NUI.

The Ngai Tahu chiefs who exercised the greatest
influence over the fortunes of their people in modern
times were Te Mai hara nui, Taiaroa, and Tuhawaiki,
better known by the whalers' sobriquet, " Bloody
Jack."   All three took a prominent part in the latter
history of the Peninsula.   Te Mai hara nui was the
highest in rank, while his cousin Tuhawaiki came
next ; but, though slightly superior by birth, both
were inferior in mental and moral qualities to Taiaroa,
a noble man, whose conduct stands out in pleasing
contrast to that of the two cousins.   For while they
will only be remembered by the story of their cruel
and evil deeds, he will always be esteemed for his

brave and generous actions in war, and his wife and
kindly counsels in peace.   Te Mai hara nui was the
Upoko Ariki, or heir to the ancestral honors of Ngai
Te Rangiamoa, the noblest family of Ngai Tahu, but
he gained still further distinction from the fact that
several other noble lines met in his person.   As the
hereditary spiritual head of the tribe, he was regarded
with pecular reverence and respect; the common
people did not dare to look upon his face, and his
equals felt his sacred presence an oppressive restric-
tion upon their liberty of action, for even an accidental
breach of etiquette while holding intercourse with
him might involve them in serious loss of property,
if not of life.   His visits were always dreaded, and
his movements whenever he entered a pa were
watched with great anxiety by the inhabitants, for if
his shadow happened to fall upon a whata or rua
(the storehouse for food) while he was passing
through the crowded lanes of a town, it was immediately destroyed, with all its contents, because the
sacred shadow of the Ariki having fallen upon it, the
food became tapu, and fatal to those who partook of
it   There was little in Te Mai hara nui's personal
appearance to mark his aristocratic lineage, his figure
being short and thick-set, his complexion dark, and
his features rather forbidding.   Unlike most Maori
chiefs of exalted rank, he was cowardly, cruel, and
capricious, an object of dread to friends and foes
alike.   At the same time he was a man of great
energy and considerable force of character.   He was
distinguished during his early years as a traveller,
being continually on the move up or down the east
coast of this island, engaged in visiting his numerous
connections   He was amongst the first to discern
the advantages to be secured by encouraging trade
with Europeans, and entered keenly himself into
business transactions with the traders who came
from Sydney to procure flax fibre.   To facilitate his

intercourse with them, he took up his permanent
residence at Takapuneko (Red House), in Akaroa
Harbor. He married Te Whe, a descendant of
Manaia, and the eldest sister of Mrs Tikao's
mother. By her he had three children, two sons,
Te Wera and Tutehounuku, and a daughter, Ngaroi-
mata. His eldest son died when a child. The next
son, on attaining manhood, went off in a whaling
ship, and was absent for many years, during which
he was mourned for as dead, and did not return till
after his father was carried off and put to death, at
Kapiti, by Rauparaha. The peaceful course of Te
Mai hara nui's life at Takupuneke was interrupted
by the outbreak of a terrible blood feud amongst his
near relations, a feud distinguished, not by the incident that caused it, but by the fearful atrocities that
were perpetrated during the course of it, deeds that
shocked even the hardened hearts of those who committed them.

KAI-HUANGA (EAT RELATION).

The Kai-huanga feud was the first serious outbreak amongst the Maoris of the Peninsula since
their conquest of Ngatimamoe. For nearly one
hundred and fifty years they had been increasing in
numbers and wealth Tu te kawa's son had revealed
to them the secret pass he had found to the West
Coast, and expeditions were annually sent across the
mountains to procure greenstone, which, when manufactured, at'racted purchasers from North and South,
who exchanged mats and potted mutton birds, and
other things, for the coveted greenstone. The
development of trade with Europeans promised a
continuance of prosperity and peaceful enterprise.
This promise was destined to be rudely broken by a
feud that not only disorganisec the entire social system of the various Maori communities here, but
nearly annihilated the population of the district.

The immediate cause that roused all this animosity, and provoked so much bloodshed, must seem to Europeans most trivial and inadequate, but there is little doubt that mutual jealousies and old grudges were working below the surface in men's minds, and forcing on hostilities which, when once begun, led to further reprisals, and so the quarrel deepened and widened after every encounter. The immediate cause of the quarrel was owing to Murihaka, the wife of Potahi, putting on a dogskin mat belonging to Te Mai hara nui, which he had left in charge of some one at Waikakahi. This act was regarded as an insult by the immediate relations of the chief, since everything in the shape of apparel belonging to him was held to be exceedingly sacred. The greatest consternation prevailed throughout the pa as soon as it became known what had happened. At length some of the men grew so exasperated at the thought of Murihaka's sacrilegious act, that they fell, not upon the perpetrator of the deed, but upon a poor servant woman belonging to a relative of hers, named Rerewaka, and put her to death. When her masters, Hape and Rangi Whakapaku, saw her dead body lying on the ground, they were much enraged, but instead of wreaking their vengeance on those who committed the murder, they went off to a village of Ngati Koreha, at Tai Tapu, in search of some member of the murderers' family. They succeeded in finding Hape, whom they killed. This man was married to Hinehorahina, of Ngati Hurihia, sister of Tawhakiterangi, one of the principal chiefs of Taumutu. His widow took refuge with her brothers, who were greatly pained at witnessing her grief for the loss of her husband, of whom she was very fond. As they watched the tears streaming down her cheeks, day after day, while she sat pounding fern root for their daily meals, they meditated over some scheme for avenging her loss. At last they decided what to do,

They collected a small war party together, and then made a sudden attack upon Waikakahi, where they killed Puiaiti and Te Moroiti, the latter being a chief of Ngati Irakehu. His death brought the Taumutu people into collision with the greater part of the inhabitants of the Peninsula, and involved them in what proved to be a ruinous struggle with superior forces. They followed up their first attack on Waikakahi by a second a few weeks afterwards, when they killed Te Rangi e pu, another Irakehu chief.

Te Mai hara nui was absent from the district at the commencement of the feud, having gone to Kaikoura to fetch a large war canoe which his relatives there had presented to him. He first heard of the outbreak on landing at Te Aka Aka (Saltwater Creek), where some persons met him, and told him that some of his family had been attacked, and several of them killed. He made no remark to his informants, but when he reached Kaiapoi, a few hours after, he said to his uncles, who resided there, "It is my turn now; Ngati hui kai is there, Ngati hui kai is here, Ngati mango is there, Ngati mango is here; Ngai tua huriri, do not move." This was an intimation that he would avenge his relatives' death, and that it was his wish that the Kaiapoi people should not interfere. There was some probability of their doing so, as many Kaiapoi families were connected by marriage with the Taumutu people. Having given expression to his determination, he proceeded on his journey towards Akaroa, followed by about twenty Kaiapoi men. On reaching Wairewa, steps were immediately taken to raise a war party, which was subsequently led by Te Mai hara nui against Taumutu. A battle was fought at Hakitai, which resulted in the defeat of the residents and the death of many persons, amongst whom was the chief Te Pori and several Kaiapoi women. More of the latter would have fallen victims, but

E

for the presence in the attacking force of the Kaiapoi contingent, who made it their business to protect, as far as they could, the lives of their kinswomen. It was in this way that Te Parure, sister of the chief Taiaroa, escaped death or dishonour. She had taken refuge with her children in a whata, but having been seen by Taununu, was pursued, and would have been captured but for Te Whakatuke, who came up just as Taununu was mounting the narrow ladder leading to her retreat, and, clasping his arms round that warrior's body, held tightly on to the ladder, and pressed him with such violence against it that Taununu was glad to desist from his purpose. Te Whakatuke, fearing the consequences of deserting his post, continued to keep guard till the engagement was over. So ended the first attack on Taumutu. Te Mai hara nui withdrew his forces, and dismissed them to their several homes.

The severe defeat sustained by the Taumutu people at Hakitai did not crush their spirits, nor weaken their determination to retaliate on the first fitting opportunity. But to accomplish their purpose it was necessary to obtain assistance, since they had received convincing proof in the late engagement that, single-handed, they were no match for Te Mai hara nui's powerful clans. Accordingly, they commissioned Hine haka, mother of Ihaia Whaitiri, a lady connected with many influential chiefs in the South, to proceed to Otakou and Murihiku, for the purpose of enlisting her friends' sympathies on their behalf, and raising from amongst them an armed force to aid them in the coming struggle. She was successful in her mission, and returned in a few months, accompanied by a considerable body of men. But they were not destined to achieve any great victory or to inflict any serious loss upon their opponents. On the arrival of their reinforcements at Taumutu, a messenger was despatched to Kaiapoi to invite the co-operation of all who wished to avenge their women killed at Hakitai. About a hundred warriors responded to the invitation, and set off at once for the seat of war. The combined forces then marched up the coast to attack Wairewa. The engagement which followed—afterwards known as Kai-whare-atua—was almost bloodless, but is memorable for being the first occasion on which firearms were used in this part of the country. The Ngati pahi, who possessed two guns, occupied a proud and envied position in the fore-front of the expedition. Though few ventured to touch the novel and dangerous weapons, all took a deep interest in their use, and hoped by their means to secure an easy victory, not so much from the execution in the ranks of the enemy likely to follow their discharge, as from the terror certain to be inspired by the report of firearms heard for the first time. These anticipations would probably have been realised, but for the chief Taiaroa, who kept far in advance of everyone, and reached Wairewa in time to give the inhabitants warning of approaching danger. On nearing the pa sufficiently to be recognised, he cried out, " Escape ! fly for your lives ! take to your canoes and go to sea, for guns are our weapons !" The mention of the dreaded guns was quite enough to create an immediate panic. Every one who could move rushed off in headlong flight, and when the Taumutu army arrived, they found the place quite deserted, and the only person they succeeded in shooting was a servant woman named Mihi nui, belonging to Pikoro. In order to understand Taiaroa's conduct on this and subsequent occasions, it is necessary to bear in mind that although he had accompanied the Southern contingent in the capacity of a leader, he was in reality a Taumutu chief, and closely related to all the Peninsula people. He was a descendant of Te rua hikihiki, who wrested that part of the country from

Ngatimamoe, but his family having removed to
Otakou, Taiaroa had become identified with the
people there. Possessing in an eminent degree the
qualities requisite to constitute an efficient Maori
ruler, he was chosen at an early age by the people
amongst whom he lived to act in that capacity, and
acquitted himself so well, that he completely super-
seded the local chiefs. His fame for courage, wis-
dom, and generosity, spread far and wide, and during
the troublous times that followed the Kai-huanga
feud, he was unanimously elected to fill the post of
chief military ruler of the Ngai Tahu tribe. Though
opposed to Hine haka's mission, he joined those who
rallied round her standard, hoping in the end to
defeat her sanguinary purpose, and to put a stop to
the fratricidal strife. On the first opportunity that
presented, he carried his purpose into execution, and
succeeded, as we have seen, in thwarting the attack
on Wairewa. Foiled in their designs, the Taumutu
forces returned home, but the Kaiapoi contingent,
after proceeding some distance on their way, began
to fear the jeers and taunts they were certain to
encounter if they returned empty-handed, so they
turned back as far as Kaitangata, where they met
and killed Iritoro, son of Whare-take-take and Hinei
Wharitia. They little imagined ths serious consequences that would ensue, or they might have selected
another victim. This man's mother was sister to
Tau nunu, a chief who had some time before migrated from the neighborhood of Kaikoura to the
Peninsula. He was attracted to these parts by the
presence of numerous and influential relations, who
were in possession of the land. Upon his arrival,
several places were assigned to him, and he selected
Ripapa, in Lytte'ton Harbor, as the site of his fortified pa. The chief no sooner heard of the death of
his nephew than he planned and carried out a scheme
of ample vengeance. The Kaiapoi warriors had

barely reached their homes before he was on the war
path, intent on surprising Whakaepa (Coalgate), a
populous offshoot from Kaiapoi. His movements
were so secret and so rapid, that he captured the pa
without a struggle, and put everyone to death. It
was not till some time after 'Tau nunu's return to
Ripapa that the Kaiapoi people learnt the terrible
fate that had befallen their friends at Whakaepa.
The whole population was roused to frenzy by the
news, and it was resolved to send as large a force as
could be mustered to punish Tau nunu; but,
receiving intelligence that Taiaroa was marching up
the coast, accompanied by a considerable body of
men armed with muskets, the Kaiapoi leaders determined to await his arrival, and get him, if possible,
to unite his forces with theirs. Their proposal was
ultimately accepted, but instead of proceeding at once
to attack Ripapa, the combined forces first marched
against Wairewa. Taiaroa repeated the warning he
gave the inhabitants on a former occasion, and
apparently with a like result, for when the besiegers
arrived, they found that most of the inhabitants had
escaped to their canoes. Pikoro was the only man
on the spot they discovered, and he was killed,
together with Tauakina, Te ata ka hua kina, and
Kaihaere, sisters of Te Mai hara nui. But Taiaroa's
well-intentioned plan for securing the safety of his
friends was not destined to be successful this time.
The Murihiku musketeers were unwilling to be again
deprived of their prey. Having, after a short search,
discovered two or three canoes, they pursued the fugitives, who, in their overcrowded vessels, were readily
overtaken, when the majority of them were either
shot or drowned. The cannibal feast that followed
this engagement was regarded at the time as peculiarly atrocious, on account of the close relationship
between the devourers and the devoured, and it was
from what took place on this occasion that the feud

came to be known in the annals of the tribe as " Eat Relation."

Leaving Wairewa, the expedition marched up the Okiri Valley, and over the Waipuna Saddle, and down the Ututu spur, to Koukourarata. The scouts in advance came there upon Te ha-nui-orangi, an elderly chief, who was sitting in the sunshine quite unconscious of the existence of danger. His youthful companions were all asleep under the trees, at a short distance off, but before they could be alarmed he was killed. The noise of the struggle roused the young men, who flew too late to his rescue, but they caught one of his assailants, Te Whaka moa moa. The rest of them took to flight, and rejoined their main body, who, hearing what had happened, decided to push on at once to Purau, fearing if they were to delay that night Tau nunu might receive warning of their approach. It was arranged that all who were armed with muskets should embark in canoes, and proceed by water to Ripapa, while the rest should climb over the hills, and assault the pa on the land side. Taiaroa, who was desirous to give Tau nunu a chance to escape, hurried forward, and was the first to get within hearing of the pa, when he shouted out, " Fly ! escape ! guns are our weapons ! " But Tau nunu had anticipated an attack, and had already taken the precaution to cross the harbor a day or two before. Many, however, adopted Taiaroa's friendly advice, and tried to escape in their canoes, but were not quick enough in getting out of musket range, for the attacking party that went round by water reached Ripapa almost as soon as their companions arrived by land, and they at once opened a destructive fire on the escaping canoes. The result was that few who tried to get away by water succeeded ; but, with the connivance of Taiaroa, many of the inhabitants passed through the assailants' ranks and reached the hills at the back of the pa, where they stopped pur-

suit by rolling great stones down upon all who
attempted to follow them.

After the destruction of Ripapa, the Otakou and
Murihiku warriors returned home, carrying with them
the entire population of Taumutu, for they feared to
leave them behind to encounter the vengeance of the
survivors of the pas that had lately suffered so
severely at their hands. But they were soon followed to Otakou by Te Mai hara nui, who, with
treacherous intent, employed every argument to
induce the Taumutu people to return home. He
assured them that all angry feeling had now sub-
sided, that his followers were appeased, being satiated
with vengeance. " Return," he urged, " to protect
your rich preserves of flat-fish at Waihora." He
was so pressing in his entreaties, and so positive in
his assurances of friendship and security, that Tawha
and the rest of the people consented to return, with
the exception of Pokeha and Tihau, who were distrustful, and remained under the protection of their
Southern friends. Having gained the object of his
visit, Te Mai hara nui did not want to accompany
Tawha, but hurried back in advance to complete his
treacherous designs. In passing up the coast he
spent a few days at Te Waiteruati (Temuka), where
he was hospitably entertained, and presented with a
quantity of potted birds. Only having sufficient
men with him to carry his baggage, he begged his
entertainers to provide him with porters to carry the
pohas they had presented to him as far as Akaroa.
His request was readily acceded to, and several men
were ordered to accompany him. The party travelled
amicably up the coast, but on reaching the head of
the harbor, Te Mai hara nui, without apparent cause
or provocation, perpetrated one of the base and cruel
deeds that have rendered his memory infamous. In
spite of the remonstrances of his friends and followers, he fell upon the unfortunate carriers, and

killed every one of them with his own hands ; and
then he cut up their bodies and sent portions to all
the different pas and hamlets on the Peninsula.

While this tragedy was being enacted in Akaroa
Harbor, Tawha and his people were journeying
towards their home, and were already nearing the
mouth of the Rakaia.   On being apprized of the
fact, Te Mai hara nui despatched a messenger to
Kaiapoi to order a detatchment of warriors to come
to his asssistance.   About two hundred obeyed the
summons, without knowing what their services were
wanted for.   The narrative of what followed, I give
in the words of Hakopate atao Tu, an old Kaiapoi
chief, still living.   "On reaching Wairewa, we met
Te Mai hara nui and a large gathering of men.   As
soon as we were seated, the Ariki rose up and made
a speech to us ; then we learnt for the first time that
we were meant to attack Taumutu.   We were ordered
to commence our march at once, and Te Mai hara
nui kept in advance of every one, to prevent any of
the chiefs who accompanied him from going forward
to meet the returning refugees and exchange pledges
of peace with them.   It was on this march down the
Kaitorete spit that our old Kaiapoi warriors first
handed a musket.   It was very amusing to watch
their efforts to conceal their nervous dread of the
weapons ; their hands trembled and shook as they
took hold of them, and at the sound of the report
that followed a pull at the trigger, they dropped the
guns upon the ground exclaiming, ' Eh he ! how
wonderful are the works of the pakeha !' But they
soon got over their fears, and learnt to use muskets
with deadly effect.   We camped the first night at
the spring midway down the spit, and the next
morning rose early and marched past Taumutu before
breaking our fast.   On the march Te Mai hara nui
caught sight of Te Rehe, a Waiteruati chief, who
accompanied the Kaiapoi contingent, and made a

rush at him with the avowed intention of taking his
life, but my eldest brother, Te Whakatuka, came to
his rescue, and an angry dispute followed.   Both
were armed with muskets, which they pointed at each
other, and dared each other to fire,   The quarrel
caused intense excitement, and there is no knowing
what the result might have been, but for the interference of some old chiefs, who came up and parted
the combatants.   Te Whakatuka was so offended
with Te Mai hara nui that he went to the rear with
his followers, and threatened to return home, but was
dissuaded from his purpose, and shortly caught up
to the army at Orehu, where they stopped to cook
food.   The place chosen for the camping ground was
in a hollow overgrown with tall rushes, between a
range of low sand hills.   Sentinels were stationed on
the high ground towards the south, and, laying our
weapons aside, we all busied ourselves preparing
food.   Before our meal was over, we noticed the
sentinels making signs, and, thinking they were
hungry and asking to be relieved, some one called
out, ‘ Come and get something to eat.’   ‘ How can
we eat ?’ was the reply.   ‘ Here they all are close at
hand.’   ‘ Who ?’   ‘ Why, the enemy.’   We no
sooner heard this than, forsaking our food, each one
picked up his belt, and fastened it round his waist,
and seized his weapons, and stood ready to meet the
foe.   Our leaders held a short consultation respecting
the order of the battle.   Tau nunu cried, ‘ I will command the coast side.’   Whakauira said, ‘ I will command the lake side.’   Te Mai hara nui said, ‘ Then
I will command the centre.’   All the warriors then
ranged themselves under their respective leaders, and
were ordered to lie flat upon the ground,   We were
not kept long in suspense.   A number of men clad
in red shirts, and armed with guns, soon appeared on
a ridge at a short distance in front of us, coming
towards us.   At the sight of such formidable antago-

nists, Te Mai hara nui's courage completely forsook
him. He became very excited, and cried out, ' Who
can overcome them ? Can these youths, inexpe-
rienced in the use of firearms, cope with those veterans ?' Then he got up quickly from the ground
with the intention of running away, but Whakatuka,
who was crouching beside him, seized him by the
legs and pulled him down again. ' Sit still,' he
said, ' and keep quiet ; wait till I stamp my foot,
and then rise.' Te Mai hara nui's teeth chattered
with fright as he sat cowering in the rushes, while
being forcibly restrained from publicly exhibiting his
cowardice. A great crowd of men, women, and
children shortly appeared, following their advanced
armed guard. As soon as the latter caught sight
of us, they uttered a warning cry and fired. Then
we all sprang to our feet and rushed forward. Those
who had guns singled out the noted chiefs whom they
recognised, and continued to fire till they fell.
Tawha was the first who was shot. He was claimed
by Tauawhara. When the Taumutu people saw
that their leader was killed, they took to flight, and
all we had to do was to follow and kill as fast as we
could. As I ran along I saw in front of me old
Upokohina, a first cousin of Te Mai hara nui, trying
to escape. He was carrying one little child on his
back and leading two others by the hand. He called
out to the man who was pursuing him, ' Do not kill
me.' Te Whakatuka, who was at a little distance,
heard him beg for his life, and asked who it was.
When he knew that it was Upokohina, he called out,
' Keep him till I come up, and take him as payment
for Tokomaru,' for he wanted to avenge the insult
offered to his friend Te Rehe and himself a few hours
before. But Te Mai hara nui, who chanced to be
close by, defeated his purpose, for, hearing Te
Whakatuka's words, he ran forward, crying out in a
loud voice, ' Spare my cousin !' Upokohina sat

down and his pursuers stood round him. When Te
Mai hara nui came up, he at once rubbed noses with
his relative, and with each of the children ; then,
without a moment's warning, he buried his hatchet
in the side of the old man's head, who fell over with
a groan ; then, withdrawing the hatchet, he struck
each of the children on the head, cracking their skulls
like birds' eggs.   Then, turning to Te Whakatuka,
he said, ' But for your exclamation I should have
spared my cousin and his children, but I could not
permit you to boast hereafter that you had either
slain or spared any of my family.   Our honor
demanded their death at my hands.' "

The slaughter at Orehu was very great, and the
cannibal feasts that followed lasted several days.   It
was the last great encounter connected with the Kai-
huanga feud, but the last victim was the chief Tau
nunu, who was killed by Kaiwhata and Kaurehe at
Otokitoki (close to the spring on the small promontory at the mouth of Lake Forsyth).   These two
persons were accompanying Taiaroa on one occasion
to the South, and finding Tau nunu alone, they tomahawked him, together with a woman named Takapau-
hikihiki.   This murder was never avenged.   The
appearance of Rauparaha at Kaiapoi put a stop for
a time to these internal quarrels, and forced Ngai
Tahu to combine together to resist the common foe,
and so ended the disgraceful Kai-huanga feud.

RAID ON PANAU (LONG LOOK-OUT).

But it must not be supposed that these places
were then occupied for the first time.   One result of
the Kai-huanga feud was to drive all who could
escape from the destroyed pas to take refuge in the
bays on the north-east side of the Peninsula.   Those
places were then so difficult of access by land, that
the refugees who took possession of them hoped to
be quite secure from pursuit.   In the course of a few

years several populous settlements sprung up, and of these Panau and Okaruru (Gough's Bay) were the chief. · The inhabitants of these settlements might have continued in peaceful possession of them, but for the repetition by some of their number of an act similar to that which originated the Kai-huanga quarrel, and which brought upon them the anger of their near neighbours, who were as familiar as themselves with the paths that led over the forest-clad hills to their several retreats. The circumstances that brought about a renewal of hostilities were as follows :—During Rauparaha's first visit to Kaiapoi, two chiefs, Hape and Te Puhirere (the latter was the father of Big William), accompanied by several other persons, some of whom belonged to Panau and the other bays just referred to, went to visit their friends at Kaiapoi. While on the way, one of their companions, a woman named Te Whare Rimu, said, " My atuas (familiar spirits) tell me that our path is obstructed ; there is darkness before us ; destruction is in front of us ; death is in front of us " Te Puhirere replied, " Well, my atuas tell me we are safe ; there is no danger." He did not know (as Big William said when telling the story) that he was being *sold to death* by his atuas for a slight he had put upon them before starting on his journey. Just before leaving home, his atua had cried out for food to be placed on its shrine. It had said, " I hunger after eel." Te Puhirere told his wife to give the atua what it asked for, but she grudged to give it the best fish, and not knowing the risk she was running by not doing so, being a new wife—the old and experienced wife being dead—she gave the atua a very small and thin eel. Her conduct exasperated the atua, who, to avenge itself, delivered Te Puhirere and his companions into their enemies' hands, by permitting them to continue their journey without warning them of the great risk they were

running. None of the party had the least suspicion
that the approaches to Kaiapoi were in the hands of
a hostile northern force. They journeyed on towards their destination till they reached the cause-
way through the Ngawari swamp, where they fell
suddenly and unexpectedly into the hands of an
ambuscade. Both Hape and Te Puhirere were
killed, but some of their companions, by jumping
into the swamp, succeeded in making good their
escape, and found shelter in the pa.

After the massacre of Rauparaha's chiefs by the
inhabitants of Kaiapoi, and his withdrawal from the
neighborhood, the survivors of the Akaroa party
returned home. When passing the spot where they
had been attacked, they found the clothing of the
two chiefs who were killed, and not liking to lose
such good mats, they picked them up and carried
them home, and appropriated them to their own use.
In time it came to be generally reported that Hape
and Puhirere had been kaipirautia, or dishonored
after death, by some persons who were known.
When a full report of what had happened reached
the ears of Te Mai hara nui, he expressed the
greatest indignation at the indignity perpetrated on
his deceased relatives by those who had dared to
wear their mats. He summoned the warriors of
Ngai tarewa, Ngati Irakehu, and Ngati hui kai, and
led them to avenge the insult by attacking in succession all the pas erected by the refugees at Panau
and elsewhere. A few only were killed ; the majority were spared, and employed by their captors as
slaves.

Two of these prisoners, who had fallen to the lot
of Paewhiti (old Martin), did not agree very well
with their master, and ran away to their friends at
Koukourata. Tamati Tikao, who was then a boy,
remembers how angry his father Taupori was because
the runaways did not seek his protection ; for he had

been invited by Ngatata to leave Kaiapoi and to
reside at Koukourarata, in order to shield him from
any attack by the Akaroa people. When the two
men who deserted from Paewhiti were seen emerging
from the bush above the Whatamaraki, every one
expected they would soon arrive at the settlement ;
but it soon became evident that they had passed on
to a neighboring village of Ngai te rangi. Taupori
could not contain his indignation at what he regarded
as a grievous slight offered to himself by the travellers, and he demanded that Ngatata should send at
once and fetch them back. His demand was complied with, and a canoe was immediately sent to convey them back. On arrival, they were placed before
Taupori, who asked them why they passed him.
" Did you not know," he asked, " that I was here
for the express purpose of protecting Ngatata and
his friends ? Did you doubt my power to protect
your lives ? I am in doubt now whether I shall not
kill you both, for the insult you have offered to me."
They then stood up one after the other, and replied
to Taupori, and succeeded after a time in soothing
his wounded pride, and inducing him to spare their
lives One of them, Te More, decided to remain
and live with Taupore, but his companion asked permission to return to his friends.

But another runaway was not so successful in
pacifying Taupori's eldest son, Te Whare rakau,
who felt injured in reputation by his distrustful conduct. Te Whare rakau had gone with his eldest
boy to Pigeon Bay to fell totara trees for making
canoes. He was engaged working on two, one called
Te Ahi aua, and the other Te poho a te Atua, when
a man named Kahuroa made his appearance, accompanied by his wife and children. When Te Whare
rakau saw him, he asked him to stay and assist him
in his work. The man consented to do so, but during
the night he went away with his family, and so

quietly as not to awaken Te Whari rakau. This made him very angry (pouri), because he had inadvertently endangered his own life and that of his son by entertaining an unfriendly guest, who might easily have killed him in his sleep. He was vexed with himself for having allowed such a person the opportunity of saying that he could, if so disposed, have killed Te Whare rakau; that, in fact, he had spared his life. On returning home he told his father and their friends, who tried to quiet him, but without avail. Some time afterwards he happened to be in a canoe, containing, amongst others, no less a personage than Momo, the great chief of Kaiapoi, and, while they were pulling along the coast, Te Whare rakau caught sight of Kahuroa on the beach. He immediately asked to be put on shore, that he might pursue him. " What !" said Momo, " would you slay your own kinsman ?" " What else can I do ?" he replied. " Why did he deceive me ? He might have killed not only me, but my son too. A little and we should both have fallen victims. For this he must die ; I cannot let him live to boast that he spared my life and that of my son." Saying this, he ran after the unfortunate man, and, having caught him, killed him on the spot.

CAPTURE OF TE MAI HARA NUI.

About a year after the raid on Panau, Te Mai hara nui was captured in Akaroa Harbor by Te Rauparaha, the noted warrior chief of Kapiti, who came, accompanied by one hundred and seventy men, in an English trading vessel, for the express purpose of securing his person. The anxiety displayed by Rauparaha for the capture of this particular chief was caused by his determination to obtain the most distinguished member of the Ngai Tahu tribe, as payment for his near relative Te Pehi, who, in his opinion, was treacherously put to death by members .

of that tribe at Kaiapoi, but who, in the opinion of those who killed him, was lawfully executed for his treacherous designs upon those who were hospitably entertaining him. Considering the circumstances that preceded the death of Te Pehi and his companions, the Kaiapoi residents had reasonable grounds, for being suspicious respecting the intentions of their visitors. For Rauparaha arrived with a large armed force, uninvited, and without warning, before their pa, and red-handed from the slaughter of their clansmen at Omihi, whom he had been provoked to attack by a silly threat uttered by one of their chiefs. The threat was, that " If Rauparaha ever dared to come upon his territory he would rip his body open with a barracouta tooth." The defiant words were no sooner reported to Rauparaha than he accepted the challenge, and having fitted out a fleet of war canoes, and manned them with his choicest warriors, he crossed the straits, and coasted down as far as Kaikoura, where he attacked and killed the vain boaster, and destroyed every pa in the neighborhood. As the population was too numerous to be put to death, he sent a large number away to Kapiti, in charge of a detachment of his canoe fleet, while he himself proceeded further south with the remainder. Landing at Waipara, he drew up his canoes, and marched overland to Kaiapoi, where his arrival caused the greatest consternation. He tried to quiet the alarm by assurances that his visit was a friendly one, and that he had only come to purchase greenstone. To convince the people of the truthfulness of his statement, he sent several of his officers of highest rank into the pa, and amongst them his esteemed relative and general, Te Pehi. By entrusting them with so many valuable lives, Rauparaha succeeded in reassuring the people, and allaying their fears. For although they learnt the sad fate of their friends at Omihi from one who escaped, they were obliged to admit the justice of their punishment, for a mortal insult such as the Kaikoura chief had offered to so renowned a warrior, could only be wiped out with blood.

For many days the inhabitants of Kaiapoi treated their guests with profuse hospitality, and dealt liberally with them in their bargains for greenstone, when all at once their worst suspicions were revived by Hakitara, a Ngapuhi Native, who had lived many years with them, and who had been staying by invitation in Rauparaha's camp. He returned early one morning with the news that he had overheard during the night, the discussion, in a council of war, of plans for the seizure of the place, and that they might be quite sure that treachery was meditated against them. His report received confirmation from the altered demeanour of their guests, who grew insolent and exacting in their demands for greenstone. The Kaiapoi Natives, after a short consultation, determined in self-defence to strike the first blow, and at a concerted signal they fell upon the Northern chiefs and put them all to death. Rauparaha was overwhelmed with grief and rage when he learnt the fate of his friends, but, not having a sufficient force to avenge them, he retired to Waipara, after killing a few travellers who fell into his hands, and there he re-embarked in his war canoes, and returned to Kapiti.

Safe in his island fortress, he occupied himself for some time in devising a scheme of revenge. The plan he at length adopted was to engage the captain of an English vessel to carry him and a body of his men to Akaroa Harbor, where he hoped to secure Te Mai hara nui. The following is the account of the voyage given to me by Ihaia Pouhawaiki, who accompanied Rauparaha's expedition :—" We sailed from Kapiti in Captain Stewart's brig. There were one hundred and seventy men, under the command

G

of Te Rauparaha, Te Rangi hae ata, Te Hiko,
Tungia, Mokau, Te mai he kia, and others.   On
reaching Akaroa Harbor we carefully concealed ourselves in the hold, while Captain Stewart refused to
have any communication with the shore till Te Mai
hara nui arrived.   For seven days and nights we
waited for that chief, who was away at Wairewa,
superintending the preparation of a cargo of scraped
flax for one of his European customers   Captain
Stewart sent repeated messages to him to hasten his
coming, and on the eighth day he arrived, accompanied by his wife, Te Whe, and his little daughter,
Nga roi mata.   He was cordially welcomed on reaching the deck by the captain, who took him below to
the cabin.   He was hardly seated before a door
opened, and Te Rauparaha entered, accompanied by
several of his companions, who at once seized Te
Mai hara nui, and taunted him with his simplicity
in permitting himself to be so readily entrapped.
After the seizure of Te Mai hara nui, the shore
canoes were encouraged to approach the vessel, but
as soon as the occupants came on board they were
led to the hatchway and thrown down the hold.
Amongst those who were caught in this way were
Apera Pukenui, the late chief of Port Levy, Paurini,
and many others.   Canoes continued to come off for
many hours, as there was no suspicion of foul play,
it being a very usual thing for Maoris to remain for
some time on board the traders that frequented the
port.   On the second day after Te Mai hara nui's
capture, Te Rauparaha attacked Takapuneke very
early in the morning.   The place was unfortified and
undefended.   About one hundred persons were killed,
and fifty taken on board as prisoners.   After the
destruction of this kainga, the vessel sailed away for
Kapiti.   During the voyage Te Mai hara nui
smothered his little daughter, Nga roi mata, appro-
priately named The Tears, lest she should become

the wife of one of his enemies.   His captors were
very much enraged with him doing so, and fearing
he might commit suicide, and escape the punishment
in store for him, they secured his hands, and then
fastened him by a hook placed under his chin to the
cross beams of the hold.   The torture occasioned
exquisite suffering, which was watched with satisfaction by his vindictive enemies.   On reaching Kapiti,
Te Mai hara nui was handed over to the widows of
the chiefs killed at Kaiapoi, who put him to death
by slow and nameless tortures."   Base as the means
adopted for his capture were, and cruel as his fate
was, it is impossible to feel much pity for Te Mai
hara nui.   His punishment was hardly worse than
he deserved, since the treatment he received at the
hands of his enemies was little more than a repetition of the cruelties he had himself perpetrated on
members of his own tribe.

ONAWE.

The remarkable pear-shaped promontory which
divides the upper end of Akaroa Harbor into two
smaller bays, is a locality possessing special interest
to the Maori annalist, not only from its having been
from ancient times the reported abode of an atua or
guardian spirit, but more particularly because it was
the site of the last occupied Maori fortress on the
Peninsula, and the scene of a terrible encounter with
Rauparaha's forces.

The summit of Onawe was called Te-pa-nui-o Hau
(the chief home of wind).   There, amongst the huge
boulders and rocks that crown the hill, and cover its
steep-sloping sides, dwelt the Spirit of the Wind.
Tradition tells how jealously it guarded its sacred
haunts from careless intrusion.   How it terrified the
unwary or too daring trespasser by demanding with
startling suddenness, and in strange unearthly tones,
" What doest thou here ?" instantly following up

the question by the peremptory command, " Turn
back !" a command which none dared to disobey
but those favored persons who possessed the gift of
spirit speech, which enabled them to hold intercourse
with supernatural beings. Unfortunately for all in
these days whose curiosity to hear a spirit's voice
might tempt them to violate the privacy of its abode,
the articulate utterances of the Spirit of the Wind
have long ceased. It has been mute ever since the
report of a musket was first heard at Onawe, and
the Maoris conclude that the loud and unaccustomed
noise scared the atua away.

When the inhabitants of Akaroa became alarmed
for their safety on account of Rauparaha's evident
intention to extend his conquests to the south of
Kaikoura, they resolved to erect a fortified pa, capable of containing all who might require to take
refuge in it. They fixed upon Onawe as the most
suitable site, though subsequent events proved their
want of judgment in selecting a position so easily
assailed.

The remains of the defensive works which still
exist attest the size and strength of the pa, and
awaken a suspicion in the observer's mind that the
Maoris received the assistance of Europeans in their
construction. But this they most positively deny.
They assert that the fortifications were entirely
designed and executed by themselves, and that any
departures from the ancient lines of construction that
may be observable, were caused by the alterations
necessary to meet the introduction of firearms. A
deep trench surrounded the pa, the earth taken from
it forming the walls, along the top of which a strong
fence was erected. All round the inside of the fence
was a covered way for the protection of the defenders. The approach to a spring on the south
side of the promontory was by a covered trench, protected by walls running parallel to each other ; but

to ensure a supply of water in the event of this road
to the spring being cut off, a number of large canoes
were dragged up into the pa, and filled with fresh
water, and covered over with matting to prevent
loss by evaporation. Ruas and whatas were stored
with provisions, and every precaution taken to enable
the occupants of the pa to sustain a siege.

The various preparations for defence were barely
completed, before the startling intelligence was
brought that Rauparaha had invested Kaiapoi with
a large military force. The inhabitants of Akaroa
and its neighborhood flocked at once into Onawe,
and prepared for the worst. Tangatahara was placed
in chief command, and under him Puaka and Potahi.
They were able to muster about four hundred warriors, most of whom were armed with muskets, the
rest having to content themselves with steel hatchets,
or the more primitive weapons used by their fore-
fathers. During the six months the siege of Kaiapoi lasted, the occupants of Onawe suffered constant
alarms from the reports that reached their ears of
atrocities perpetrated by Rauparaha's foraging parties. This condition of suspense was brought to a
close by the capture of Kaiapoi, and the arrival of a
party of fugitives with the news of its destruction,
and the important intelligence that they had left
Rauparaha in the act of embarking his men with the
avowed intention of conveying them round to attack
Onawe. Every one was now on the alert, and many
were in dread expectation of what was to follow.
Shortly after receiving this timely warning, the sentinels descried at a very early hour one morning, a
large fleet of war canoes pulling up the harbor.
Rauparaha evidently purposed to surprise the place,
but his design was frustrated by the watchfulness of
the defenders. Finding his plan had failed, he
retired, ordering part of his force to camp in Barry's
Bay, and part at the Head of the Bay. Ngatitoa

landed near the short wharf in Barry's Bay, where
they commenced to prepare for cooking their food ;
while Ngatiawa landed near where Mrs Shadbolt's
house stands, and prepared to do the same. Innumerable fires were soon blazing on the little heaps of
stones, gathered into the shallow basin-shaped holes
scooped in the ground, and on which, when sufficiently heated, the food would be placed, and covered
with matting and earth to cook. Observing that
Rauparaha had divided his forces, and that between
the two divisions lay a thick wood, and a stretch of
swampy ground, it occurred to Tangatahara that by
falling suddenly upon Ngatiawa, now they were off
their guard, he might overpower them before Ngatitoa could come to their assistance. He accordingly
sallied forth from the pa, and skirted along the edge
of the rising ground on which Mr Callaghan's house
now stands. But the enemy's sentinels posted in
the wood quickly discerned his intentions, and raised
the alarm by running to the top of the hill and calling loudly upon Ngatitoa to come to their help.
Their cries were heard, and their comrades at once
rushed forward, firing as they came floundering
across the muddy beach that separated their camp
from the promontory. Checked by the failure of
this attempt to surprise the enemy, Tangatahara
turned to meet the advancing Ngatitoa, and returned
their fire. Tahatiti was the first Ngai Tahu shot.
On seeing him fall, his companions began to retreat
slowly towards the pa. Big William, then a boy
about twelve years old, ran back to report the fatal
result of the enemy's fire. On reaching the gap in
the cliff, near the gate of the pa, he caught up to
Tama, who, having been wounded in the knee, was
hobbling towards a place of shelter While the
retreating band of Onawe warriors were standing
about the gate, a number of Kaiapoi captives suddenly appeared amongst them, accompanied by their

captors. Their appearance very much disconcerted
the defenders of the place, who were loth to fire upon
their kinsmen, and yet realised the danger of permitting any of the enemy to approach too near. Rauparaha himself, accompanied by quite a crowd of
Kaiapoi notabilities, came boldly up to the walls,
where he had a very narrow escape, for Puaka,
recognising him, pushed his musket through a loop-
hole, and levelled it at him, and must have shot him
dead but for Tara, Pita te Hori's eldest brother,
who was standing by Rauparaha, and pushed the
muzzle of the gun aside. The Kaiapoi captives,
partly at the instigation of their conquerors, and
partly moved by a jealous dread lest Onawe should
escape their own fate, urged the inhabitants to sur-
render. In the disorder and confusion occasioned by
this unexpected parleying, some of the Northern
warriors got inside the gates, and commenced killing
every one about them. A panic ensued, and for
some minutes Onawe was the scene of the wildest
confusion and bloodshed, the shrieks and cries of the
dying mingling with the loud and furious shouts of
the victors. Big William relates how, terror-stricken
by the fearful sights and sounds that surrounded him
on all sides, he sought a hiding-place in one of the
covered trenches, but, having been seen, was followed
by a young Ngatiawa warrior, whose handsome face
made an indelible impression on his memory. Finding he was pursued, he picked up a spear and prepared to defend himself, and as the young man ran
towards him in a stooping position, he thrust the
spear at his face, and succeeded in piercing his cheek,
and nearly putting out his eye. Unexpectedly
checked in this manner, the Ngatiawa called fran-
tically for a gun to be brought to shoot his assailant,
but another warrior running up the trench behind
him, seized William, and, having tied his hands and
feet, carried him down to his canoe, and eventually

carried him off to Kapiti, where he grew so much into favor with his master, that he was treated more like a son than a slave, and finally allowed to return to his home in Akaroa.

Amongst those who escaped were two refugees from Kaiapoi—Aperahama Te Aiki and Wi Te pa. They happened to be outside the gate when the slaughter began, and at once sought shelter in the scrub that covered the hill sides to the water's edge. They were observed by two men in charge of one of the northern war canoes, who pulled to the beach just under their hiding place, exclaiming "Our slaves, two for us," And they might have been caught, but for the courage of Wi Te pa, who fortunately had a loaded gun with him. Creeping down through the bushes, he stood concealed just above high water mark, and as the man in the bows was preparing to jump on shore Te pa fired, and nearly blew the top of his head off; his companion, seeing what had happened, pushed the canoe back again into deep water with all speed, and the two fugitives made their way to the hills, where they were joined by the late Pita Te Hori and others, and having evaded the parties sent by Rauparaha in pursuit, succeeded in making good their escape to the south. The majority of the inhabitants of Onawe were either killed or carried away into captivity. In the evening of the day on which the pa was taken, the prisoners were all examined, and the old men and women were picked out and put to death on the flax flat, now Mr Callaghan's paddock, in Barry's Bay. There the bodies were cut up, and so much carried off to the camps as the northern warriors required as a relish for their fern root.

MAORIS REORGANISING.

The capture and destruction of Onawe almost annihilated the Maori inhabitants of the Peninsula.

Of the few survivors, some had the courage to return
to their homes, after the departure of the northern
invaders, but others, unable to overcome their fears,
fled for refuge to Otakou, where they remained till
induced to join the expedition organised by Taiaroa
and Tukawaiki to attack Rauparaha on the shores
of Cook's Straits.   Before the capture of Kaiapoi,
Taiaroa had escaped with about two hundred followers, purposing to return with a larger force for
the relief of the besieged pa, but before he could
execute his design the place was taken, and the
subsequent capture of Onawe put a stop for a time
to his movements ; but having learnt that Rauparaha paid periodical visits to the settlement he had
formed on the shores of Cook's Straits, he determined
to go there and seek to avenge the injuries done to
Ngai Tahu.   He was cordially assisted in carrying
out his designs by Tuhawaiki, Karetai, and other
chiefs, who headed the populous communities which
still existed in the south.   But though active in
organising the first expediton, Taiaroa did not
accompany it.   It consisted of two hundred and
seventy men, under the command of Tuhawaiki and
Karetai.
    They proceeded in war canoes from Otakou to
Queen Charlotte's Sound, where they were successful in surprising Rauparaha, who had a very narrow
escape from destruction,   For in the frantic efforts
made by his men to launch their boat, on discovering that they had fallen into a Ngai Tahu ambuscade, the keel was torn off, and the boat rendered
useless.   Rauparaha, finding his followers falling all
around him, and being unable to reach his canoes,
which had got afloat, without running the risk of
being detected and pursued, sought concealment in
the kelp near the shore, where, by occasionally lifting
his head under cover of the broad leaves as they
swayed backwards and forwards with the waves, he

H

was able to breathe. He remained in his hiding place till the first fury of the attack was over, and then he swam to a canoe, which remained in the offing waiting to pick up any who might escape. Paora Taki, the old Native Assessor at Rapaki, always maintains that he might have killed Rauparaha on this occasion, if he had been properly armed, but unfortunately on the way up the coast he had been induced by a powerful friend to exchange his gun for a very simple weapon, which was nothing more than a sharp-pointed stake. In the confusion which followed the rush on Rauparaha's men, both sides got mixed up in one close crowd. Some one brushed roughly past Paora, who, on turning round, saw it was Te Rauparaha himself. He had on a parawai mat, and was walking rapidly towards the water's edge, with his arms folded across his breast, and holding a greenstone mere in his right hand. Paora, not daring to attack him with the simple weapon he possessed, tried to secure some inferior foe, and the first he encountered was a woman, whom he pushed over and pinned to the sand by a thrust through her thigh ; he then called loudly for the loan of a tomahawk to despatch his prey. A passing warrior, attracted by his cries, seized the woman by the hair, and was about to plunge the weapon into her skull, when he recognised her as one of the captured Kaiapoi people. " Why, Paora," he said, " it is your own aunt." Poor Paul tried to make amends for his rough treatment of his injured relative by a more than ordinary amount of nose rubbing, the Maori equivalent for kissing. After another successful encounter with their enemies, Ngai Tahu returned home.

Encouraged by the success of the first expedition, known as Oraumoa iti, a second, on a much larger scale, was resolved upon, to be known as Oraumoa nui. Some little time was spent in making preparations, and, when they were completed, it was found that upwards of four hundred warriors had assembled to take part in it. Taiaroa assumed the command, and, having despatched a portion of his forces by water, he marched up the coast, gaining slight accessions to his numbers at each stage.

On the way an incident occurred which throws some light on the motives which prompted those deeds of apparently senseless barbarity which so often darken the pages of the internal history of Maori tribes. Accompanying Taiaroa's expedition was a chief noted for his harsh and cruel disposition, Te Whakataupoka by name. On reaching Taumutu, this man was with difficulty dissuaded from killing the surviving remnants of the hapus destroyed by Rauparaha, whom he found gathered there. The reason he gave for wishing to perpetrate such a cruel deed was, that all his own friends and relations had been killed in the encounter from which these people had escaped, and he regarded their escape as having been purchased at the cost of those who perished, and therefore demanding the vengeance of surviving relatives. His inhuman proposal was resisted by Tu te hou nuku, the long-lost son of Te Mai hara nui, who had arrived in a whaling ship at Otakou just as the second Oraumoa expedition was leaving, and who, approving of its object, had at once joined it. Tu, unlike his father, was of a merciful and kindly disposition, and bestirred himself to protect the lives threatened with destruction. He sent off at once to Wairewa for his cousin Mairehe (Mrs. Tikao), and the few remaining members of his family still to be found there. On their arrival, Te Whakataupoko found that he could not carry out his sanguinary purpose, as he would have been forcibly restrained from doing any harm to the sacred persons of the Ariki's family, who formed part of the remnant that escaped from Te Rauparaha, and whose presence

protected their less influential fellow-sufferers from
destruction.

DEATH OF TU TE HOU NUKU.

It would needlessly prolong this narrative to relate
the encounter between the several forces under Taiaroa and Rauparaha.   Suffice it to say that the
Southern expedition was successful.   But a sad
disaster befell it when returning, which resulted in
the loss of many valuable lives   Taiaroa's fleet,
which consisted of twenty-nine canoes, was mainly
composed of vessels specially adapted for ocean
voyaging, formed by lashing two ordinary war canoes
together, and further strengthening them with a
deck ; but the canoe in which Tu te hou nuku and
many of the oldest chiefs embarked was only an
ordinary war canoe, quite unable to cope with the
winds and waves of stormy Rau Kawa.   When
rounding Cape Campbell, the fleet encountered a
tremendous storm, and though Tu and his companions handled their canoe with all the skill of
experienced seamen, it capsized before reaching the
shore, and all but an old woman named Mawhai
were drowned.   She managed to escape by clinging
on to the canoe till it was washed up.   Their comrades, who witnessed the accident from the beach,
were unable to render them any assistance, but after
it was all over they waited in the neighborhood till
the bodies were cast up.   On finding the remains of
Tu te hou nuku, they prepared at once to conduct
his funeral rites, which were superintended by Te
Wera.   He commenced by killing the poor woman
who had reached the shore alive, as an offering to
the manes of the deceased.   He then cut up the
canoe, and with the fragments burnt the body of the
young chief.   The actual handling of the corpse was
assigned to Rangitihi, the husband of Wakatau's
sister, who was in consequence subjected to the incon-

venience of being fed for a long period by the hands
of his wife, Te Wera. His own hands having become
tapu from contact with the sacred body, he dared not
touch anything in the shape of food, cooked or
uncooked, nor engage in the cultivation of the soil,
for a whole year afterwards As Tu te hou nuku
left no children, Te Mai hara nui's line became
extinct at his death.

CONCLUSION.

The depopulated Peninsula would have continued
without Maori inhabitants up to the date of colonisation, but for the great change wrought in Rauparaha's warriors by Christianity. Those fierce and
cruel men, having been led by the teaching of the
Rev. Mr Hadfield, the present Anglican Bishop of
Wellington, to embrace Christianity, gave convincing
proof of their sincerity by releasing all their Ngai
Tahu captives, whose compulsory labors were a great
source of wealth and profit to them. But they not
only gave them their freedom, they even allowed
them to return to their own land, and, in order to
ensure them a safe reception from those who might
during their enforced absence have usurped their
estates, several notable Northern chiefs accompanied
them home. Port Levy, Akaroa, Gough's Bay, and
Wairewa could again count their inhabitants by
scores, if not even by hundreds, while several small
hamlets were formed in other places round the coast.
Port Levy became the principal centre, and there
many important Maori gatherings took place, both
before and after colonisation began. It was there
that Rauparaha's son and nephew spent some time
instructing the people in the doctrines of Christianity,
and teaching them to read and write in their own
language, endeavoring as far as they could to repair
the wrongs done to Ngai Tahu by Rauparaha and
his warriors. It was there that the northern chiefs

, met Taiaroa and other influential Southern chiefs,
and exchanged pledges of peace and good will.   The
reoccupation of Kaiapoi, just before the arrival of the
Canterbury Pilgrims, tended to thin the Maori population of this district, which has been still further
reduced by the fatal effects of European diseases,
rendered more destructive than they would otherwise
have been, from the Maoris having been forced to
crowd together on the limited areas reserved for
them ; where, surrounded by constantly accumulating
heaps of pollution, deprived of the healthy excitement
of hunting and travel, deprived of all political
influence, without any fixed aim or object in life, a
prey to ceaseless regrets and chronic depression of
spirits, they have fallen easy victims to every form
of epidemic that has appeared amongst them.

Knowing the disorganised state into which Maori
society had fallen just before colonisation began, the
public are too ready to credit that event with whatever improvement may be apparent in the present
condition of the Natives, and to conclude that the
Maoris must be in every way better off than they
could have been without the settlement of the country.
But, as a matter of fact, it was not to colonisation,
but to their own acceptance of Christianity, that the
Maoris owed the restoration of peace and order.
When the first colonists arrived, the Maoris were a
Christian nation.   Without saying a word in dis-
paragement of the colonists, who as a whole have
honestly endeavored to treat the Maori fairly, it
cannot be denied that whatever benefits the Maoris
have derived from colonisation have been the result
of *indirect rather than any direct efforts* made by the
colonists for their good.   Beyond being spared the
prospect of a violent death, it is hard for a Maori to
see that he has gained anything ; and even that
benefit would have been secured to him under the
reign of law established by the reception of Chris-

tianity. Provision for the education of their children, and for the proper care of the sick and needy, was stipulated for by the Maoris when parting with their lands, so that no credit is due to the Colonial Government for what has been done towards fulfilling the conditions of the original deed of purchase. But, whatever faults may be charged against our administration of Native affairs, and however disastrously our mistakes may have affected the interests of individuals of the Native race, it is gratifying to know that the more intelligent amongst them regard their misfortunes, not as the result of any intention on our part to injure them, but rather as the inevitable result of being brought suddenly into contact with a civilisation so far in advance of their own simpler mode of life.

The relations between the English and the Maori inhabitants of the Peninsula have always been of the most friendly kind, and although they do not hesitate to charge us with complicity in the murder of their great chief, Te Mai hara nui, they have never shown the slightest disposition to retaliate, and there is no instance on record of any European being killed by Maoris here, or even suffering violence at their hands. The rarity of convictions for criminal offences speaks well for the general good conduct of the people, and the universal testimony borne to their honesty and kindliness of disposition by their English neighbors, show how deeply they have imbibed those Christian principles on which the only real civilisation rests. Though their numbers have dwindled down from thousands to the insignificant total of two hundred and fifty, and the relative numbers of the two races inhabiting these parts are reversed, may the Maoris never have just cause to regret that they trusted the English.

No. 2.—EUROPEAN ACCOUNT OF THE MASSACRE IN AKAROA HARBOR.

The following narrative of the Maori massacre was published in the *Auckland Herald*. It was written by a Canterbury resident, in reply to a tale told by John Marmon, a celebrated "Pakeha Maori," whose history of the affair was published in the northern capital. The compiler of these stories gives it space here, because he wishes to place before his readers everything that is known on the subject :—

"In your weekly issue of Jan. 20, I notice your comments on one of the most shocking stories in Maori history, as told by the late John Marmon, and which you believe to be substantially accurate. You further state that Captain Stewart, the well-known discoverer of Stewart's Island, New Zealand, was master of the vessel that took Te Rauparaha and his party to Banks Peninsula, and that his name will always be infamous for his connection with the atrocious massacre there. In justice to the memory of the dead, I feel it my duty to correct your statement, and not to allow the name of one of our earliest pioneers to be handed down to posterity in connection with that sad affair.

"Now, sir, Captain Stewart, the well-known discoverer of Stewart's Island, and Captain Stewart, master of the brig Elizabeth, were *not* one and the *same* person. The former was for many years master of a trading and sealing vessel, sailing out of the port of Sydney. In one of his sealing expeditions he discovered the island which now bears his name. In his old age he retired from the sea, and took up his abode with an old friend, a Mr Harris, of Poverty Bay, with whom he lived until the day of his death, which occurred in the year 1843 or 1844. He was a man much respected, and on his visits to

Auckland could be easily recognised. No doubt there are a few old settlers still living that have seen, as well as myself, a very tall man walking up Shortland street, in full dre-s of Stuart tartan (Scotch plaid), and who will recognise in the description Captain Stewart, the discoverer.

" Marmon states that Captain Stewart, on his arrival in Sydney, was arrested and put in prison, where he remained six months. This is not true. I may state that I arrived in Sydney in April, 1833, when everything connected with this notorious voyage was quite fresh in everybody's memory I have heard it related over and over again It appears Captain Stewart, after leaving New Zealand, made his way to Sydney. Soon after his arrival the news got spread about, and finally reached the ears of the Government, but, whether from having no jurisdiction, or for want of sufficient evidence, I cannot say, no immediate action was taken in arresting Captain Stewart. In the meantime, and while the Government were deliberating, Stewart cleared out of Sydney, and sailed for a port in South America. This was the last heard of Captain Stewart or the brig Elizabeth in these colonies.

" As to Marmon's account relative to conversing with Captain Stewart and John Cowell after their return to Kapiti, I should say it is a fabrication ; for to my knowledge Marmon had been living in Hokianga, where he died, for nearly fifty years. I have never heard of his living at any time in the South. Again, it is the first time I ever heard John Cowell's name in connection with Captain Stewart or the brig Elizabeth.

" In referring to Captain Stewart and his infamous voyage, I may relate the story as I heard it at the time I speak of, viz :—In the early days of New Zealand there was a great chief named Te Pahi (head of the tribe to whom Te Rauparaha belonged),

I

who was taken to Sydney, and from thence to England, where he was presented to King George, who
was very kind to him, and made him several presents,
and told him when he returned to his country to be
good to the white man. On Te Pahi's return, he
was full of what he had seen in England. He
appears to have been a very good man, and anxious
to tell of the wonderful things he had seen to other
tribes. He went with a small party in a canoe to
Akaroa (Banks Peninsula), to pay a friendly visit
to the chief, Te Mairanui. On his arrival, he and
his party were treated very kindly. Not having any
suspicion of the treachery in store for him, they all
went into the pa, when Te Mairanui and his men
fell on them and killed every man. When the news
reached Kapiti, there was great excitement amongst
Te Pahi's tribe, of whom Te Rauparaha (after Te
Pahi's death) was head. Of course, as was the custom then, the tribe were bound to have their revenge
on the first opportunity. This opportunity offered
when Captain Stewart made his appearance. Whether
Captain Stewart was aware of the real intention of
the Natives is a mystery, but for certain he was promised a large quantity of flax. On the arrival of
the vessel in Akaroa, the Natives, as was the custom, soon came on board to trade, among them the
chief Te Mairanui and his daughter, a girl from ten
to twelve years of age. During this time Te Rauparaha and his party were in the ship's hold, keeping
out of sight. As soon as the decks were full of men
from the shore, Te Rauparaha's party rushed up
from below, and killed all they could, with the exception of Te Mairanui and his daughter, whom they
took alive. Te Rauparaha and his men then went
on shore, took the pa, and killed all they came
across. It was rumoured that human flesh was
cooked in the ship's coppers, but this appears to be
doubtful. The brig then sailed for the island of

Mana, in Cook's Straits.   On the passage Te
Mairanui was lashed to the mainmast, and his little
daughter allowed to walk about the deck.   The
story goes that one day Te Mairanui called his
daughter to him, and, using these words, said,
' They are going to kill me, but they shall not kill
or make a slave of you.'   With that he took hold
of her and dashed her brains out against the combings of the main hatchway.   On the arrival of the
brig at Mana, Te Mairanui was taken ashore, and
killed in this way : He was hung up by the heels,
a vein cut in' his throat, and as he bled to death,
they caught the blood in a bowl and drank it.   I
have never heard (as Mr Travers asserts) that a
red-hot ramrod was pushed through his neck, or that
Te Mairanui's wife was taken by the party of Te
Rauparaha.   I have not read Mr Travers' work on
' The Life and Times of Te Rauparaha,' but I question very much whether he was better informed than
myself.

   " Marmon says that Te Rauparaha and his party
went overland from Cloudy Bay to Banks Peninsula.
Now, this of itself is sufficient to throw a doubt over
his whole version.   And, again, he must have been
quite ignorant of the geography of the Middle
Island of New Zealand, or he must have known
that it was impossible in those days to travel the
distance without canoes.   Then for Te Rauparaha
to bring away fifty slaves was another impossibility.
How could he cross the many rapid rivers ? where
could he get food from for them (there was little or
no fern root, as in the North Island) ? are all questions to be asked.   Then, again, Rauparaha's settlement or pa was on the North Island.   He had no
settlement or pa in those days on the Middle Island,
being always in fear of Bloody Jack and his tribe,
from whom he had several narrow escapes.   At one
time they had a desperate fight in Fighting Bay,

close to Port Underwood, in Cloudy Bay, which is called to this day Fighting Bay in memory of the fight referred to, so that it is very clear that Te Rauparaha would have to take his departure for his own settlement on the North Island, and this could not be done without canoes. Then, again, Natives in those days never travelled any distance by land when they could go by water in their fine large war canoes, carrying from fifty to a hundred men. If Marmon's version is true, Rauparaha had full satisfaction or revenge for his brother being killed, in killing the unfortunate natives and taking away the fifty slaves. He would not have gone a second time. It is the first time that I have ever heard John Cowell's name in connection with Captain Stewart.

"I may state that I arrived in New Zealand in May, 1836, in the whaling ship Louisa, of Sydney, Captain Haywood We anchored under Mana Island, in Cook's Straits, where the ship remained during the bay whaling season, from May to October. Te Rauparaha was our chief, or we were under his protection, for which he was well paid in blankets, &c. Although he was a terror among the natives, he was always very good to the whites ; in fact, in one instance I have to thank him for saving my life It happened in this way : I was ashore with a boat's crew, filling water casks, when Te Rauparaha's son, a lad about sixteen to seventeen years of age, was very troublesome to our men, and annoyed them so much that one of our crew, in a hasty moment, struck young Te Rauparaha in the face, and made his nose bleed. Now, to draw blood from a chief was one of the greatest crimes that could be committed, and the transgressor very seldom escaped with his life. When the Natives saw the blood, they were very much excited, and came rushing upon the crew, flourishing their tomahawks. We all thought our last hour had come. Old Te Rauparaha, hearing the noise, came out of his hut to see what was up. On hearing the particulars, he told the natives not to touch the white men, for his son was in the wrong. He must take his own part, and fight the Pakeha—very good, one Maori, one Pakeha. It ended in a stand-up fight, in which, to our delight, young Rauparaha got a good thrashing, and we were thankful to get off with our lives. However, young Rauparaha soon forgot it, and we were ever afterwards the best of friends. Had not old Rauparaha been at hand, I am afraid it would have been rather a serious matter for us."

No. 3.—GEORGE HEMPLEMAN AND HIS PURCHASE OF AKAROA.

It this paper we publish the text of a memorial forwarded in 1843 by the late Mr Hempleman to George Grey, Esq., then Lieutenant-Governor of the Colony. As will be seen, Mr. Hempleman claims to have been the first purchaser of the greater part of Banks Peninsula, including what was then Wangoolou, but is at present known as Akaroa. It will of course be apparent that if these claims had been substantiated, Captain Langlois' subsequent purchase would have been illegal. Of one thing there can be no doubt, and that is, that the Maoris sold the land twice over, and no doubt would have done the same thing ten times, if they had had the chance. Further on will be found the story of George Hempleman and his claims to Akaroa. The following is the memorial referred to :—

To His Excellency George Grey, Esquire, Lieutenant-Governor and Commander-in-Chief in and over the Colony of New Zealand, &c.

The Memorial of George Hempleman, of Peracke, in the Province of New Munster, Master Whaler and Mariner.

HUMBLY SHOWETH

That your memorialist on or about the month of March, in the year 1837, purchased of certain Natives, the occupiers thereof, the tract of land hereinafter described, and in the month of November, 1839, when full and complete payment was made to all the parties interested, and at that time assembled for the purpose, received from them a certificate of such purchase, which certificate is in the words and figures following :—

" November 2nd, 1839.

This is to certify that Captain Hempleman has purchased the extent of land from Bloody Jack as undermentioned :—From Mowry Harbor south to Flea Bay north, including Wangoolou, as agreed by the undermentioned, viz., by payment of one big boat, by name the Mary Ann, including two sails and jib.   Extent of land fifteen miles east, south inland.

Signed by

JOHN TUHAWAIKE.
TOBY X PARTRIGEE.
JACKEY X WHITE.
ALLON X TOMMY ROUNDHEAD.
TYROA X
KIKAROREE X.
WALKATOWREE X AHANE.
KING JOHN X.
JACKEY GAY X BANGANA X.

And witnessed by

SIMON CRAWLEY.
JACK X MILLER.
ALFRED ROBERTS.
JAMES X CREED."

That your memorialist has at times been resident on the land so purchased, and has also fenced and cultivated a portion thereof, and also established and worked a whaling station thereon.   That the chiefs of and in that neighborhood have been always, and are now, ready and willing to admit the sale of such lands to your memorialist, and his rightful claim thereto.

That on or about the month of April, 1840, your memorialist caused to be addressed a statement to the Colonial ecretary for the Colony of New South Wales, and forwarded the same to Sydney in the same month, in which statement his claim to the said lands was set forth. agreeably with the provisions of a certain Act of the Legislative Council of New South Wales, empowering the Governor of that Colony to appoint a Commission to examine and report on claims to grants of land in New Zealand.

That some time afterwards, viz., about November, 1842, your memorialist was informed by the Chief Police Magistrate of Akaroa that your memorialist's claim was not among the gazetted claims to land published at Auckland, whereupon your memorialist immediately wrote to the Colonial Secretary at Auckland a letter setting forth his claim, together with a copy of the statement which had been addressed to the Secretary of New South Wales.

That your memorialist received a reply thereto, stating that the claim had not been received in the Colonial Secretary's office, and inviting him to produce any proof in his power that the letter to the Colonial Secretary of New South Wales was actually forwarded at the date specified.

That your memorialist with such invitation obtained a declaration from one Alfred Roberts (the person who wrote the statement to the Colonial Secretary of New South Wales setting forth his claim) of the facts before mentioned.   A copy of this declaration is annexed hereto

That in February, 1840, when Captain Fitzroy was in Wellington, your memorialist addressed a memorial to His Excellency, wherein, after setting forth the facts hereinbefore referred to, he prayed that he would be pleased to take the case into his favorable consideration, and grant your memorialist permission to prove his claim.

That Captain Fitzroy, through his private secretary, replied to your memorialist that the Commission having returned from Banks Peninsula, could not then go again ; an officer would inquire into the case.

That no steps whatever or instructions, as your memorialist has been informed, have been taken or issued for the investigation of his claim, the delaying which is to him a source of great loss and anxiety, and

Your memorialist humbly prays your Excellency to permit an investigation to be made into his claim, in order that he may receive a Crown grant upon his establishing a right thereto, or that you will grant to him such relief as under the circumstances may to your Excellency seem meet.

Copy declaration referred to in the foregoing memorial.

I, Alfred Roberts, of Wellington, in the Province of New Ulster, in the Colony of New Zealand, boatman, do solemnly and sincerely declare that I did in the month of April, in the year 1840, by the request and at the dictation of George Hempleman, then of Perake, in New Munster, in the said Colony of New Zealand, master whaler, write a certain letter setting forth the said George Hempleman's claim to certain land therein mentioned, and situate in the district of Perake aforesaid, which he, the said George Hemplemen, had purchased of certain native chiefs who had declared themselves the owners and possessors thereof and who had conveyed the same lands by deed dated November 2, 1839 ; and further, that I did direct such aforesaid letter to the Honorable C Leas Thompson, Colonial Secretary for the Colony of New South Wales, and did forward the same by brig Nimrod, which sailed for Sydney in or about the month of April, in the aforesaid 1840, and I make this solemn declaration conscientiously believing the same to be true, and by virtue of the provisions of an Act made and passed in the 6th year of the reign of His late Majesty, entitled an Act for the more effectual abolition of oaths and affirmations taken and made in various departments of the State, and to substitute declarations in lieu thereof, and for the more entire suppression of voluntary and extrajudicial oaths and affidavits, and to make other provisions for the abolition of unnecessary oaths.

(Signed) ALFRED ROBERTS.

Declared and subscribed at Wellington aforesaid, this 15th day of December, in the year of our Lord one thousand eight hundred and forty-three.

(Signed) M. RICHMOND, C.P.M.

Examined with the copy memorial and declaration in possession of the Commissioner, Col. Campbell.

December, 1853.

After his purchase of the Peninsula from Bloody Jack and the other Maori chiefs, George Hempleman appears to have lived quietly at Peraki, making occasional whaling trips, and visiting Sydney to exchange the oil for other commodities. He seems to have seen the occupation of Akaroa by the French with indifference, and to have had no dispute with them whatever about their taking the land. When,

J

however, about the year 1852, he found out that the
Peninsula had been included in the Canterbury Association block, and that the English Government had
given that Association some right over the land
which he looked upon as his private property, he
made a complaint to the Lieutenant-Governor in
Auckland that his rights had been infringed. The
result of his complaint was, that in the first session
ever held of the New Zealand Legislative Council,
the second ordinance passed was to the effect that
all claims made by persons professing to have purchased lands from the Natives, prior to the English
occupation, should be at once enquired into.

Colonel James Campbell was appointed the Commissioner to investigate the Middle Island claims.
Appended is his report on Mr. Hempleman's claim :

No. 39

NEW ZEALAND.

Report of the Commissioner appointed to examine
and report upon the claims to grants of land
under the Ordinance of the Legislative Council
of New Zealand, Session 1.   No. 2.

Claim No. 39.

Claimant's name.................George Hempleman.
Address ....Peraki Bay.

Natives' Names from whom Purchased or Obtained.

Tuhawaika (or Bloody Jack) and other Native
chiefs, with their tribes assembled (see original certificate forwarded), when a deed of sale was executed
by the above chiefs and others.   John Miller and
William Simpson, examined as witnesses in the case,
were present on the occasion (see proceedings pages
13, 14, and 15), when the Natives unanimously
admitted the payment they received, and the alienation of the land in question, of which the following
are the boundaries.

Boundaries.

From Mowry Harbor (as then called), situated on the northern extremity of the Ninety Mile Beach, between that harbor and Flea Bay, and from thence as a base line extending fifteen miles inland, or across Banks Peninsula, that is to say, within a nearly square figure, three sides of which are each fifteen miles in length, including Wangooloa, now called Akaroa Harbor. (See accompanying map).

Date of Alleged Purchase.

Made in 1837, but completed 2nd November, 1839.

The payment made to the Natives for the land appears to have been a small trading vessel, named the Mary Ann, of about ten tons burden, previously employed in conveying whale oil and bone from New Zealand to Sydney, a quantity of tobacco, blankets, and other slops, etc. Estimated value of the whole at the time, £650.

Commissioner of Crown Lands Office,
Akaroa, March 3rd, 1853.

Sir,—As I have nearly concluded my investigation of all claims to land in Banks Peninsula, and as Mr. Boys is proceeding as rapidly in the necessary surveys as the difficulties thrown in his and my way will admit of, I have to request, as there is now no necessity for delay in its final adjustment, you will bring the case of Mr George Hempleman before His Excellency the Governor-in-Chief I am so dissatisfied with the report I made on the 19th March, 1852, upon Mr Hempleman's claim, and more particularly with what I then recommended to be done for him, that I beg they may be cancelled. And to this I conclude there can be no objection, as His Excellency has not as yet come to any decision as to his case. Therefore, in justice to him, I beg leave to forward another report and recommendation, which

I hope will be approved of by His Excellency. As I
may now say that all the claims but Mr. Hempleman's to lands in Banks Peninsula have been satisfied, I have also to request, in order to obviate the
necessity of Mr. Boys returning to Akaroa, that I
may be authorised to employ him surveying the
lands";to be appropriated to Mr Hempleman, so that
1 may be enabled to make out Crown grants of them
for him ; and in doing so I shall take care that
there be reserved for town purposes the whole of the
available lands in French Farm Bay, and any other
lands I may consider necessary for Government or
other purposes, such as Native reserves, &c. As to
the latter, I have been anxiously expecting to hear
from you. I shall, however, be glad to know as soon
as possible if His Excellency would wish me to prevent Mr. Hempleman from selecting any of the lands
which Mr. Godley, though he knew they were subject
to claims or contracts to be fulfilled, has conveyed to
Canterbury colonists and others, not only in Akaroa,
but also in other, parts of Banks Peninsula, which
are within the block purchased by Mr. Hempleman
from the Natives. You are aware that notwith-
standing Mr Godley's conveyance of it to Mr Watson, he (Mr Hempleman) still keeps possession of
Peraki Bay, and of which, I conclude, he is, along
with other lands, to have a Crown grant. This being
done, of course the remainder of Banks Peninsula
which is not disposed of will be at the disposal of
the Canterbury Association.—Yours, etc.,

JAS. CAMPBELL,
Commissioner Crown Lands.

The Hon the Colonial Secretary,
Wellington.

P.S.—I think it advisable now to inform you that
soon after I had the honor of receiving your letter of
the 26th January last, having no hopes of Captain
Simeon making any communication to me, I con-

sidered it would be best that I should write myself
to him on the subject of it.   I forward a copy of my
letter to him, and I beg you will acquaint His Excellency that I shall as soon as ever I am able, make
known to you the result of the efforts I shall make,
in order if possible to make an effort to effect an
arrangement with Capt. Simeon.   But I do not see,
in the present state of the Canterbury 'Association's
affairs, what he can do for the colonists.   I, however, feel myself by the task assigned me, both most
responsibly and unpleasantly situated.

JAMES CAMPBELL,
Commissioner of Crown Lands.

Report.

The Commissioner has the honor to report for the
information of His Excellency the Governor-in-Chief,
that having carefully considered what is contained
in the foregoing proceedings, and the evidence taken
in the claim No 39, he is of opinion that the said
George Hempleman made a *bonâ fide* purchase from
the Native chiefs, whose names are attached to the
deed of sale, forwarded herewith, and their tribes
assembled, of the tract of land, the boundaries of
which are given on the other side.

Recommendation.

And the Commissioner therefore respectfully begs
to recommend, in accordance with the 6th clause of
the Land Claims Ordinance, that a Crown grant
may be given to George Hempleman of two thousand
and six hundred and fifty acres of the land situated
within the block which he purchased from the
Natives.   And it is further recommended that
George Hempleman should only be allowed to select
the above extent of land in such parts of the said
block as may be approved of by the Commissioner.

JAMES CAMPBELL,
Commissioner of Crown Lands.

No. 39.   George Hempleman.

Acres 2650, the extent of land which, under the
6th clause of the Land Claims Ordinance, the Commissioners are authorised to recommend to be allowed
to a claimant.

Title.

Purchased from Tuhawaiki and other Native
chiefs, with their tribes assembled, when a deed of
sale was executed by the said chiefs and others, and
when the Natives unanimously admitted the payment
they received and the alienation of the lands, of which
the following are the boundaries :—" From Mowry
Harbor, as then called, situated at the northern
extremity of Ninety Mile Beach, between that harbor
and Flea Bay, and from thence as a base extending
15 miles inland, across Banks Peninsula, that is to
say, within a nearly square figure, three sides of
which are each 15 miles in length, including Wangooloa, now called Akaroa Harbor."

Date.

Purchase was made in 1837, but not completed
until 1839.

Requires Crown grant.

Description of Land selected by Geo. Hempleman.

Peraki Bay....................	500 acres
Flea Bay	500 ,,
Land unappropriated by the Crown, situated between German and Robinson's Bays, being within Akaroa Harbor	650 ,,
Land unappropriated by the Crown, situated at the head of what is properly called Akaroa Harbor, and extending on to and including what is usually called Barry's Bay............	1000 ,,
Total..................2650 acres	

N.B.—The Crown grants could not be filled up at Akaroa before the Commissioners and Government Surveyor had to leave Banks Peninsula, the winter being too far advanced, and the weather become too inclement for surveying operations. The surveys, however, can be made in the spring, or as soon as the weather will permit.

JAMES CAMPBELL,
Commissioner of Crown Lands.

Copy of Report on No. 39.

The Commissioner has the honor to refer His Excellency the Governor-in-Chief to the investigation, report upon, and favorable recommendation as to George Hempleman's claim, which he forwarded on the 19th March, 1852, and also to his communication dated the 3rd March last, upon the subject. To that communication, as also to the Commissioner's whole proceedings in the investigation of George Hempleman's claim, he begs again to refer His Excellency. The Commissioner has also the honor to refer to opinion, dated 15th December, 1852, given by Judge Stephen, the original forwarded to the Civil (Colonial?) Secretary, as to George Hempleman's case, in which His Honor says, " Unquestionably the contract referred to by you " (in the case submitted to the Judge for his opinion, a copy of it also forwarded to the Civil Secretary), "if confirmed by the Commissioner's reports, would take the land as found by the report out of the block granted by the Crown to the Canterbury Association."

The Commissioner having carefully considered what is contained in his proceedings above alluded to, and the evidence taken by him in support of claim No. 39, he is of opinion that the claimant made a *bonâ fide* purchase from the Native chiefs, whose names were affixed to the deed of sale in

the presence of their assembled tribes, of the tract of
land thrown in the said claim, and the Commissioner begs respectfully to recommend, in accordance
with the 6th clause of the Land Claims Ordinance,
that Crown grants should be given to claimant of
two thousand six hundred and fifty acres (2650
acres) of the land situated within the block which
claimant purchased from the Natives, as described
in claim No. 39.

> JAMES CAMPBELL,
> Commissioner Crown Lands, etc.

George Hempleman was not at all pleased with
Mr. Commissioner Campbell's report. He considered
that he had fairly bought the fifteen square miles of
country for which he dealt with Bloody Jack and the
other chiefs, and that the Government should give
him a Crown grant. He went to Wellington shortly
after the report was made public, to press his claim,
and he refused to accept the 2650 acres in compensation. The Government, as a matter of course, stood
by the report of their Commissioner. In the meantime the Government gave instructions to have the
2650 acres surveyed, and Mr. Boys was sent instructions to that effect, as will be seen by the following
letter :—

> Crown Lands Office, Christchurch,
> August 23rd, 1853.

Sir,—As I am desirous of not interfering with
surveys which it may soon be requisite to make up
the country, and regarding which I have fully com-
municated with Government, I have to request that
at your earliest convenience you will be so good as
to arrange that the lands shown beneath, situated in
Banks Peninsula, may be surveyed for Mr. George
Hempleman, of Akaroa, for whom Crown grants of
them will as usual be prepared.

Directions will be given to Mr Hempleman to

attend to and point out where, within the localities specified, he may select in blocks the extent of land pointed out, but of course you will take care that he is not allowed to interfere with or encroach upon any lands for which you are aware that Crown grants have already been recommended by me to be given to other persons, and I beg you will confine him to Government regulations as regards frontages and all. necessary roads, etc., to be reserved for Crown and public convenience.

No 1—Peraki Bay........................ 500 acres
No. 2—Flat Bay........................... 500 ,,
No. 3—Lands unappropriated by the Crown, situated between German and Robinson's Bays, and situated in the Akaroa Harbor......... .... 650 ,,
No. 4—Lands unappropriated by the Crown, situated at the head of what is properly called Akaroa Bay...... 500 ,,
No. 5—Lands unappropriated by the Crown, situated in what is usually called Barry's Bay, and, if necessary, extending from thence towards No. 4 500 ,,

Total........................... 2650 acres

The whole of these lands having been saved from any proceedings whatever of the Canterbury Association, under their first Act of Parliament, 14th August, 1850, you will pay no attention in making the necessary surveys to conveyances of any portions of them to the Church, etc , or to individuals, by the agent of the Canterbury Association.—Yours, etc.,

JAS. CAMPBELL,
Commissioner.

John C. Boys, Esq.,
    Government Surveyor.

Before Mr. Boys, however, had time to put the

work in hand he was recalled to Wellington, and
the matter was left in the hands of Mr Justin
Aylmer, the present Resident Magistrate, who was
then Mr. Boys' assistant. Mr. Aylmer, however,
resigned almost immediately afterwards, and after
some negotiations, Hempleman is said to have
signed an agreement that he would take 250 acres
where Mr. George Breitmeyer's farm is now situated,
in German Bay, and 250 acres in Barry's Bay,
where Mr. Birdling's property now is, to settle the
whole thing. This statement, however, George
Hempleman strongly denied, and the Government,
so far as we are aware, never produced any docu-
mentary evidence that he had done so. Hempleman
must have had a certain right to these properties,
for they were actually sold for him. The following
letter, written by Hempleman to Sir George Grey in
1876, shows his views on the subject, and makes it
quite clear that he had not parted with the whole of
his claim for the 500 acres in question :—

Wellington, Nov. 16th, 1876.

Sir George Grey,

Sir,—I have the honor to hand you enclosed
herein copies of two letters relating to Mr George
Hempleman's claim in Banks Peninsula. The one
from Mr James Campbell to Mr J. C. Boys,
states, as you will perceive, the whereabouts of the
estate then in the possession of the claimant ; the
other, written by J. E. Fitzgerald, Esq., and directed
to your Excellency, is not correct in every particular.
The writer states that the Commissioner neglected
or refused to examine certain individuals, whose evidence would materially effect the case for the prosecu-
tion. Such was not the case , nearly all, if not quite
all, were examined, including several English and
Native witnesses. He also states that the inhabitants of Akaroa sent in a petition against the deci-

sion of the Government.   Four of the signatures
were Messrs Aylmer, Watson, Doyley, and D. Watkins.   Mr. Golden, Collector H.M. Customs, first
started the petition, and the four above-named
persons possessing fifty-acre sections in the town of
Akaroa, were afraid that Mr. Hempleman would
select their land, hence the petition.   Mr. Fitzgerald
also states that the claimant was at that time reeling
about Christchurch intoxicated.   Mr. Hempleman
arrived in Christchurch late in the evening, and left
again early next morning, allowing very little time
to make himself known in that manner.

When Mr J. C. Boys received instructions from
James Campbell, Esq , to lay out the land for Mr.
Hempleman, he at once made arrangements with the
claimant to proceed with it.   Unfortunately as soon
as arrangements were made, Mr. Boys had to leave
for Wellington, and so it was put in the hands of
the assistant surveyor, Mr. Aylmer, son of the before-
mentioned person.   He immediately resigned his
position, and so the matter fell through.   The next.
thing the claimant heard was that he was to receive
250 acres instead.   The claimant also signed the
requisition under protest.   Sincerely trusting that
justice will at last be administered.

I have the honor to be, Sir,
Your very obedient servant,
G. HEMPLEMAN

Sir George replied to this letter from Kawau on
December 5th, stating that it was not a matter for
him to decide, and referring Hempleman to the
Government.

From his earliest residence in the Peninsula, in
the year 1835, up till some years after the arrival
of the Canterbury Pilgrims, George Hempleman
kept a very minute diary of all his doings.   A great
deal of it consists of unimportant matters, being a

record of the everyday work of the men and the state
of the weather. There are occasional entries, however, with regard to the squabbles with the Natives
and his dealings with them, that are of great interest.

He seems to have had a great dislike and con-
tempt for the Maoris He kept several Native
servants, who were practically in a state of slavery,
and he used to ill-treat these so badly, that the
severe thrashing he administered reached the ears of
the Government, and on the visit of the Britomart
to Akaroa, Captain Stanley, who was in command
of that vessel, ordered him on board, with the whole
of his dependants, and read an official letter to him,
warning him against his proceedings, and informing
him that if the cruelty were continued, steps would
be taken to punish him severely. It is not known
whether this remonstrance had very much effect, and
no one knew that he had received such a document
till it was found after his death amongst his papers.
There were, however, some excellent traits in his
character. He was twice married, his first wife
being a German, who died at Peraki and was buried
there. His second wife, who lived in German Bay
with him, suffered severely from illness, being bed-
ridden for many years, and during the whole of that
time Hempleman nursed her with a tenderness which
surprised those who knew the many asperities of his
character. He was born at Altona, the principal
city of Schleswig-Holstein, in 1799, and died on
February 13, 1880, being therefore 81 years of age
at his decease. He was a sailor by profession, and
being of humble origin, had to go before the mast,
gradually rising till in 1835 he had the command of
a whaling brig, which came here on a cruise from
Sydney. In that year he left a party of whalers in
Peraki, and on his return from Sydney in a few
months, he made his celebrated purchase from Bloody

Jack and the other Natives, particulars of which I
have already recorded.

Hempleman lived in Peraki for many years, but
afterwards removed to German Bay. The last few
years of his life were spent in the hospital, this
matter having been arranged by the Government for
his greater comfort. Whilst there he met with an
accident, which was undoubtedly the primary cause
of his death, for his iron frame would otherwise have
probably enabled him to continue his conflict with
the Government up to the present time. It appears
that a fellow resident at the hospital named McGregor, in a fit of insanity, seized hold of old Hempleman, pulled him out of bed, and threw him on the
fender, giving him a very severe shaking, and inflicting other severe injuries. From this time Hempleman never fully recovered, the last days of his life
being occupied in preparing his case, which the
Government had arranged should be heard before
the Middle Island Native Land Purchases Royal
Commission, consisting of Messrs T. H. Smith and
F. E. Nairn, who were to hold their sitting early in
March. Mr. Izard was to have appeared for Hempleman, but it was destined that before the Court sat he
should have passed away. On Friday, February 13,
when visiting his old friend M. Malmanche at his
orchard, he suddenly fell and expired whilst eating
a peach.

Hempleman was a remarkable looking man.
Firm determination was expressed in every linea-
ment, from his prominent nose to his iron chin.
His frame was a fitting adjunct to such a head,
being large, square, and bony, showing a great power
of endurance. He was well known all over the provincial district, and was very genial, being very fond
of company, and never tired of repeating his stories
of byegone days. He was very exact in these nar-
rations, seldom varying in any important point.

Like most old whalers, he was fond of a glass, and
occasionally exceeded, his favorite beverage being
rum. He was enthusiastically fond of the sport of
pig hunting, and his gaunt figure was usually accompanied by a pair of brindled bull and mastiffs, and a
long stick. When overcome he lay down for a
sleep, these dogs would not let a soul approach, and
sometimes stopped people from passing along the
road. One strange peculiarity of his was, that he
had totally forgotten his own language, not being
able to understand a single word of German, which
he must have solely spoken till he was twenty-five
or twenty-six years of age. He was continually
travelling to Wellington during the session, to urge
his claims, and his figure was nearly as well known
in the lobbies of the House as that of the Premier.
The Hon. Mr. Mantell was an earnest advocate of
Hempleman's claims, and took a great deal of
trouble in the matter. During Hempleman's visits
to Wellington he used to spend a few days with his
friends in Christchurch on the way, and during one
of these visits, whilst resting on one of the parapets
of the Victoria Bridge, he fell over into the river,
and was locked up for attempted suicide. The
police, however, soon discovered that Hempleman
was not the sort of man to swallow any quantity of
cold water voluntarily, and allowed him to proceed
on his way to Lyttelton. He bequeathed his
wretched legacy of defeated claims to a grand-
daughter, named Miss Kate Welsh, who has, we
learn, been advised that she has a claim, but understand she has no intention of prosecuting it. So
ends the story of George Hempleman's claim.

No. 4.—GEORGE HEMPLEMAN'S DIARY.

The compiler has had placed at his disposal a
number of log-books, which comprise the diary of
George Hempleman. They are yellow with age,
dating from November, 1835, at which time Captain
Hemplemau sailed from Sydney to Banks Peninsula,
on a whaling voyage, in the brig Bee. It was on
the 29th November that the brig left Pinch Gut,
where she had been lying, and, after a short anchorage at Watson's Bay, finally cleared the Heads, a
terrible thunderstorm from the southward prevailing
at the time. No damage, however, was done, and
the vessel got clear of the coast without mishap.
The usual events of a voyage followed, but on
December 20th a poor woman who had stowed herself in the fore-hold "for love of Mr Wright's
nephew," as it is quaintly put, was discovered. She
was of course sent back to Sydney by the first opportunity, which happened to be in a whaling barque
called the Governor Bourke, with 1200 barrels of oil
aboard.

There were many vessels spoken, and most of them
seem to have had a lot of oil aboard, showing how
plentiful whales were in those days. The Bee, however, seems to have been a very leaky craft, for they
had to pump ship every two or three hours. On
Monday, December 21, they got a supply of vegetables from Lord Howe's Island On January 11th,
1836, the first whale was captured. A sperm
whale that yielded thirty-one barrels was caught on
January 25, but the leak kept increasing, and on
the 30th they tried to discover where the water came
in by breaking out the run, but were unsuccessful.

On Saturday, the 6th of February, the East Cape
was made, and the ship hove to for Natives to come
aboard with pigs and potatoes. She got a good lot,
and then stood away to the southward. On Wed-

nesday, the 17th, to quote the log, " Strong breezes
and squally.   Made and shortened sail as required,
and lay-to till daylight ; then stood in for the harbor,
to come to an anchor in 4½ fathoms water, clay bottom," The harbor was in Banks Peninsula, but
whether or not it was Akaroa is a moot point.
Some persons are of opinion it was Port Levy.   At
any rate, wherever it was, they found a convenient
place for hauling the brig ashore, and, stripping off
the copper, found several bad places.   Wherever the
harbor was, it must have been close to Akaroa, for
on March 27th we read that two boats were sent to
" Wangaloor," as it is spelt, and on April 15th a
boat was sent to Pigeon Bay to cut spars for a
house.   On the 18th of April they commenced
building a house of " timber and flags," the latter,
no doubt, being raupo.   Maoris helped them at the
work.   On the 27th of the same month the American ships Friendship and Nile arrived.   From this
time whales seem to have been very plentiful, for
there are almost daily records of their being taken.
The Caroline, ship, Captain Cherry, arrived on May
20th, so the harbor, wherever it was, must have been
quite lively   Some of the whales gave them a good
deal of trouble, for we hear of the boats being stove
in, and of narrow escapes ; but fish, as they called
them, were very numerous indeed, no less than ten
being caught in one week.
     On Friday, July 15th, they finished their shore
works, and all hands were employed getting ready
the vessel for sea, and on the 16th they sailed.   They
got a number of whales outside, and returned to the
harbor to try them out.   At length, on Sunday, the
24th of the same month, the vessel put to sea.   The
voyage back to Sydney was very uneventful and quiet,
and on the 9th of August the pilot came on board,
and the same evening the good brig Bee, with her
valuable freight, dropped anchor in Sydney Harbor.

The records in Hempleman's diary of the events of 1839 are very unsatisfactory.   There are bare statements, no doubt intelligible to those who knew all about it, but to us, living so long after, many bear no coherent meaning.   Some of the most interesting passages in the diary refer to the murder of some Northern Natives, who came from Queen Charlotte's Sound, and who were working with Captain Hempleman.   It appears there were two boys named Jacky and Tommy, who worked in the whale-boats, besides several women living with Hempleman's men.   One of these women was actually killed, and Simpson in speaking of it always refers to it regretfully, because he says he could have saved her life by buying her for a blanket, if he had only known.   Bloody Jack being at feud with the Northern Natives, and knowing some of them were in Hempleman's camp, came down to kill them, and did actually kill one boy.   It appears that this boy Jacky was walking up the Peraki hill with some of the white whalers when they met the Maoris.   Jacky was carrying a basket of potatoes, which he dropped instantly and ran for dear life ; but they were too quick.   One soon overtook him, and stunned him by striking him on the back of the head with a greenstone mere mere, and Bloody Jack then shot him through the head with a musket.   The other boy, as will be seen by the diary, was ransomed, and there is a tale to the effect that Hempleman kept him stowed away in a cask for days, and so enabled him to escape the vigilance of Bloody Jack and his followers.   We append a few extracts from the log verbatim, thinking it best not to alter either spelling or composition in any particular :—

" Saturday, October 26—Fine weather throughout.   At 10 a.m. one boat's crew to the river, in search of provisions ; at 2 p.m. one out fishing ; carpenter employed as yesterday.

L

" Sunday, October 27.—Fine weather throughout.
People employed shooting in the bush, one boat's
crew at the river.

" Monday, October 28.—Fine weather throughout.
At 9 a.m. the captain went out fishing and returned
at 6 p m. with the boat's crew from the river, who
brought a good supply of pigeons ; carpenter employed as yesterday.

" Tuesday, October 29.—Fine weather throughout. One boat out fishing, but returned shortly,
the wind being too strong ; carpenter employed as
yesterday.

" Wednesday, October 30.—Strong winds throughout, from S.W. At 10 a.m. one boat's crew went
to the river ; carpenter employed as yesterday.

" Thursday, October 31.—Fine weather throughout. At 10 a.m. the boat's crew heard the report
of guns up the river, and found it to be two Maoris
from Bloody Jack, who was in Oashore Bay, with
fifteen boats. At 11 a.m. walked up the hill to
Maori Harbor, where the boat was hauled up, when
were greatly surprised at seeing about one hundred
natives, who came with the intention of killing the
boy Jacky, which they did in the most barbarous
manner, when having got to Maori Harbor, they
refused us our boat, we then walked over the hill to
the next bay, where they kept us as prisoners ;
carpenter employed as yesterday.

" Friday, November 1.—Fine weather throughout. The river party still as prisoners, being in
great suspense, not knowing whether they were to
live or die, still kept as prisoners ; carpenter employed as yesterday.

" Saturday, November 2.—Fine weather throughout. This day the river party were escorted to
Peracy Bay by fifteen of Bloody Jack's boats who
came ashore at 10 a m. and hauled their boats up,
on their first landing, they discovered the other boy

Tommy when in the act of killing him a chief named Tyroa prevented them by claiming the boy, and shortly after came upon the captain for payment for the boy, which was a new six-oared boat, which the captain consented to, knowing it to be the only way of saving the boy's life ; carpenter stowed away in the bush.

"Sunday, November 3.—Fine weather throughout. Bloody Jack and his crew still ashore, who asked the big boat as payment for the place, which the captain gave, with three new sails ; carpenter still in the bush.

"Monday, November 4—Fine weather. At 10 a.m. Bloody Jack and his gang started for Wangaloa ; at 11 a.m. one boat out fishing ; at half-past ten a m. carpenter came out of bush. This day took two white men on, who came with gang from Otago.

"Tuesday, November 5.—Fine weather throughout. One boat out all day fishing ; carpenter employed at Tonguers boat.

"Wednesday, November 6.—Fine weather throughout. One boat out all day fishing ; carpenter employed as yesterday.

"Thursday, November 7.—Strong winds from the N. One boat out fishing ; at 8 a.m. saw five of Bloody Jack's boats pass the heads bound to the southward ; carpenters and sawyers at work."

Such is the brief record existing of a tragedy that is a favorite subject for discussion amongst many of the Peninsula veterans.

No. 5.—" HEADED UP."

(CONTRIBUTED BY THE REV. J. W. STACK.)

Some of the Akaroa residents probably remember a wall-eyed old Maori, who lived at Wainui twenty years ago Among my notes I find the account of his imprisonment at Peraki, as told me by his cousin, the late Henare Pereita, of Kaiapoi. Though somewhat similar to a story already given in the published extracts from the Pireka log, it relates to quite another event. It is interesting as illustrating the merciless manner in which the managers of whaling stations sometimes behaved in those far off times, when they were obliged to take the law into their own hands. The story was as follows :—

"While I was living with my friends at Onuku, in Akaroa Harbor, I heard that a relative of ours, named Puaka, had been seized by the pakeha chief (Hempleman) of the whaling station at Pireka, and put into an empty oil cask, and headed up. In vain I begged Tukiauau and Mantai to go and demand his release ; for some reason or other they would not, so I went with Mohi Patu and our white man Jim to attempt to obtain it myself. We were all rather afraid about our errand, as the pakeha was known to be a hot-tempered man, and we were not quite sure of escaping without punishment, if our interference aroused his anger, as he had forty white men around him ready to do what he told them. On reaching the station we sent a message to say that we wished to speak to the chief. While waiting for the interview, we got into conversation with the ‘ hands ’ about the place, and learnt some particulars from them about our friend’s capture. Presently we heard calls for us to go up to the house We went up feeling very nervous and uncomfortable. Hempleman asked our business, and

when we told him that we wanted to see his Maori
prisoner, greatly to our surprise, he at once consented. Taking up a hammer that was lying near
his feet, he walked up to a great cask that stood a
few feet from his house, and knocked off the hoops
round the top of it, and removed the head, then
over-turning the barrel without any seeming regard
for its contents, he told Puaka to come out. Then
slowly and with difficulty there crawled out a horrid-
looking object, with matted hair and filth-besmeared
body. The stench from the cask was quite over-
powering, and we all shrunk back from it. Then
Hempleman told us to carry the man to the front
of his house, but only Mohi could venture near him,
and he did so by holding his breath. We could not
restrain our tears at the sight of our friend, and I
went for some water to wash off the filth ; but it was
long before we got him anything like clean, and then
his captor came and fastened him by the leg to an
iron bar at the side of the house. When Puaka
was able to speak to us, I asked him what he had
done to incur such a terrible punishment. He said,
' I happened to be at Wairau when the pakehas
attacked Rauparaha, and the Wairau massacre
followed. I was so alarmed at what I witnessed on
that occasion, that I hurried down the coast with all
speed, to escape the consequences that I feared would
follow from the pakeha's vengeance, but without re-
vealing to any one on the way the cause of my hasty
flight It was not till I reached Otago that I dared
to open my lips about what happened at Wairau.
A stay of three months in that far off place calmed
my fears, and I prepared quietly to return home ;
but on my way to Akaroa I passed along the coast
from Wairewa, instead of going up the valley. On
reaching Pireka I was recognised by the hands, and
taken before Hempleman, who said that he had
lately heard of my hurrying past him without giving

the alarm, and as he, in common with the Maori
inhabitants of the Peninsula, lived in constant dread
of being surprised by Rauparaha and his northern
·warriors, he vowed to punish me in such a way as
would deter any other Maori from copying my
example. Whereupon he took the head out of an
empty oil cask, placed food and water in it, and then
put me into it and fastened the lid. The only air
and light I could get was through the bung-hole.
Here I have been kept for many weeks, never allowed
to get out, or to have my cell cleaned, the head of
the cask being occasionally removed, when it was
necessary to supply me with food and water. Having heard my cousin's piteous tale, I told him a plan
I had devised for securing his escape, since Hempleman positively refused to let him go. I said that
when he felt a little stronger he should ask to be
allowed to join a boat's crew , and as it was the
practice for the crews to pull out to sea very often,
on returning to land somewhere along the shores of
the bay he would soon have an opportunity of getting into the woods unobserved. When once clear
of the station he was to make for a particular point
opposite Onuku, and there light a fire. Having
given him these instructions, and seeing that he was
fast recovering from the effects of his confinement in
such cramped quarters, I returned home. Not long
afterwards I observed the smoke of the signal fire
agreed upon between us, and at once paddled my
canoe over to meet the fugitive. I learnt from him
that he owed his liberty to having acted on my
advice. At first we feared pursuit, but Hempleman
took no further notice of the matter, and we afterwards met as very good friends."

No. 6.—THE FRENCH SETTLEMENT OF AKAROA.

In this and following numbers an account is given of the foundation of the French Colony in Akaroa, and the causes that led to it. The subject is a most interesting one, and so it has been endeavored to procure information from every available source. This number is taken from "Odd Chapters from New Zealand History," originally published in the *New Zealander*, and there entitled

"THE NANTO BORDELAISE COMPANY."

"Though, perchance, somewhat out of chronological order, the attempt to form a French settlement in the Middle Island may follow, pertinently, in these papers, the narration of the intention to found a semi-French kingdom in these Islands. That the French Government had serious intentions of establishing colonies in the South Pacific, and a penal colony in New Zealand, is apparent from the angry debates in the French Chamber of Deputies on the 27th, 28th, and 29th of May, 1844, when M. Guizot, the Minister of Foreign Affairs, declared that after ' repeatedly repudiating the sovereignty of New Zealand, the British Government was induced, by the proceedings of a rich and powerful company (the New Zealand Company), to adopt measures by which the acquisition of that sovereignty had been completed, at a time when vessels from France were on their voyage to New Zealand for the like purpose.' M. Guizot was, however, misinformed, as the sovereignty was proclaimed prior to the despatch of the vessels mentioned.

"In August, 1838, a Captain L'Anglois, the master of a French whaler, purchased, he asserted, from the Natives on Banks Peninsula, a block of land defined in the claim as follows :—' All Banks

Peninsula, with the exception of the Bay of Hiku-
raki and Oihoa on the south, and Sandy Beach
north of Port Cooper ; the supposed contents 30,000
acres.' The block included the whole of the head of
the Akaroa Harbor and the site of the present town.
Two deeds exist, in the French language, purporting
to convey this cession of land, but they were *probably* not executed—but of this there is no certainty
—until the return of Captain L'Anglois and M. de
Belligny in 1840, after the signing of the Treaty of
Waitangi ; neither was there any evidence, either
Native or European, that such a purchase had been
completed in 1838, save that of one George Fleuret,
who deposed to the belief ' that an agreement was
then made by Captain L'Anglois for the purchase of
some quantity of land.' Fleuret was desirous of
remaining on the Peninsula when the Cachelot (the
vessel in which he was serving) went away ; but on
the captain's remonstrance with him, that he could
not stay there alone, and that he (the captain)
intended to return, he continued the voyage, and
returned with the other immigrants in the Comte
de Paris in August, 1840. On his consenting to
return, on his first voyage, the captain showed him
' a paper,' which he said was a contract or agreement,
signed by a native named Chigarry, (?) for the disposal of, or promise to dispose of, land to him
(Captain L'Anglois) upon his return to New Zealand.' He also added in his evidence that he saw
the captain ' give some pantaloons and cloaks to the
Native Chigarry, and others, which he understood
was on account of the payment he had promised the
Natives for land.' The full amount of the purchase
money, in kind, was to have been £240, of which
amount only £6 was paid by the captain, in 1838.
Upon the captain's return to France, he ceded his
right and title to his reputed purchase to a company,
consisting ' of two mercantile houses at Nantz, two

at Bordeaux, and three gentlemen of Paris, who
formed a company called the Nanto-Bordelaise
Compagnie, reserving to himself an interest to the
amount of one-fifth in the said company, and giving
up the deed of sale from the Natives, as his subscrip-
tion of 6000 francs to become a partner to the
amount of one-fifth in the company.' There is a
certified copy of this deed, which is of some length,
to be found in the proceedings of the New Zealand
Company, but it carries no native signature or mark,
as would have been the case had it been completed.
We are told by M. S. de Belligny, who styled himself the company's agent, that the object of the
expedition was 'the colonisation of the Middle
Island of New Zealand, and for fishing upon its
coasts, and that the company was formed before it
possessed the slightest knowledge of the intention of
the English Government to take possession of the
said island.' A similar amount of ignorance, however, was not manifested on the English side of the
Channel, as the *New Zealand Journal* in February
of the same year, prior to the departure of Captain
L'Anglois on his second voyage, remarks : ' If the
French Government should send her political prisoners to British New Zealand, let it be clearly
understood that they are free the instant they set
foot on British land.   France can exercise no jurisdiction over them there, and supposing the *projet*
should ever ripen into action, which is very improbable—should the sons of France accept the hand of
friendship, which we are quite sure will be held out
to them, the New Zealand community will be the
better of their peculiar intelligence and skill.' This,
it should be remembered, was a comment on an
article in the *Journal du Harve* on the question
whether the Middle Island was a suitable place for
the *deportation* of criminals, the company having
agreed to cede to the Government a portion of their

acquired territory for this purpose—it being in ' an excellent position for defence as well as climate.' The company had a capital of one million francs (£42,000), a sixth of which was only paid up, but the Company had agreed to cede to the French Government one-fifth of its territory ' to establish a penal settlement.' Accordingly the ship Comte de Paris sailed from Rochefort, commanded by Captain L'Anglois. Louis Philippe was an interested party in the company, and gave ' a grant of money and picked men from the Royal Navy as a subsidy to the expedition. The emigrants, who were 63 in number, although stated in the *Journal des Debats* to number 100, comprising 30 men, 11 women, and 22 children, complained while on board, and after arrival, of the treatment they received on their passage—as other immigrants have since that early date so frequently done. But those French pioneers had certainly a considerable reason for thus murmuring, for although the good ship Comte de Paris had a complete whaling crew—men enough to man four six-oared boats and work the ship at the same time,—the captain made the emigrants work in the same manner as the crew, with the exception of their not being compelled to go aloft and furl or make sail. The immigrants on landing were to have been ' furnished with the necessaries required by the climate, and the implements necessary for the carrying out the mission they were commissioned to fulfil, and to have provisions to serve for twelve months, counting from the time of landing, and five acres of land per adult.' Those conditions, it appears, were not carried out in their integrity.

" Five days previous to the arrival of the Comte de Paris, H.M.S. Britomart arrived at the Peninsula, and took possession of the island in the name of the Crown : whether legally or otherwise is a moot point, as the French flag had been planted on the Penin-

sula in 1838 by Commodore Cuille, of the Heroine.
Three days later the French frigate L'Aube, commanded by Commodore Lavaud, arrived, and on
August the 13th, two days later, the immigrants
also, having been on board from the latter end of
February. Among the stores brought were six long
24-pounders, which, upon Captain Stanley's remon-
strating with Commodore Lavaud, were not allowed
to be landed. Mr. Robinson, who came from the
Bay of Islands in another vessel, was left there as
magistrate, and from the *Gazette* we learn that the
Commodore was particularly hospitable, and offered
to send his carpenter on shore to build a house for
Mr. Robinson, and insisted upon that gentleman's
living on board the L'Aube during her stay in the
waters of the Peninsula, which offer, of course, was
gratefully accepted until the completion of the magis-
terial residence. On the 19th the immigrants landed
in ' a sheltered, well-chosen part of the bay, where
they could not interfere with any one,' and commenced, with the characteristic industry of the
French workman, to erect houses and cultivate land ;
and so successful was *one* of the cultivators, that the
Constitutionnel of the following year, commenting on
the progress of the Colony, stated that one of the
colonists, who had planted himself a league from
Akaroa, had, with the aid of his wife, from two acres
and a half of land, cleared, in five months, 1500f.
by the sale of vegetables. The English inhabitants
of the Peninsula, at the time of the landing of the
French immigrants, amounted to 84 adults, and
their children, so from this source the 1500f. would
probably partially come. At the end of the year the
immigrants had not procured any stock, but were
living on preserved and salt meats, with what vegetables they could get from their ' small gardens,'
while the commodore of the L'Aube had commenced
building a store for them, to protect their property

from the weather. It must be remembered that the
frigate stayed at Akaroa for a lengthened period,
and the Commodore thereby arrogated to himself the
domination of the settlement, but avowed most distinctly to Captain Hobson that he ' disclaimed any
national intrusion on the part of his Government,
but he supported the claims of the company as private individuals, asserting this to be the only *bonâ
fide* purchase of that district which had been made
from the Natives.' It was at this time (November,
1841) that the Governor made the proposal that the
company should be given similar terms to the New
Zealand Company, and put in possession of a block
of land, in proportion to their outlay of capital, in
the extreme northern district of the North Island,
' in the district of Kataia, where there is a good
harbor, with an abundance of fine land with an undu-
lating surface, well adapted for vineyards.' This
proposal was not adopted, and early in the following
year (1842) Monsieur Maillères arrived in England
to make arrangements with the Government, with a
view to the settlement of the claim and the company's title ; when the ' Colonial Land and Emigra-
tion Commissioners' found that an expenditure by
the company of £11,685 had been incurred,
including, of course, the subsidy obtained from
Louis Philippe. In 1845 Lord Stanley authorised
an award should be given to the company of 30,000
acres, their claim not having been brought before the
Commissioners appointed to inquire into land claims.
    " This paper and narrative cannot be better con-
cluded than by quoting a paragraph from Mr.
Mackay, in his second volume on Southern Native
affairs :—' The New Zealand Company purchased
the claims of the Nanto-Bordelaise Company, and,
in virtue of other subsequent arrangements, whatever
lands the New Zealand Company possessed have
reverted to the Crown ; but through all these pro-

ceedings the original question as to what extent the
Native title has been extinguished by the French
Company has never been decided.'

" After the cession of the territory to the New
Zealand Company, the French Government offered
to take the emigrants free of charge to Tahiti, and
give them the same amount of property as they
possessed in New Zealand, but they all declined the
offer."

THE STORY OF THE FRENCH COLONISATION OF AKAROA.

As a fitting narrative to follow the last, the compiler has selected the following account of the French
settlement, principally written from information furnished by Mr. Waeckerlie, one of the original settlers,
who came in the Comte de Paris.

About the year 1820, the adventurous seamen
who had hitherto captured the whale in the Northern
Ocean, found that the fish were fast decreasing in
number, and turned longing eyes to the vast waters
of the South Pacific, which voyagers had told them
swarmed not only with many varieties of the whale
tribe found in the north, but also with the huge
sperm, whose oil was of great value, as well as the
spermaceti found in its head. A few soon ventured,
and their good reports and great success induced
many to follow their example. At first the Cape of
Good Hope was chosen as the centre of the operations of those daring men, whose lives were in continual peril, but whose profits were enormous ; but
year by year they fished further and further, and the
coasts of Australia and New Zealand were soon
made the scene of their dangerous avocation.

About 1835, before the first representative of
England (Captain Hobson) had taken up his residence in Auckland, an adventurous French mariner,
named Captain L'Anglois, came on a whaling cruise

to these seas. Amongst the many harbors that he
visited was the beautiful Bay of Akaroa, the perfect
safety of whose sheltered waters went straight to the
heart of the rough seaman, after the fierce gales he
had encountered in the stormy southern seas. The
luxuriant vegetation that everywhere fringed the
inlets, showed that the soil was of exceeding fruit-
fulness ; the mighty pines that towered above their
meaner fellows gave promise of a vast supply of timber ; whilst the innumerable kakas, pigeons, and
other native birds, that woke the echoes of the bush
with their harmonies and discords, and the fish that
swarmed in the waters of the bay, showed that an
abundant supply of nutritious food would always be
obtainable. So charmed was Captain L'Anglois
with the tranquillity of the spot, that, with a true
Frenchman's love of France, he coveted it for his
country, and determined to found a colony on this
scene of primeval loveliness. It was in the year
1837 that he first had an opportunity of taking the
premier steps in this direction, by purchasing all that
part of the Peninsula from the Maoris which lies
between Peraki and the Akaroa Heads. Mr
Waeckerlie did not know the name of the chief from
whom Captain L'Anglois purchased the land, and
the price paid for it, but doubtless the amount was
a comparatively small one.

In 1838 Captain L'Anglois returned to France,
and on his arrival he told some of his countrymen of
the purchase he had made, and the result was the
formation of a company to colonise his estate. The
company appears to have been encouraged by the
French Government, for an old ship of war called
the Comte de Paris was lent to Captain L'Anglois
to take out any persons who might be desirous of
settling on his land, and another armed ship, called
the L'Aube, was sent out to New Zealand before-
hand, under the charge of Commodore Lavaud, to

protect the colonists on their arrival.   All this, however, was done quietly, for the English had already
settled in parts of the islands, though New Zealand
was not proclaimed a British Colony till 1841.   It
was not till the middle of the year 1839 that the
company was formed, under the name of the Nantes ·
Bordelaise Company.   The principal people taking
an active part were Captain L'Anglois, and his
brother, M. Jacques L'Anglois, and M.M. St. Croix
and Eugene de Belligny.   In August, 1839, the
company advertised for emigrants in Havre de Gras,
offering a free passage and the occupation of five
acres of land on arrival, which would become the
freehold of the occupier in five years, if cultivated
within that time, but if not cultivated it would
revert to the company.   Each emigrant was also promised provisions sufficient to last eighteen months
after landing in the settlement.   There does not seem
to have been much enthusiasm shown, for it was the
1st of January, 1840, before some thirty persons left
Havre in a steamer bound to Rochefort, whence the
Comte de Paris was to sail for the new colony.
After an eight days' passage, they arrived at Rochefort only to find that the Comte de Paris was not
nearly ready for sea.   On the 8th of March, 1840,
everything was ready for a start.   A good many
more emigrants had joined at Rochefort, so that at
that time there were 65 on board, which, with the
officers and crew, made the total number of souls on
board the Comte de Paris 105   There were six
Germans amongst the emigrants.   M. St. Croix de
Belligny, who is, it is said, living in Auckland, acted
as agent for the company, and by his great affability
and skill he appears to have won universal goodwill.
There were no stock on board the vessel, not even so
much as a cat or dog, but there were choice collec-
tions of all sorts of seeds, and a number of carefully
selected grape vines.

The start was a most unfortunate one, for the
steamer that towed the vessel out missed the channel, and the Comte de Paris stuck in the mud, and
had to be lightened of part of her cargo before she
could be got off. However, on the 19th of March
these difficulties were surmounted, and a fair wind
soon took the vessel out of sight of France The
first part of the passage was not eventful, but was
very uncomfortable, for the Comte de Paris not only
sailed very slowly, but steered very badly. The
weather, too, was very rough, and all on board were
glad when a short stay was made at an island in the
tropics (probably one of the Cape de Verdes), where
fresh provisions, including a bountiful supply of
bananas, were procured Four months after starting,
when off the coast of Tasmania, a terrific storm of
thunder and lightning was experienced. The lightning first struck the main topgallant and topmasts,
and they both carried away. The seamen were terrified at the catastrophe, and great confusion ensued.
Immediate orders were given to take all sail off the
mizen mast, but fortunately they were not immediately obeyed, or there would have been great loss
of life, for a second flash struck the mizzen mast,
and it carried away about eight feet from the deck,
and the vessel broaching to in the trough of the sea,
nearly capsized. Captain L'Anglois and his crew
were, however, equal to the emergency. They cut
away the wreck and rigged jury masts, and a month
later they were off the Peninsula. Here two of the
emigrants died, and, as their friends were desirous
that they should be buried on land, the vessel
anchored in Pigeon Bay, where the remains of the
unfortunate colonists were interred on the beach. It
was a primitive burial, and all trace of the graves
has long since been swept away. Captain L'Anglois
was anxious, before entering Akaroa Harbor, to
ascertain if Commodore Lavaud had arrived there,

and taken possession of the place, as previously
arranged ; so he despatched a whaleboat from
Pigeon Bay for that purpose. Four days later the
boat returned with the distressing intelligence that
there was no sign of the frigate   On the 14th of
August the Comte de Paris sailed from Pigeon Bay,
and anchored at Akaroa Heads on the 15th, and
dispatched another boat up the harbor in search of
the lagging Commodore. This time the search was
successful, for they found the vessel had arrived, and
the frigate's launch was sent to tow the Comte de
Paris up the harbor. Very lucky it was for those
on board that such was the case, for there was a heavy
sea running at the Heads, and one of the flukes of
the anchor had broken, and the vessel had drifted
close to the rocks. However, the frigate's boat soon
had her in tow, and once inside the Heads all difficulties were passed, and the following morning found
her safe anchored off the future town of Akaroa.
All on board were delighted and astonished at the
delightful prospect, and the colonists were determined
not to spend another night on board the ship, so all
the spare sails and canvas were taken ashore, tents
were hastily rigged, and the wearied voyagers reposed
that night where the *Akaroa Mail* office at present
stands.   The morning of the 17th was calm and
beautiful, and the colonists were pleasantly awakened
at the first dawn of day by the notes of innumerable
birds.
   A strange circumstance had been noticed by the
new arrivals in coming up the harbor   When the
Comte de Paris was towed past Green's Point, near
where Mr W. B. Tosswill's residence now stands,
all on board saw a small group of men surrounding a
flagstaff, from which flew gaily in the morning breeze
" the Union Jack of Old England." Such a sight
naturally surprised and disturbed the new comers, but
they were told it meant nothing, but was merely a
                              N

piece of vain glory on the part of two or three
Englishmen who happened to be whaling in the
vicinity. The real facts of the case, however, were
by no means so unimportant as was represented. It
appears that Commodore Lavaud, on his way from
England, touched at Auckland, and that whilst his
vessel was lying in the calm waters of the Waitemata, Captain Hobson, who then represented British
interests in the north, though New Zealand had not
yet been made an English Colony, entertained him
right royally. It appears that in an unguarded
moment the Commodore let out the secret of the
French expedition to Akaroa, and what was more
injudicious, spoke with rapture of the beauty of the
Akaroa Harbor, the fertility of the soil, and other
natural advantages. Now Captain Hobson was a
man of action and of foresight. He saw that New
Zealand had a great future before it, and was anxious
that when it was made a jewel of the British Crown,
it should be without a flaw. He then called in
stratagem to his aid, and whilst the gay Frenchmen
were enjoying themselves ashore after their weary
voyage, a small brig of war, named the Britomart,
was secretly despatched, under the charge of Mr
Robinson, who was instructed to make the best of
his way to Akaroa, and if possible hoist the English
flag there before the French arrived   Meanwhile,
Commodore Lavaud appears to have been in no hurry
to reach his destination, for he knew the sailing
qualities of the Comte de Paris, and did not think
she could arrive here till the end of August. Besides,
the company was good, and he knew Akaroa was
only a beautiful wilderness at the best, so it was
early in August before the L'Aube sailed down the
east coast and passed through Cook's Strait on her
way to the Peninsula. Meanwhile, Mr Robinson
and his expedition had not had a very good time of
it, and it was with very desponding hearts that on

the 14th of August they reached Akaroa, for they
feared the French must have been before them and
taken possession of the place.   What was their
delight, then, to find that no foreign keel had
ploughed the waters of the bay.   No time was lost,
the English flag was at once hoisted, and the country
claimed for the British Crown.   It was not a moment
too soon, however, for the following morning Commodore Lavaud arrived, just a few hours too late.
But the new colonists knew nothing of this.   The
Commodore held a conference with Mr. Robinson,
and it was agreed that whilst the French man-of-war
remained in the harbor, the English flag should not
be hoisted, and the fact of their having taken possession before the arrival of the French be kept a secret,
for fear it should lead to disturbances between the
English and the new comers.   The secret was well
kept, and though of course many rumors were current,
it was not till years afterwards that the arrivals by
the Comte de Paris were aware that they were living
in an English, and not a French Colony.   As soon
as possible after the landing the land was allotted to
the settlers.   As before stated, the bush came down
almost to the water's edge in many places, so there
was little clear land.   It was therefore arranged to
divide the land facing the sea into $2\frac{1}{2}$ acre blocks,
giving one to each emigrant, and to let them select
their other $2\frac{1}{2}$ acres where they liked, it being the
condition of the tenure that the land should be cultivated within five years of the arrival, or revert to
Captain L'Anglois.   The colonists all avoided selecting land in the bush, but took up the clearings which
they found here and there, which were then covered
with toi toi.   They lived altogether in the tents for
about a month, but by that time they nearly all
removed to the wharès they had built on their respective sections.   The six Germans who were amongst
the emigrants found that they could not get their

sections altogether in Akaroa, so they determined to
explore Captain L'Anglois' estate further. They
found a beautiful bay with plenty of clear land a little
higher up the harbor, and asked permission of the
Commodore to locate themselves there. Permission
was granted, five acres were parcelled out for each,
and the bay was christened with the name it still
bears of German Bay. The Germans built a great
V hut, 40ft long by 30ft wide, of timber and rushes,
with proper divisions, and in this they passed a very
pleasant winter. Commodore Lavaud built a magazine in Akaroa, just where the Court House now
stands, and this was used for the storage of provisions and tools, and also for a hospital. Everything went peacefully along, the seeds germinated
well, the vines flourished, and the colonists were
content with their prospects. The French settlement was of course under French law, which was
administered by Commodore Lavaud. Mr Robinson
was the English Resident Magistrate, but his office
was almost a sinecure.

REMINISCENCES OF THE FIRST FIVE YEARS.

It has been previously related that a Mr. Green
resided, when the French colonists arrived, at the
point near Mr. Tosswill's, where the British flag was
seen flying by the new arrivals. Mr. Green was in
charge of some six or eight head of cattle belonging
to Mr. W. B. Rhodes. Mr. Rhodes was well
acquainted with New Zealand, and had had numerous transactions, both with the earliest settlers and
the Natives. Some six months before the French
arrived, he had been in Wellington, and from thence
he went to Sydney, then the most settled part of
Australasia, and had purchased a number of the
best cattle he could procure, which he brought over
in a vessel belonging to him, and placed in various
localities under the charge of persons in his employ-

ment. Mr Rhodes was one of those who, at a very
early period, recognised the vast capabilities of these
islands, and foresaw that in the time to come they
would support a large population, and his foresight
was deservedly rewarded later on, by the amassing
of a very large fortune. These cattle were not
allowed to be sold at any price, and were simply
allowed to increase as fast as possible. The cows
were not milked, the calves running with them, and
one can imagine with what great longing for milk,
beef,· and butter, they were viewed by the colonists,
who at that time had not a single head of their own.
Mr. Green did something else besides looking after
the cattle—he used to purchase any grog he could
from the whaling vessels that visited the port, and,
as there was no hotel, it was a standing joke with
the colonists to say that they were going to have a
drink of milk at Mr. Green's, when they went there
in search of something which they considered far
more exhilarating. In a couple of years Mr. Green
left Mr Rhodes to start an hotel, and was succeeded
by Mr. Reid, and a short time after Mr. Joseph
Rhodes came to superintend the place, and also
another in Flea Bay, where some more cattle had
been placed. He sold the first cow, which realised
the enormous sum (for an ordinary milker) of £43.
Such was the first start of dairy farming in Akaroa.
Cows were, however, soon to become more plentiful.

In 1841, M. St. Croix de Belligny went to Wellington about matters connected with the new settlement, and to get a supply of money. Towards the
end of the following year he went to Sydney, and
brought back a bull and ten or twelve cows, and also
one little entire horse, the first that ever set foot in
Akaroa. This last excited the extreme admiration
of the Maoris, and they coveted him exceedingly.
This was rather a good thing for the French Association, for the third and last payment for the land

was then due to the Natives, and the horse was made
a part of it. It may here be mentioned that the
payment for the land was nearly all in kind, very
little money passing. The Comte de Paris brought
out a large number of gaudy old faded uniforms,
gold lace, cocked hats, and other trumpery rubbish,
which was eagerly accepted as ''utu'' for the land
by the unsophisticated aboriginals. One must not
forget to mention, however, that in this last payment
was included a small schooner, built by Mr Sinclair,
for which the Association gave that gentleman two
hundred acres in Pigeon Bay, in that inlet now
known as Holmes' Bay, where the property of Mr.
Holmes is at present situated. M. de Belligny,
like Mr. Rhodes, let his cattle go on increasing at
first, but on leaving the Colony in 1845, he sold
them at the lowest price he could possibly afford,
which was from £20 to £25 per head, and very
glad indeed were the settlers to get them. The
colonists, however, had had both milk, butter, and
beef before this, though they had had to pay a good
price for them. The first steer calved in Akaroa by
M. de Belligny's cows was killed in 1844, some
eighteen months after the cattle arrived from Sydney. Mr Waeckerlie was the butcher, and every
pound of the beef brought 2s. 6d. per pound, and
more would have been gladly given, for fresh beef is
never so well appreciated as by those who have been
years without it. The first milk and butter came
from Pigeon Bay. Messrs. Hay and Sinclair came
over to that place in 1841 from Wellington, and
brought some cattle with them, and they found a
market for all the butter they could make, at from
2s. 6d. to 3s per pound. The price was afterwards
lowered to 2s , and Mr. Hay used to walk over
about once a week with twenty or thirty pounds,
which he always disposed of at that price.

Mr. Green was the first hotel keeper ; after he

left Mr. Rhodes he built a commodious hotel at
Green's Point, and procured a license The building
was a very substantial one, 40ft. by 30ft., and the
timber for it was cut by Mr. Waeckerlie.   It was
only one storey high, but most conveniently arranged,
and was very well patronised, more especially when a
whaler came in, when there were "high jinks"
indeed.   The building was afterwards bought by Mr.
George Tribe, and taken by him to Lyttelton, and
placed on Norwich Quay, where it was burnt down
in 1854 or 1855.   After selling this building, Mr.
Green bought a piece of land from M. Belligny.
agent for the French Association, and put up
another and larger hotel in the more central position
now occupied by Armstrong's Buildings, just opposite the present Government Wharf.   As soon,
however, as circumstances warranted it, there was a
French hotel, M. de Belligny's servant being the
proprietor.   The building he put up for that purpose
is the house where Mr C. M. Henning at present
lives, and, like Mr. Green's, his enterprise was a
most successful one.

  There was of course no grain of any kind grown
the first year or two, and the colonists were depen-
dent on their supplies from outside sources.   They
were supplied in this manner.   Once a year the
French man-of-war on the station visited either
Valparaiso or Sydney, and came back with what
was required.   On the first of these trips, in 1841,
the vessel was delayed by contrary winds, and the
colonists were in consequence reduced to sore straits
for flour, rice, and other farinaceous food.   Tea, too,
was at a premium, but the latter was certainly a
luxury, and many supplied its place with the outa-
whai or manakau.   Their potatoes, too, were not
yet fit for digging, so that they really were incon-
venienced, though of course there was no danger of
starvation, with the bush teeming with birds and the

harbor with fish, in addition to their own stores.
However, news came that a whaler was in at Port
Cooper, and it was immediately determined to send
round an expedition to procure the much longed for
flour. M. Fleury took the command, and manned
a whale boat with five or six men and started for
Port Cooper. The winds were, however, peculiarly
adverse, and he never got any further than the Long
Lookout Point, for the sea was too heavy and
threatening, and he was afraid the boat would be
swamped. After making the most persevering
attempts for two or three days, the party had to
take their boat into the nearest bay, and walk home
to Akaroa. Very weary indeed were the adventurers
when they started, and the walk through the then
almost unexplored country was a very rough one, so
that on their arrival back they were nearly dead with
fatigue. No one ever saw or heard anything after
that of the whaler in Port Cooper, but a few days
afterwards the man-of war arrived, bringing abundance of the much-coveted stores to the Colony.
From that time the supply of flour never ran short,
for in 1843 and 1844 every one began to grow their
own wheat. Little patches were sown in the clearings, and gave the most enormous returns, eighty
bushels per acre being considered only an ordinary
crop. One piece of five acres, on the spur between
Akaroa and German Bay, gave a most enormous
yield, and, from what was then considered its vast
size and extraordinary prolificness, it was the admiration of the colonists Potatoes, too, did exceedingly
well, and soon became very plentiful.
    The same frigate did not always stop on the sta-
tion. Two years after the landing, another frigate,
commanded by Captain du Boissy, arrived to relieve
the L'Aube. It was optional with Commodore
Lavaud whether he should go Home in his own or
take charge of the new arrival, but he liked Akaroa,

and chose the latter course. Two years later, in 1844, Commodore Berard arrived in another vessel. He was the senior officer to Commodore Lavaud, and so could do as he pleased, and, although Lavaud wished to remain, he sent him Home. Commodore Lavaud does not appear to have been at all well liked. He was too much of a martinet, and his decisions were in many cases extremely arbitrary. His successor was a very different man, and by his great kindness and general ability soon won the good will of the settlers. Mr. Robinson, the English Magistrate, too, left in 1842 or 1843, and was succeeded by Mr. John Watson. Mr Robinson's house was where Wagstaff's Hotel now stands. He bought five acres from the French Association there, and put up a dwelling-house which was used as an R.M. Court. Mr Robinson was not at all liked by the colonists, but his successor, Mr Watson, was universally esteemed both by English and French for his great impartiality in the administration of justice, and his great general kindliness.

When the settlers arrived, there were not many Maoris in the neighborhood of Akaroa   It is true there were pas at Onuku, Wainui, and Tikao Bay, but these had only some fifty or sixty inhabitants altogether, and they were a most weak, harmless lot, whose leading vice appeared to be the habit of begging incessantly for everything they saw.   In 1843, however, there were a good number in Port Levy, Pigeon Bay, Little River, and Kaiapoi, and it was then first reported that these were going to unite and make an attack upon the infant Colony during the absence of the frigate at Valparaiso for stores. Of course, with the man-of-war in harbor, the colonists knew they were quite safe, but they did not by any means like the idea of being attacked whilst she was absent. However, one thing was certain, the vessel must go for stores, and so the

o

best possible arrangements were made for defence, in case of an attack being made. A garden had been established at French Farm by Commodore Lavaud, for the growth of vegetables for his crew, and here fifteen or sixteen of the sailors were left, under the command of a quartermaster. Some five or six more men, all that could possibly be spared from the ship, were stationed at Akaroa. Their precautions, however, were not confined to this, for it was determined to erect three block-houses as places of retreat in case the Maoris came. The sites for these block-houses were selected as follows :—Where Bruce's Hotel now stands, near the beach just at the back of the present Town Hall, and in German Bay. They were very strongly built, the upright timbers being 8ft. by 8ft., whilst the planking was of black pine, four inches thick. They were two storeys high, the upper storey overlapping the lower, as we see in the old English houses in Chester and elsewhere, in order that those above could fire down on any Maoris who attempted to fire the building below. A ditch 4ft. wide at the bottom and 8ft. at top was also dug round the walls, the earth out of which was made into a sloping bank against the sides of the house, and the ditch was filled with water. The only admittance to these houses was by a drawbridge across the moat, and thence by a ladder to a door in the upper storey, there being no entrance at all from below. When the drawbridge was up and the ladder raised, those within were nearly perfectly safe from any attack the Maoris could have made, for the 4in. boards would stop any bullet from an ordinary gun. As a matter of course there were loopholes here and there for the defenders to fire from if the place were besieged.

These block-houses were never used but once, and that was during the absence of the ship, when the news was brought that some 250 Natives were coming from the North to attack them. The rumour spread rapidly, and the more cautious removed their wives and children and more precious goods into the block-houses, and slept there at night. Sentinels were also posted to give notice of the Maoris' approach, and the men were drilled and armed with a carbine, cutlass, and two pistols each. At last the word came that from 60 to 100 strange Maoris were actually on their way from Pigeon Bay. All the people then living in German Bay went into the block-house, and when the Maoris found them so well prepared, they of course announced that they came as friends only. They passed on and went into Akaroa, meeting the leaders of the colonists near the present site of the Town Hall. They announced that they came not as foes, but as friendly visitors, and were accordingly welcomed and had some food given them, after partaking of which they entertained their hosts by giving one of their war dances in grand style, and then they went on to the Kaik at Onuku. As a whole the colonists behaved very well during their trial ; but one gentleman caused much amusement. This was rather a diminutive Frenchman, whose counsels were of blood and thunder before the Maoris arrived. He argued that it was no good going in for half measures ; that they must put their foot down and show the Natives what they could do. He scorned the idea of anything approaching a compromise, as degrading to a band of resolute Europeans, and said if they were only firm the savages must yield. When the Maoris really did came, however, a change came over the spirit of the heroic man, and as he gazed at the fierce tattooed faces, sinewy limbs, and great bulk of the Native warriors, his face grew whiter and whiter, and at last he was unable to bear their terrible aspect any longer, and sneaked off into the block-house, much to the amusement of his comrades.

He was the only man that showed the white feather ;
but the week the Maoris stopped was a time of
anxiety, and the greatest possible caution was exercised, for all feared that the least relaxation of
watchfulness would be the signal for an attack.
One night Mr. Green fired a shot, and produced
quite a panic, every one fancying the struggle had
come at last. However, after a week's peaceful
sojourn at Onuku, Wainui, and Tikao Bay, the
strange Natives went away, most of them going
back *viâ* Little River

There was one pleasant custom observed during
these early days, which was, that every family gave
a feast to the rest of the colonists annually. These
meetings were pleasant ones indeed ; whilst the
older colonists related their experiences to each other,
the younger danced and made love in just the same
manner as they do now-a-days. At the end of the
five years the colonists all got their five acres. Many
of them had never fulfilled the conditions laid down
by the French Association, but that was not allowed
to stand in the way, and an English Crown grant
was promised and given to all who applied.

There were sometimes disputes between the French
officers, and one of these culminated in a duel, which
was fought in the present Lavaud street, Akaroa, in
the end of 1845 or beginning of 1846. The combatants were the Commissioner and Dr. Renaut, the
doctor-in-chief of the French man-of-war Le Rhin,
which Commodore Berard commanded. The people
on shore were of opinion that something most extraordinary must be going on, for the combatants,
accompanied by their friends, went round the place
early on the morning of the duel, discharging every
little liability due to the townspeople. The duel was
fought on the sandy beach opposite where Mrs.
Scott's shop at present stands. The distance (25
paces, was carefully and solemnly measured by the

seconds in the presence of a group of officers, and
the weapons, which were pistols, were carefully loaded
and presented to the duellists. Lots were then
drawn for the first fire, and the Commissioner won.
Taking a steady aim, he fired, but the cap was
defective, and did not ignite the priming. Dr.
Renaut then raised his pistol and fired low. The
bullet cut the trousers and grazed the right thigh of
the Commissioner, but did no further damage. No
doubt irritated by his narrow escape, the Commissioner called out angrily to reload, but the seconds
declared that wounded honour was fully satisfied, and
refused to allow the combat to proceed further.
There was another circumstance which also tended
to stop further hostilities. The Commodore was of
course as well aware of what was going to take place
as any officer in the Le Rhin, but etiquette forced
him to appear unconscious. During the time the
preparations for the duel were being made, he was
pacing in front of the old Roman Catholic Church,
at the back of the site of Mr. O'Reilly's stables, but
before they fired he stepped behind, so as not to see
the duel. Directly he heard the shot, however, he
hastened to the scene of the combat, and of course
the mere fact of his presence prevented its being
carried further. The causes leading to the duel are
not known, but are believed to have arisen from a
trivial disagreement.

No. 7.—EARLY DAYS.

In Pigeon Bay there resided a family named Sinclair, who owned the property now held by the
Holmes in Pigeon Bay. In the early days this
family and the Hays came from Wellington about

the same time. Mr. Sinclair, on his first arrival
built a vessel, and went on a voyage with his son-in-
law. We have not been enabled to ascertain their
proposed destination, but they never were heard of
again. Mrs. Sinclair was therefore left with two
sons and three daughters, and with these she worked
on and made a good living. She was an exceedingly
hospitable, kind old lady, and gave many a night's
lodging to a traveller in those early days, who would
otherwise have had to spend the night amongst the
bush. One daughter married a Captain Gay, who
was commander and owner of a vessel. After a
certain time had elapsed, the family sold out to Mr.
George Holmes, and started a regular family ship,
and went to British Columbia. Not liking that
place when they arrived there, they went to Honolulu, in the Sandwich Islands, where they bought an
island for themselves. They prospered there exceedingly, and are now owners of one island and a half.
Some of the family have bought land in the North
Island Frank Sinclair occasionally pays New Zealand a visit, to take away the best bulls, rams, and
entire horses he can get, to improve the stock in his
island home. The family are now rich, and are
shearing from 80,000 to 100,000 sheep. A description of this island was written by Miss Bird, and a
few extracts may prove entertaining. She says :—
    " I must now say a little about my hosts, and try
to give you some idea of them. I heard their history from Mr. Damon, and thought it too strange to
be altogether true, until it was confirmed by themselves. The venerable lady at the head of the house
emigrated from Scotland to New Zealand many years
ago, where her husband was unfortunately drowned,
and she being left to bring up a large family, and
manage a large property, was equally successful with
both. Her great ambition was to keep her family
together, something on the old patriarchal system ;

and when her children grew up, and it seemed as if even their very extensive New Zealand property was not large enough for them, she sold it. and, embarking her family and moveable possessions on board a clipper ship, owned and commanded by one of her sons-in-law, they sailed through the Pacific in search of a home where they could remain together.

"They were strongly tempted by Tahiti, but some reasons having decided them against it they sailed northwards and put into Honolulu. Mr. Damon, who was seamen's chaplain, on going down to the wharf one day, was surprised to find a trim barque, with this immense family party on board, with a beautiful and brilliant old lady at its head, books, pictures, work, and all that could add refinement to a floating home, about them, and cattle and sheep of valuable breeds in pens on deck. They then sailed for British Columbia, but were much disappointed with it, and in three months they reappeared at Honolulu, much at a loss regarding their future prospects.

"The island of Niihau was then for sale, and in a very short time they purchased it of Kamehameha V. for a ridiculously low price, and, taking their wooden houses with them, established themselves for seven years. It is truly isolated, both by a heavy surf and a disagreeable sea passage, and they afterwards bought this beautiful and extensive property, made a road, and built the house. Only the second son and his wife live now on Niihau, where they are the only white residents among 350 natives. It has an area of 75,000 acres, and could sustain a far larger number of sheep than the 20,000 now upon it. It is said that the transfer of the island involves some hardships, owing to a number of the natives having neglected to legalise their claims to their *kuleanas*, but the present possessors have made themselves thoroughly acquainted with the language, and take the warmest interest in the island population. Niihau is famous for its very fine mats, and for its necklaces of shell six yards long, as well as for the extreme beauty and variety of the shells which are found there.

" The household here consists, first and foremost, of its head, Mrs Sinclair, a lady of the old Scotch type, very talented, bright, humorous, charming, with a definite character which impresses its force upon everybody ; beautiful in her old age, disdaining that servile conformity to prevailing fashion which makes many old people at once ugly and contemptible ; speaking English with a slight old-fashioned, refined Scotch accent, which gives *naïveté* to everything she says ; up to the latest novelty in theology and politics ; devoted to her children and grandchildren, the life of the family, and, though upwards of seventy, the first to rise and the last to retire in the house.   She was away when I came, but some days afterwards rode up on horseback, in a large drawn silk bonnet, which she rarely lays aside, as light in her figure and step as a young girl, looking as if she had walked out of an old picture, or one of Dean Ramsay's books.

" Then there are her elder son, a bachelor ; two widowed daughters with six children between them ; and a tutor, a young Prussian officer, who was on Maximilian's staff up to the time of the Queretaro disaster, and is still suffering from Mexican barbarities.   The remaining daughter is married to a Norwegian gentleman, who owns and resides on the next property.   So the family is together, and the property is large enough to give scope to the grandchildren as they require it.

" They are thoroughly Hawaiianised. The young people all speak Hawaiian as easily as English, and the three young men, who are superb young fellows, about six feet high, not only emulate the natives in feats of horsemanship, such as throwing the lasso, and picking up a coin while going at full gallop, but are surf-board riders, an art which it has been said to be impossible for foreigners to acquire. " The natives on Niihau and in this part of Kauai call Mrs. Sinclair ' Mamma.' Their rent seems to consist in giving one or more days' service in a month, so it is a revival of the old feudality. In order to patronise native labor, my hosts dispensed with a Chinese, and employ a native cook, and native women come in and profess to do some of the house-work, but it is a very troublesome arrangement, and ends in the ladies doing all the finer cooking, and superintending the coarser, setting the table, trimming the lamps, cutting out and ' fixing' all the needlework, besides planning the indoor and outdoor work which the natives are supposed to do. Having related their proficiency in domestic duties, I must add they are splendid horsewomen, one of them an excellent shot, and the other has enough practical knowledge of seamanship, as well as navigation, to enable her to take a ship round the world! It is a busy life, owing to the large number of natives daily employed, and the necessity of looking after the *lunas*, or overseers. Dr. Smith, at Koloa, twenty-two miles off, is the only doctor on the island, and the natives resort to this house in great numbers for advice and medicine in their many ailments. It is much such a life as people lead at Raasay, Applecross, or some other remote Highland place, only that people who come to visit here, unless they ride twenty-two miles, must come to the coast in the Jenny, instead of being conveyed by one of David Hutcheson's luxurious steamers. If the Clansman were ' put on,' probably the great house would not contain the strangers who would arrive."

P

No. 8—ARRIVAL OF THE FIRST ENGLISH SHIP.

The Monarch, commanded by Captain Smale, chartered by Messrs. Robinson (formerly Resident Magistrate at Akaroa) and Smith, who was the first person who placed sheep on Mr Buchanan's run at Little River, was the first English ship that ever came to Akaroa. She arrived on April 2, 1850, and the following is a full account of her trip, published in the *Akaroa Mail* in 1877 :—

" It is now twenty-eight years ago since we first turned our thoughts towards New Zealand. The idea speedily ripened into resolve, and finally we took our passage in a small barque named the Monarch, of 375 tons register, the owners, Messrs. Robinson and Smith, coming out with her. The crew consisted of the captain, David Smale, three officers, six A.B. seamen, and an apprentice, while the passengers numbered fifty-two, including a doctor. With a small vessel, a short crew, and a few adventurers, for such we might be termed in those days, we set sail for Auckland, but Akaroa was to be our destiny, and there we proved to be the first direct English settlers in what is now called Canterbury. The town of our adoption, Akaroa, now boasts of a periodical publication, and it has been thought that an epitome of our voyage, and the subsequent career of some of those ante-pioneers to the Canterbury settlement—ante-diluvians as we have been jocosely termed—might prove interesting to the readers of that journal.

" We left Gravesend on the 22nd day of November, 1849, putting into Cowes, Isle of Wight, whence we resumed our voyage at 6 a m. on the 27th, and, with a fine light breeze, ran down the Channel that day, losing sight of land as the shades of night closed in, and hid it from our gaze. With Madeira came our

next view of *terra firma*, but we were not able to
indulge in more than a fleeting glance, as our captain
deemed it advisable to keep as near mid-ocean as
was practicable. So onwards in our course until
about three days' sail from ' Rio,' when we fell in
with a smart-looking craft, the Pilot Fish, bound to
that port from Liverpool. The breeze was light, and
enabled us to sail in company for two days, during
which, by nautical means, we held a long conversation
with her captain, who, on changing his course, promised to report us, a promise which we afterwards
ascertained he had faithfully fulfilled, and, with one
other exception, his was the only vessel we sighted
on our passage out. All went well until, having
rounded the Cape, a fine wind favoring us, we sailed
from there to the meridian of Hobart Town in twenty-
one days, which was considered a smart trip. A few
days previous to our reaching this longitude, it was
discovered we were getting short of provisions.

"Many and loud were the expressions of annoyance
and discontent when this discovery was made known
to us, so much so that the owners decided upon running for Hobart Town. The wind, however, proved
dead against the carrying out of their decision, and
being a fair one for our proper course, the idea was
abandoned, after four days of beating about, and we
once more resumed our voyage to Auckland. The
same evening that we bade farewell to the distantly
seen shores of Tasmania, a fearful squall struck our
vessel, forcing her through the water at such a speed
that the rudder was broken away before sail could
be shortened. In addition to this serious mishap,
the stern windows were dashed in, and the saloon
flooded with about three feet of water. With great
presence of mind, two of the passengers, an elderly
gentlemen (Mr. Wray) and his daughter, seized
feather beds, and managed to hold them over the
broken windows until the sailors succeeded in batten-

ing them down. In this rudderless, and therefore
helpless state, we were driven before a gale of wind
down the west coast of New Zealand. Fortunately,
the weather abating, we were enabled to fix a temporary rudder, and, in about a fortnight from the
time of our severe handling by the elements, found
ourselves sailing past the Snares. All went well
with us until nearing Cape Saunders, when our
temporary rudder fell from its bearings, leaving us
once again at the mercy of wind and tide, and our
escape from shipwreck and destruction on that bold
rocky promontory was little short of a miracle.
Soundings were taken at once, only twelve fathom of
water being discovered beneath us, while a light
breeze, dead on shore, was slowly, but surely, drifting
us on to the rocks. Consternation prevailed, but
despite the confusion, the boats were got ready for
lowering, and the anchor was let go with the hope of
arresting further ingress. ' The best laid plans of
mice and men gang oft agree,' and never was the
quotation more aptly verified than in our case, for
no sooner was the anchor dropped, than it was discovered that it had not been shackled to the chain,
the whole of which, however, was paid out, and served
in some degree to check our drifting. It was night,
and only here and there could a star be seen to cheer
us. The looming headland looked down dark and
threatening from above. Around us the surging,
seething billows rushed madly on, to dash themselves to foam against the rocks beyond ; while,
through the rigging, the breeze seemed to sigh and
moan a funeral dirge to our ill-fated ship.

"Hope had fled, and grim despair had taken possession of us all, for there was no chance of extraneous
aid, and the coastal steamers which now ply so
frequently between our ports, and run up and down
the coast, were not then in existence, when, as is
often the case just about midnight, the wind suddenly

veered round to an exactly opposite quarter, and
speedily drifted us away from the land into comparative safety.   Then arose sincere and hearty thanks-
givings for deliverance in the hour of peril to Him ·
who rules not only the winds and waves, but also
the destiny of His creatures.

"With the appearance of day, the only spar we
had on board was fixed so as to steer the vessel, and
under sail we set out for the nearest, or any, port
that could be found.   On the 27th day of March,
1850, we made the heads of Akaroa Harbor, into
which the owners had determined to enter, but the
wind proved unfavorable for so unmanageable a rudder, and, in an almost starving condition, we were
compelled to lie to for almost a week, before a fair
wind arose for taking us in.   On the 2nd day of
April we entered the heads at about 7 a.m., and to
our great delight saw a boat coming down the harbor
towards us.   The occupants soon boarded us, and
amongst them was an old sea captain, who, knowing
the harbor, had come to pilot us up to the anchorage,
not forgetting to bring with him some eatables, consisting of new bread, butter, and watercress, which
were portioned out, and devoured with voracious
eagerness.   It should have been stated that, on the
day previous to our entering the heads, a boat with
one of the officers and a crew of volunteers from
amongst the passengers had proceeded down the
harbor, and reported our arrival and condition, which
was no doubt the cause of the boat with supplies
coming to meet us.

"We let go anchor at one o'clock the same day,
and in an hour afterwards many of us landed, thankful enough to be on *terra firma* again after our long
and perilous voyage.   Here and there might then
have been seen small groups of the new arrivals
wending their way to seek new friends amongst the
strangers, astonished to find, instead of the tradi-

tional cannibal of New Zealand, Europeans, like
themselves, representatives of England, Scotland,
Ireland, France, Savoy, and Germany, who proffered
a most hearty welcome, and seemed right pleased to
see us, while a few Maoris, to all appearance tame
and civilized, joined in the cordial reception accorded
to us by all. Fortunately, among our pssengers
was a young man who could speak French fluently,
and this proved of great service to us. Eventually
a kind of patois was established, which enabled us to
deal with our new friends, and such was their kindness and hospitality, that after twenty-seven years
sojourn in this colony, we still look back with feelings
of the keenest gratitude and pleasure to the welcome
we received at their hands. We partook of tea on
the day of our landing at Bruce's Hotel. The table
was well furnished, and the cooking excellent. As
may easily be imagined, we did ample justice to the
substantial repast set before us, and enjoyed it as
only those can who, for a long time, have neither
tasted fresh meat, nor, indeed, a proper meal. For
this, our first meal in our new country, we each paid
two shillings and sixpence. As night came on, we
returned to the ship, and this daily routine was kept
up for about a fortnight, during which we, each day,
wandered farther away in the different valleys, becom-
ing at the end of this period so enamoured of the
place, that no less than forty of the passengers agreed
to remain. Akaroa was then in all its pristine
beauty, so enchanting in its climate, and so picturesque in its scenery, that one could not resist the
fascination and the feeling that it was all that could
be desired ; but we soon found the beauties of the
place could not alone satisfy the wants of man, for,
owing to the sudden influx of population caused by
our arrival, provisions became scarce, and the serious
question arose as to whether we had acted wisely in
determining to remain. The ship being yet in the

harbor, we had still an opportunity of escape, when
news reached us of the arrival at Wellington by the
Lady Nugent of the agent for the 'Canterbury
Association,' tidings which filled us with a vague
hope of better things to come, and so, reluctant to
leave a spot which had strangely insinuated itself
into our affections, we finally decided to remain. On
the 15th of May, 1850, the Monarch, having had a
new rudder made and fixed, sailed away without us
for her original destination, Auckland.   During her
stay in harbor, four of her crew were drowned from a
small boat, when returning to the ship from ashore,
where they had been having a spree, all being more
or less intoxicated.   We were now left to our own
resources, and to shape our course in the best way we
could.   But, before taking leave of the vessel for
good and all, it may be well to add a few particulars
about the live stock we were enabled to successfully
bring out with us.   But few were landed alive out
of the original stock.   The deer, pheasants (save one
brace), partridges, and hares given by Lord Bray-
brooke died on the passage out.   We landed, however, one pure bred bull, two ditto heifers, one pure bred
mare, and a brace of pheasants, all belonging to Mr.
Smith.   As Canterbury was not known in those
days, the mare was sent on to Nelson, and was one
amongst the first, it not the first, that won a prize
in the Colony ; the bull and the heifers remained in
Akaroa ; and the pheasants were let loose in Pigeon
Bay.   We also brought out vegetable, tree, and farm
seeds of all kinds. kindly given us by Lord Mans-
field's gardener.   It may also be of interest to mention that Mr. Bruce was our pilot into Akaroa, and
Big William the first Native on board.

" There is always, in narratives of this kind, a
certain delicacy in mentioning the names of others :
but to some extent it is necessary to do so.   Only
a few, however, need be mentioned.   Some soon-

removed to other parts of the country, while others
turned their thoughts and best attention towards
what seemed to each most desirable, and which they
thought would best further their own interests, as
well as those of their adopted land. Among those
who settled down may be mentioned the Haylocks,
Pavitts, Farrs, Vogans, Parkers, Rule, Green, and
Hilleur. After a while the Haylocks decided to
erect a flour mill, to be driven by water power. This
was accomplished, and the building was named after
the street in which it was erected, the ' Grehan Mill.'
The Pavitts built the first saw mill in Canterbury at
Robinson's Bay, where they had purchased land.
Both these mills were of much service to Akaroa,
and their erection may be regarded as a great achieve-
ment under the then existing circumstances, for there
was no foundry in those days, and only one man, a
whitesmith, who knew anything ot ironwork. Nothing daunted, however, by the many and great
obstacles, the mills were completed, and, though
some parts were of somewhat rude construction, the
desired end was attained. Mr. S. C. Farr acted as
engineer to this primitive saw mill, and, afterwards,`
was engaged for the second mill of the same kind in
the province, named the ' Cumberland Saw Mills,'
situate in Duvauchelle's Bay.

"My self-imposed narrative now draws to a close.
scenes changed, circumstances altered, some rested
from their labors and passed on to fairer regions ; a
few remain, who are with us still, while others, faithful to the old spot, though removed some little distance from it, like to occasionally visit us.   Scme
have done little to mark their course, and, when they
pass away, will be forgotten ; but there are others
who have left their mark upon the rocks ot time, not
soon to be erased.   Their aim has been usefulness ;
—they have been, in every sense of the word, good
colonists,"

No. 9.—EARLY REMINISCENCES.

The Monarch brought some pheasants, which were turned out at Pigeon Bay, but went over to Port Levy. They did not do well at first, failing to increase much, till some Chinese pheasants were added to their ranks, after which they soon became numerous. Besides the pheasants, some cattle were brought out by Mr. Smith.

There were fifty-two passengers on board; most were bound to Auckland, at which port the Monarch intended to call first, but forty of these were so delighted with the appearance of Akaroa, that they resolved to remain here. At this time little progress had been made since the first settlement by the French. The English were few and far between, though, of course, a good many whalers, French and American, visited the harbor.

Mr. Watson was the Resident Magistrate, and Messrs. Farr and family, Parker and family, Pavitt and family, two Vogans, Haylock and family, Rule, Green, and Hilleur, were amongst the principal passengers by the Monarch.

Amongst the earlier settlers were Messrs. Bruce, P. Wood, Reed, McKinnon, and others. The two latter squatted on the land afterwards purchased by the Rev. W. Aylmer.

Messrs. Farr, Pavitt, Haylock, and their families, with the two Vogans, settled within the township of Akaroa. Mr. Pavitt, sen., and his family went to Robinson's Bay, where Mr. Saxton now lives, the elder sons going sawing in the bush. The houses were of the most primitive description, the block-houses being then gradually falling into decay. Bruce's Hotel had by far the most imposing appearance. Bruce kept it beautifully clean, having it washed down every morning as if it was a ship. He was an old sailor, formerly the owner of a cutter

which traded from the South.   On Mr. Bruce's first
trip here, Captain Smith, late of the Wairarapa, was
on board, and a Maori woman.   The vessel, when
lying inside the heads in calm weather, with all sails
set, was suddenly capsized in a squall.   The Maori
woman, who was down below at the time, was
drowned, but the rest succeeded in getting in a boat
belonging to the vessel ; and Bruce was so struck
with the appearance of the place that he determined
on settling here, and started the hotel which now
bears his name.

Paddy Wood, another " old identity," kept an
hotel where Mr. Garwood's store now stands.   These
two publicans were continually quarrelling, but this
was nearly entirely owing to Wood's fault, who was
very rough and disputatious.   Bruce was a most
affable man, and many a tale is told of his kindness
and generosity.

Where the private part of Bruce's Hotel now
stands, there was originally a store, built by Messrs.
Ellis and Turner.   These two men, like the publicans, could not agree, so after a lengthy series of
quarrels they determined to separate, and divide the
property.   Here, however, a difficulty arose with
regard to who should have the building.   At last
they hit upon the most original plan of dividing it,
and cut it fair down the centre with a cross-cut saw,
each party boarding up his own end.

Another store stood where the iron gate near Mr.
Garwood's shop is at present situated.   This was
built by a man named Duvauchelle, and was afterwards used as a lock-up, and at the end of its career
in that capacity became a hospital.   It now forms
the older portion of Mrs. Watkins' store.

The late Dr. Watkins' dwelling-house was then
situated on the beach, and was also near Garwood
and Co.'s store.   It was moved in pieces up to its
present position.

Mr. Waeckerlie had a flour mill close to where the Chinamen's house now is. A good deal of wheat was grown, principally by the Natives. The first willow, supposed to be a slip from the one overhanging Napoleon's grave at St. Helena, was planted in German Bay by Mons. de Belligny. It is from this tree that all those that beautify Akaroa, and the borders of the Avon in Christchurch, originally sprang. This same gentleman also planted the first walnut trees, which have so increased and multiplied. The first willow was cut down by Mr. Lucas, who appears to have been utterly devoid of sentiment, and, when reproached with his Vandalism, said that he did not see any difference between one willow tree and another!

The Canterbury settlement was first started in 1848, by an association in England, composed of men of influential position, who were deeply impressed with the necessity of a thorough reform in the management of the colonies. Their object was to establish a model colony, in which all the elements of a good and right state of society should be perfectly organised from the first. Unity of religious creed being deemed essential, the settlement was to be entirely composed of members of the Church of England ; religion and the highest class of education were to be amply provided for ; and everything was to be ordered and arranged so as to attract men of station and character, and a high class of emigrants generally, to embark their fortunes in the undertaking. The scheme was carried out by men whose hearts were in the work, among whose numbers the names of John Robert Godley and Lord Lyttelton are conspicuous. In their hands the enterprise lost nothing of the high character that was first impressed upon it, although many modifications of the original plan were found desirable, and judiciously carried into effect. The principle of religious exclu-

siveness was necessarily soon abandoned, and the
first ideas of the projectors may have been imper-
fectly realised in other respects, but it is only just to
acknowledge the debt of gratitude that Canterbury
owes to its founders, as even the measure of success
that crowned their efforts is appreciable in the tone
and spirit of its people at the present time.

The first party of emigrants, numbering 791, left
England on September 7th, 1850, in four ships, and
arrived at the port, now called Lyttelton, almost
together, in December of the same year. Mr.
Godley, the agent of the Association, was already in
New Zealand, and considerable preparations had
been made at the Port for the immigrants' reception.
When the Canterbury Pilgrims (as they were called)
first viewed their new country from the summit of
the volcanic hills that skirt the seaboard, they saw
before them a bare expanse of plains, stretching from
thirty to sixty miles to the foot of the dividing
ranges (the backbone of the country), broken only
by a few patches of timber, and with no other sign
of civilization than the solitary homestead of the
Messrs. Deans, who had settled there some years
before. The only approach to the level land was
over the mountains, about 1200 feet in height, or
round by sea to Sumner, and thence by the Heath-
cote River to Christchurch, as the chief town was
named. Those who can look back from the Canterbury of to-day to the time when they commenced to
spread over the country, to bring their new land
under the plough and spade, must feel astonishment
as well as pride at the really wonderful results
that little more than thirty years have produced.
Looking over the Plains now from the Port hills,
the eye is delighted with the beautiful panorama
spread out before it. The whole face of nature has
been changed. In place of the once bare Plains,
with nothing to mark the distance or break the

monotonous expanse of level grass land, the spec-
tator sees before him a timbered country, with well-
grown forest trees, smiling homesteads, well-culti-
vated fields, and cheerful hedgerows stretching far
and wide in every direction ; here and there a river
glistening in the sun, and the city of Christchurch,
only six miles distant, almost concealed amidst the
trees.

The first settlers that arrived here under the Canterbury Association were Dr. Watkins, the late Mr.
D'Oyley, Mr. Matson (manager for Captain Muter),
the late Mr. Dicken, the late Mr. Funnell, and Mr.
Hammond, of German Bay. The next arrival was
that of the Rev. W. Aylmer and his family, who
brought with him Mr. Moore, Mr. Morgan and his
family, the late Mr. Augustus Porter (brother to
Mr. John Porter), and Miss Catherine Edgeworth,
now Mrs. Garvey. He was the first incumbent of
Akaroa, but previous to his arrival two clergymen
of the Church of England did temporary duty—the
Rev. Mr. Thomas and the Rev. Mr. Fenton (cousin
of Mr H. H. Fenton). On Mr. Aylmer's first
arrival, the only building available was Commodore
Lavaud's original house, containing four small rooms,
and a round house built of clay, that used to stand
at the back of the present Court House This was
close packing for ten people. Mr. Justin and Mr.
H. Aylmer used to live in the round house. Mr.
and Mrs. Aylmer and part of the family walked
over from Pigeon Bay, but Mr. Justin Aylmer and
ten others had the pleasure of coming in a cutter of
17 tons burden, named the Kaka, commanded by
Captain Kane, now of Timaru. The trip took no
less than a week, the last night off the Akaroa
Heads being very stormy and disagreeable, as, owing
to the crowded state of the little craft, the hatches
could not be kept on. So long was the delay in the
vessel's arrival, that Mr. Bruce sent out a boat to

look for the Kaka, and one of the crew of that boat was Mr. Gerald Fitzgerald, lately Resident Magistrate at Hokitika.

The first schoolmaster in Akaroa was Mr Wadsworth, who came out in the same ship with Mr. Garwood. He was a very capable man and much liked, but he soon left, and entered the civil service in Victoria, where he now holds a good position.

The first Church of England service was held in the French Magazine, which was also used as a Court House, and stood on the site of the present Court House, and the seats were borrowed from the Roman Catholic Chapel. Shortly after this, Archdeacons Paul and Mathias paid a visit to Akaroa, for the purpose of holding a wholesale marriage and christening of the Natives. The Maoris flocked in in great numbers, apparently delighted at the idea. Many of the children had been baptised before by clergymen of various denominations, but they had it done over again to make all sure. Some of the ladies left long strings of their children outside the building whilst they went in to be married.

In these earlier days a brig named the Mountain Maid used to visit Akaroa and other New Zealand ports periodically. She came from Sydney, and was the property of Mr. Peacock, father of the Hon. John Peacock. The Mountain Maid was a perfect floating warehouse, from which the settlers drew their supplies. She had everything on board, " from a needle to an anchor," and her decks used to be crowded by busy purchasers whenever she arrived.

Some time in the year 1852, Colonel Campbell was sent down by Sir George Grey as Commissioner, to enquire into all land claims. He had with him Mr. J. C. Boys, of Rangiora, as surveyor, and Mr J. Aylmer as assistant surveyor. Colonel Campbell did not make things at all pleasant for the Canterbury Association settlers. He was a disappointed man, having taken great interest in the foundation ot the settlement when in London, and fully expecting to be appointed first agent, a post that was afterwards given to Mr. Godley. Mr. Robinson, the first Resident Magistrate, while putting forward certain claims of M. de Belligny (whose agent he was), produced deeds that were remarkably awkward for the Rev. W. Aylmer. One of these claims plainly showed that fourteen acres of land on which Mr. Aylmer's house now stands once belonged to M. de Belligny. Mr. Robinson, when Mr. Godley first arrived, presented this deed to him, which Mr. Godley threw into his safe and would not look at, and afterwards sold this land as part of a fifty acre block to Mr. Aylmer. When one says sold, one means that it was selected by Mr. Aylmer, with Mr. Godley's consent, for all land was bought in England at £3 per acre, and its locality was afterwards chosen with a right of exchange. This fourteen acres of land was some that M. de Belligny had received compensation for, both in money and land. The reason for this was that it had been considered necessary to get the land back from M. de Belligny for the township. In the Association charter these words occur : " Save and except all lands purchased and exchanged with M. de Belligny." M. de Belligny had been away a long time before this. Of course Mr. Aylmer, having built his house on the land, was placed in a very awkward position, and he went to Wellington in Mr Peacock's brig to see Sir George Grey. After hearing his case, the Government of the day consented to give him a Crown grant, and so the affair was settled

This was only one of the disputes that arose, war raging between Mr. Watson, the Resident Magistrate, and the Commissioner. Sir George Grey paid a visit to the Peninsula in this year (1852), and endeavored to make peace, but with small success.

Mr. Watson told Sir G. Grey that he had no animosity
towards the Commissioner, so Sir George Grey
suggested they should shake hands and make it up,
upon which Mr. Watson said, " Bedad, your Excellency, I'd sooner not," and he did not.   Manners
were then very primitive.   On this visit of Sir
George's he had come in unexpectedly one night,
having walked from Pigeon Bay.   He went to bed
at Bruce's Hotel, and Mr. Bruce thought this a fitting time to push some claims of his own ; so he
walked into Sir George's room, sat coolly down on
the side of the bed, and poured his troubles into His
Excellency's ears—one does not know with what
success.

Out of these disputes respecting land arose a duel.
It took place between Mr C. B. Robinson, the first
Resident Magistrate, whose second was Mr. Cooper,
now Collector of Customs at Timaru, and Captain
Muter, whose second was the late Mr. Crosbie Ward.
It was fought in a bush track in Holmes' Bay.
Pistols were the weapons used.   At the first shot
Mr. Robinson fired in the air, but Captain Muter
aimed at his opponent, though he did not hit him.
Captain Muter was anxious for a second shot, but
Mr. Robinson declared that if so, he would certainly
do his best to shoot his adversary.   The seconds
then interfered, being of opinion that wounded honor
was fully satisfied, and the affair was brought to an
end.   Captain, now Colonel Muter, left Akaroa soon
after and rejoined his regiment, and much distinguished himself during the Indian Mutiny.   The
vessel in which he went Home from India was burnt
at anchor, after her arrival in British waters, and in
this fire Colonel Muter lost considerably.   He afterwards edited an Anglo-Indian paper.   While on the
subject of duelling, one may mention that a bloodless
one was fought at the Head of the Bay in 1863.
The weapons in this case were also pistols, and the

combatants were the late Mr. Michael Brennan Hart and a Mr. Woodley, one of the Monarch's passengers. No life was lost, and there are great doubts as to what the pistols were loaded with.

The New Zealand Constitution was granted in the year 1852. For the Akaroa district two members were required for the Provincial Council. There were three candidates, the late Mr. Sefton Moorhouse, Mr. Robert H. Rhodes, and the Rev. W. Aylmer. Before the polling booth was opened, Mr. Moorhouse drew the attention of the returning officer, Mr. Watson, to the fact that if an elector intended to vote for two members, he must do so at the same time, that is, he could not first vote for one and then go out, and afterwards vote for another. This had a great effect on the election, as, owing to one of Messrs. Rhodes and Moorhouse's supporters voting for Mr. Rhodes first, and afterwards returning to vote for Mr. Moorhouse, the latter vote was objected to by Mr. W. Aylmer's agent, and the returning officer agreed with him. This made the number of votes between Messrs. Aylmer and Moorhouse exactly the same, and the returning officer giving his casting vote for Mr. Aylmer, he was elected in the second place, Mr. Rhodes having a majority over the others. Mr. Moorhouse petitioned the Provincial Council to upset Mr. Aylmer's seat, and Messrs. Pollard and Calvert appeared in the case, one on either side. The result of the case was that Mr. Aylmer's election was declared valid.

To show how primitive the people of Akaroa were in these days, and the little amount of public money that was being spent, it may be mentioned that the whole of the inhabitants, headed by the Resident Magistrate and Parson, turned out to repair the road from Bruce's to Waeckerlie's.

About this time a sad accident occurred. Two men (one of them the father of Mr. H. Magee) were

R

going over the ranges at the back of Akaroa, when
one missed the other. Magee's mate came back to
Akaroa, but could give no account of Magee, so a
search party was instituted. Magee was found lying
dead at the foot of a precipice. Many rumours were
current about this affair, the dead man being discovered in a remarkable position.

No. 10.—A LADY COLONIST'S EXPERIENCES.

Mr. and Mrs. Peter Brown left Glasgow in October, 1839, in the ship Bengal Merchant, bound to
Port Nicholson with immigrants, under the New
Zealand Association. The Bengal Merchant was
commanded by Captain Emery, and had on board
about a hundred passengers. She was the first emigrant ship that ever left Scotland for New Zealand.
The passage was a fine weather one, and the passengers were all well during the voyage. The events
were few and far between, consisting of the birth of
one child, a marriage, and the death by sunstroke of
a boy. No land was touched at till Port Hardy was
reached, where a few hours' stoppage took place, and
the Maoris were seen for the first time by the new
colonists, who were astonished at their primitive
costume, one red shirt being the only European
clothing amongst the whole hapu. Port Nicholson
was reached early in February, 1840, and the new
comers landed at the Petoni Beach. There were
very few Europeans living in the place, only one lot of
immigrants having landed previously, some fortnight
before. The immigrants were not by any means
delighted at the appearance of their adopted home.
There were no houses, those on shore living in tents

or small makeshift whâres of the most wretched
description. Such a thing as sawn timber was
unknown, and all the fittings of the ship were landed
and made into three buildings, one for a hospital,
another for the company's stores, and a third for the
ammunition. There were a good many Natives
about, and they were of course utterly uncivilised,
much shocking the new comers, who were frightened
with their wild dances in honor of the arrival of the
Pakehas. There were no licenses at this time, and
the consequence was, that every one who could buy a
gallon of grog started a small hotel on their own
account. The Natives were in consequence often
much excited by the drink, and used to lose control
over their actions.

Mrs. Brown and most of those who came by the
Bengal Merchant went to the Hutt Valley, and took
possession of some land close to the river. The
river was an excellent one for washing clothes after
the long voyage, and it can be imagined how gladly
they seized the opportunity Whilst thus employed
an adventure occurred. They were in the habit of
drawing the water with a bucket and a rope attached
to it. Unfortunately, one day the rope slipped from
Mrs. Gilbert's hand, the bucket sinking to the bottom
of the river. Seeing a Native paddling his canoe on
the river, Mrs. Brown made signs to him to hook it
up with his paddle. Instantly he threw off his mat,
and, jumping into the river, he seized the bucket,
refusing to give it up without "utu." Not being
able to understand his language, they could not find
out what he wanted. They offered him food, but he
refused. Mrs. Brown then seized the bucket, and
ran off with it, but, turning round, saw the Maori
following her, quite naked, with his tomahawk raised
in his hand. She threw the bucket from her, telling
him she would tell "Wideawake," the Maori name
for Colonel Wakefield. He kept the bucket in his

hand, till at last they came to terms for a flannel shirt. Being rather alarmed at this, they left this lonely place and came to live in Petoni. A few months afterwards the Maori made his appearance there, and laughing heartily at the story, told Mrs. Brown's husband how he had frightened her.

Mr. Hay (father of the present Pigeon Bay family), who was a passenger, also settled in Petoni, and so did Dr. Logan, the ship's doctor. The arrangements made by the Association for settling the new comers were exceedingly bad. They had been told on leaving Scotland that they were going to a land flowing with milk and honey, but discovered that there were neither of these commodities ; in fact, the Bengal Merchant had on board the first cow ever landed in Wellington. Those purchasing one hundred acres in England had been given a cabin passage, but when they asked for their land it could not be given to them, as it was not yet surveyed. The British Government, too, objected to Crown grants being given till it had been shown that the Natives had been paid five shillings an acre for the land. The consequence of this was that every one squatted where they liked, with the pleasant knowledge that they might be turned off at any moment. The surveyors, amongst whom were Mr. Deans, who afterwards went to Riccarton, were commencing operations. They laid out the town first, and each purchaser of one hundred acres rural land got his town section of an acre, but for the rest of their purchase they had to wait till the claims of the Natives had been adjusted. The result of this unsatisfactory state of things drove many away. For instance, Messrs. Hay and Sinclair left, and settled in Pigeon Bay, and others scattered far and wide.

, Mr. and Mrs. Brown and the others who had squatted on the banks of the river Hutt, soon found out their mistake in going to live so near to that treacherous river. On the 1st of June, 1840, Mrs. Brown's first son was born, and that same night heavy rain set in, and the following morning the river had overflowed its banks, and the flood was over two feet high inside the house. The bed in which Mrs. Brown was lying began to float, and as it was impossible to move her, it was proposed to suspend the mattress to the rafters of the house. As this latter, however, was a very temporary erection, made of small scrub in its rough state, tied together with flax and daubed over with mud, Mrs. Brown objected, fearing the whole structure would give way and she would be drowned. Her entreaties were at last listened to, and she was left where she was. Fortunately, when the tide turned the river began to fall gradually, so the suspension was never carried out. This flood destroyed many goods, and utterly disheartened the colonists. During that day and the following no fires could be kept alight to dry anything, and altogether misery was the order of the day.

At Petoni and the Hutt the people from each vessel were in the habit of making a separate settlement, as it were. Of these one was known as the Cornish Row, being at the Hutt. One of the people in these whâres set his house on fire, and, as they were all built very close together, the whole row was burnt, and one ship's immigrants left homeless. To add to their discomfort, on that same night the colonists experienced their first earthquake. It was a very severe one, and terrified the new comers exceedingly, but luckily no one was hurt. In fact, the houses were of such a frail description, that if they had fallen bodily on any one, he or she would have been none the worse. The only food was the Company's rations, eked out with an occasional piece of fresh pork from the Natives. There were no

vegetables but some wretched Maori potatoes and
Maori cabbage.

Mr. Peter Brown was a baker, and soon after this
he went to Petoni, where he was baking for a Mr.
Duncan, a fellow-passenger. Shortly after this the
settlement was shifted some seven miles round the
beach, from Petoni to Thorndon, and the old huts
were abandoned, and more substantial buildings
erected, The road from Petoni to Thorndon was
very wild, there being a few Maori settlements scattered along it. At one of these, named Wharepouri,
Mrs. Brown had another Maori adventure. She was
coming from town to Petoni rather late, and, when
she came to Wharepouri, found the tide was in, and
asked the Maoris to carry her across the creek. For
some reason they would not do so, though she offered
them all the cash she had. They kept asking her
for more, and pointed out the night was fast approaching. She told them her child was at Petoni,
and she must go on, but they only mocked her. At
last, finding all her entreaties useless, she leaped in
herself, and, though the water was up to her waist,
scrambled through. This dreadfully disgusted the
Maoris, who by this action lost their " utu " altogether, and the whole pa came out and shrieked and
yelled at her, telling her the " typo would seize her
by the legs." It can be imagined what an uncomfortable walk home Mrs. Brown had in her wet
clothes.

After three years, Mr. Brown got an offer from
Mr. Connell to take charge of a bakery at Akaroa,
where there were then a good many residents. He
accepted the offer, and he and Mrs. Brown left Wellington in 1843, and sailed for Akaroa in the
schooner Scotia. On board the vessel were Mrs.
Knight and child. Mrs. Knight was afterwards
named Mrs. Webb, and settled in Laverick's Bay,
and the child is the present Mr Knight, now residing

at Laverick's.   The trip took a long time—over a
fortnight—for a head wind forced the vessel to lay
for a time in Cloudy Bay.   However, all went well,
and they landed at Akaroa in May, 1843, the first
person to welcome them ashore being Mr Bruce, the
proprietor of Bruce's Hotel.   Akaroa was then a
dense bush down to the back of Bruce's Hotel, large
pines and totaras standing nearly to the water's
edge, and Mrs. Brown was delighted at the extreme
beauty of the place, which was then in its primeval
loveliness.   There were of course a few clearings
here and there, where the French people had squatted,
but they were small, as each family had only five
acres allotted to them.   The great majority of the
population were French and German, there being
only some five or six families of English, Irish, and
Scotch.   There were, however, three hotels at this
early date.   The principal was of course Bruce's
Hotel, and there was another where Mr. C. Henning
now lives, called the French Hotel, kept by a Mr
François.   The third one was at Green's Point,
being the oldest established of them all.   The town,
however, growing towards German Bay, Mr. Green
found he was out of the world at Green's Point, and
built a new hotel on the site of the present Armstrong's Buildings ; in fact, the existing buildings
are the old hotel.

Amongst the hotelkeepers, the most celebrated
person was Captain Bruce.   He was a sailor man,
having been the captain of a large merchant vessel
called the Elizabeth, owned by Johnny Jones.   He
had a cutter of his own called the Brothers, which
used to collect whalebone and oil on the coast between
Akaroa and Dunedin.   One day, as he was coming
into the Akaroa Heads, the cutter capsized in a
squall, and left poor Captain Bruce destitute.   He
was, however, a man of resources, and soon started
Bruce's Hotel, which he made a great success, his

excessive geniality and knowledge of the sea attract-
ing all the sailors from the whalers. He was a
capital townsman, being the life and soul of the
place, and might be seen almost any day with his
glass in his hand, looking out seaward for the arrival
of fresh vessels.

The whaling vessels used always to come in for
supplies about Christmas-time, and it was no un-
common thing to see a dozen in harbor together at
that time, and, as will easily be imagined, a brisk
trade was done with the residents for fresh provisions of all kinds. During the rest of the year,
however, the arrivals were few and far between, and
there was often great scarcity of certain stores, and
the arrival of a small vessel from Wellington, which
was really the depôt for everything from England,
was quite an event. There being no outside trade,
with the exception of the occasional traffic with the
whalers, the residents really depended on their gardens for their existence. There were no butchers,
but everybody kept pigs, and when one person killed,
it was divided all round, the compliment being
returned. There were also great herds of goats running on the hills. These were owned by a great
many people, and used to be got in at intervals,
when the different owners would mark the kids with
their own mark, and some would be killed for the
general use. The pigs were an intolerable nuisance,
as they were not kept shut up, but wandered where
they liked, doing a great deal of damage. When
Governor Grey visited the place in 1847, the inhabitants petitioned him to put a stop to this indiscrimi-
nate pig keeping in the streets. He granted the
petition, ordaining that all pigs in the town of
Akaroa should be kept in confinement. Finding
this was rather expensive, many of the residents took
to the hills with their pigs and their cattle, where
they could run them undisturbed. Mr. McKinnon

and Mr. Lucas got Mrs. Brown to ask Governor
Grey whether they might be allowed to squat on the
hills, and he replied in the affirmative, saying they
had better go there " and breed children and cattle
as fast as they could." This permission was taken
abundant advantage of. At that time there was no
settler on the south side of the harbor, though Mr.
George Rhodes had stations at Long and Flea Bay.
Mr. McKinnon went to Island Bay, and Mr. Lucas
to Land's End, and, as they did well, many others
were encouraged to follow them. Mr. Wright went
to Wakamoa next, and Hempleman was living at
Peraki on a whaling station, Job Price at Ikeraki,
and Mr. Wood, better known as " Paddy Wood,"
at Oauhau. These latter were all whaling, and kept
little stock for their own use. There were great
droves of wild pigs on the hills, and in the whaling
season these used to come down in hundreds to feed
on the blubber.

Mr. Connell went to Nelson, and left Mr. and
Mrs. Brown out of employment. Mr. Wood persuaded Mr. Brown to go as cook and baker to
Oauhau, but they had no idea of how rough it was.
They went round in a whale-boat. There was a
great swell on outside, though the weather was fine
in Akaroa. Not a word was spoken the whole way,
and when they got in Mr. Wood said that he was
never in a worse sea. The place was terribly rough,
and, as there was no firewood, the food had to be
cooked with whales' blubber. They ran short of
provisions, and the men got discontented, and the
station was left a month before the usual time, much
to the gratification of Mr. and Mrs. Brown, who
spent a very wretched three months there.

Of course at this time there were no surveys and
no Crown grants, and Hempleman asserted that
nearly the whole of the Peninsula was his, so that
any one lived rent free. There were no very large

Maori settlements ; Little River and Taumutu were
the principal pas, but a good many were living in
Pigeon Bay and Port Levy. The Akaroa Natives
were at Tikao Bay and Onuku, and were very
friendly with the Europeans. Tuhau was the leading chief, and one of his two wives is still living.
Tikao was chief of the Tikao Bay Maoris ; but a
younger brother, also bearing the same name, is now
in command. It will thus be seen that year by year,
though by slow degrees, the settlement of the Peninsula was proceeding, and population spreading from
the town itself to the adjacent hills. The French
and Germans got Crown grants of the land they had
been originally given, on their taking out letters of
naturalisation, and thus a great many new subjects
were gained to Her Majesty.

Bishop Selwyn used to come round periodically
and visit the settlers and the Maoris. The first
Presbyterian service was held by the Rev. C. Fraser
in Mrs. Brown's house, near where Mrs. Rhodes now
lives, but it was long afterwards before they had the
first resident minister, who was the Rev. Mr. Grant,
who afterwards went to Christchurch, and, as many
of our readers will remember, was subsequently lost
in the Matoaka.

No. 11.—BILLY SIMPSON.

Probably the oldest living white resident on the
Peninsula now lives at our Akaroa Hospital. He
has been a fine-looking man. The features are
marked, determined, and regular, and his high,
broad forehead shows that his brains were of no
mean order. There is a deep scar on the right
brow, on which hangs a tale, of which more here-

after. Age and hardship have made him a mere
skeleton, but there is still great vitality apparent in
his bright eyes, which kindle when he is spoken to
of old times. He has been, as most of the readers of
the *Mail* know, residing at Mr McPhail's, at Island
Bay, but recently an attack of illness rendered it
necessary to bring him to Akaroa for medical aid.
Simpson is an old sailor, who was born in Berkshire
just seventy years ago, according to his own account,
though many fancy he is much older. He was
early apprenticed to the owner of some vessels running in the West India trade, and he spent his time
in the ordinary manner. When he had completed
his time, he shipped for Sydney in a large ship
called the Mary Ann. This vessel was built for
troops, and took out the 28th Regiment to New ·
South Wales. Her commander, Captain Smith, is
described by Simpson as a perfect brute, and dire
were the quarrels that took place between him and
the men. This gentleman was familiarly known as
" Pirate Smith," and Simpson warmly asserts that
he had as good a right to fly the death's head and
cross bones flag as Captain Kidd ever had. Arrived
in Sydney, the crew struck and went ashore, refusing
to go aboard the Mary Ann again. Brought up
before the magistrates, the option was given them of
sailing in the vessel or forfeiting their wages and
clothes. They all preferred the latter alternative, and
stopped in the Colony. It was at a time when whaling was the principal occupation of sailors in these
seas, and in Sydney Simpson soon fell in with Captain Hempleman, who, finding him a good hand in a
whale-boat, engaged him to go with him for a trip
in the brig Bee, as boat-steerer, with one and a half
shares. This was in the beginning of 1835, about
forty-seven years ago, so Simpson must have been
about twenty-three years of age at the time.
    Captain Hempleman had been in command of

several big ships before this time, though quite a
young man, but had left a large vessel, an English
whaler, named the James Calvert, at the Sandwich
Islands, owing to some dispute, and therefore had,
much against his will, to accept the command of the
brig Bee, a small and inconvenient vessel compared
to those he was accustomed to. Long and Wright
were the names of the owners of the Bee, and they
fitted her out for a cruise to New Zealand, where
whales were then reported as specially plentiful. One
reason that Captain Hempleman accepted the command of the Bee was, that he was permitted to take
Mrs. Hempleman aboard. They would not allow
her to be aboard the larger vessels, and he did not
like leaving her ashore, so he took a short trip as
mate in the ship Norwood, of Sydney, and then took
command of the Bee, and, amongst other hands,
shipped Billy Simpson, the hero of this memoir.
Mrs. Hempleman, the first, who afterwards died at
Peraki, was an English girl, who had came out as
an immigrant to Sydney.

The voyage of the Bee to New Zealand, and what
success they met with, has been previously recorded
in these stories, and Simpson says the account is a
most correct one. The place where the whaling was
carried on, the name of which is not mentioned in
the log, was Peraki, but Simpson is very indignant
about it being said that they cut poles for the houses
in Pigeon Bay, for he vows they never went there.
On mature reflection, however, he says he remembers
that Port Levy was then called Pigeon Bay, and
that it was there the poles were cut. The trip of the
Bee was a very successful one, and Hempleman was
so pleased with Peraki that he determined to return
to it if possible. On his arrival in Sydney he was
still more anxious to do this, from the fact that
Messrs. Long and Wright raised the old objection to
his carrying his wife aboard the vessel. He there-

fore persuaded a Sydney firm, named Clayton and
Duke, to let him establish a whaling station on shore
at Peraki. He was to be visited at intervals by
vessels, which would bring provisions and take the oil
away that had been collected. It was just Christmas
time in the year 1836 when the schooner Hannah set
sail from Sydney with the first white men who had
ever attempted to form a settlement on the then
savage, wooded, and mountainous tract of country
known as Banks Peninsula.

The Hannah had another shore whaling party to
land in New Zealand, besides Hempleman's. The
destination of the other was Poverty Bay, but the
schooner went to Queen Charlotte's Sound. There
they stopped for five or six weeks, and though the
one party left them to go to the North, they had a
good many additions to their ranks, many of the
men forming connections with Maori women. There
were four boats' crews in the party, some thirty white
men in all, Mrs. Hempleman being the only white
woman. About a dozen Maoris accompanied them
from Queen Charlotte's Sound. The Hannah went
first to Akaroa, where she stopped two days, before
proceeding to land the party at Peraki. There were
no whalers in these waters at the time, and the few
Maori whâres were deserted, for it was just after the
massacre by Rauparaha, and he had laid all the
plantations waste, destroyed the pas, and driven the
few people who escaped death or slavery into the
interior. As, therefore, there were no provisions to
be got from the Natives, or any object to be gained
by stopping in the harbor, the Hannah sailed for
Peraki the second morning after her arrival, and that
same day landed the party at their future home. It
was fine autumn weather, and many aboard were
pleased with the idea that it was St. Patrick's Day
(being the 17th of March, 1836) when they landed.
They soon got their things ashore, and commenced

building their whâres. They used to sleep in casks for some time, and they were much delayed by going after whales, before they had the trying works and their own houses put up. Hempleman's house was of sawn timber, brought from Queen Charlotte's Sound. There was no time for planting. It was just arranged that one boat should be on the fishing ground at daybreak one morning, and another the next, and of course when whales were got they had to be tried out. Very few amongst the men knew anything about whaling at all. Captain Hempleman was a really good hand, but he was always drinking. A sad accident, too, depressed them much. Mr Beers, or Boan, was an excellent headsman, in fact, got most of the whales that were caught. One day his boat was upset in returning to the shore, and he and three of the hands were drowned. Two of these were Sydney natives, fine fellows, who knew their work, and could ill be spared in the little settlement. Beers, it is thought, might have escaped easily, as he was a good swimmer, but he had a heavy monkey jacket on at the time, and in swimming after the hands to get them to the boat, so that they could hold on, the coat became saturated with water and dragged him down. He was very deeply regretted indeed.

At this time Simpson heard from the Maoris a good many tales regarding Rauparaha's invasion, and he had previously been shipmates in the Bee with one of those who escaped. The account he gives of the matter, as related to him by the Maoris, is as follows :—Some time antecedent to these events, a Ngatiawa chief named Pahi had visited Europe. He was much impressed with the customs of civilised nations, especially with the fact that wars were usually made against people speaking a different language. He brooded deeply over this idea, and when he returned, he formed the ambitious idea of doing away with the inter-tribal discords, and making the Maoris a strong, united people, capable of waging war on other places beyond New Zealand, and of repelling any foreigners. In the North, amongst his own people, the idea was well received, but he then wished to go through the South, and for that purpose announced his intention of coming across the straits to Taiaroa, who was the leading chief of all these tribes, though he resided in Otago. He came across, but the old feeling of hatred to the Northern tribes was still strong, and when he got to Kaiapoi he was treacherously murdered by a rangitiera named Tangatahira. The great Northern chief Rauparaha vowed revenge, and right royal "utu" he took for the assassination of his friend. Rauparaha induced the captain of a trading brig, named the Martha, to take himself and a number of his warriors to Akaroa. He had no money to give him, but he proffered a few of those preserved human heads which were then such a common article of traffic, being sold as curiosities for the museums of the old world, and he promised to fill the vessel with pigs and flax as " utu." Directly the Maoris landed, however, they immediately began to massacre all the Natives they could meet, and all the survivors fled to a stiongly fortified pa at the end of that Peninsula running out between Duvauchelle's and Barry's Bays, now in the occupation of Mr Birdling. The position was a strong one, and it was several days before the attacking force gained an entrance to the pa, but when they did, a most horrible carnage ensued, many of those taken being killed in the most terrible manner. The Maori who was with Simpson in the Bee told him that the conquerors seized many of the children, and, cutting their throats from ear to ear, eagerly drank the hot life blood as it flowed from the terrible wounds. They held high and hideous festival on the bodies of their dead foes, and Simpson says he has

himself seen the huge copper Maori in which they
roasted several corpses at a time. Bloody Jack
was the Maori who held the command in defending
the pa. He was not a chief, but his great fighting
qualities had placed him at the head in this time of
desperate danger. He and many others escaped
after the last successful assault, and found a refuge
in the bush. Every plantation and whâre that the
merciless victors could find, they utterly destroyed,
so that famine should be the lot of the wretched few
who had escaped them.

When their horrible work was done they went
aboard the brig, and one cannot help thinking that
Captain Stewart, who was the commander of the
vessel, was rightly served for aiding the Maoris by
carrying them on their bloody errand, when, instead
of flax and pigs, these savages brought aboard a
number of their wretched victims. He (Captain
Stewart) remonstrated, but was warned that his fate
would be a terrible one unless he obeyed Rauparaha
in all things ; and there is little doubt he would have
been killed, had they not required his skill to take
the vessel back to Kapiti, which was their destination. The voyage must have been a fearful one for
captain and crew, for the Maoris kept murdering
their prisoners, and cooked their flesh in the ship's
coppers, greatly to the horror of the sailors, who
insisted on them being at once destroyed when the
Maoris left the ship.

One terrible incident seems to stand out in bold
relief. When the Martha came up the harbor,
Rauparaha and his men hid themselves under the
hatches, and told Captain Stewart to make signals
to the shore that he wanted to trade, in the hope
that some unsuspicious Native might be lured aboard
and become their victim. The experiment succeeded
only too well. A chief of importance seeing the
signal, and thinking the Martha was an ordinary

trading vessel, came on board with his daughter, and
was instantly seized and bound.   During the terrible
time of the massacre ashore they were left in the
hold of the vessel ; but when these demons were once
more clear of the land they loosed him and taunted
him with the horrible and bestial tortures and indigni-
ties they were going to inflict on his daughter as well
as himself.   Determined if possible to save the poor
girl from the indescribably horrible fate in store for
her, the gallant prisoner managed to snatch a tomahawk from one of their fiendish persecutors, and
killing the miserable girl with a single blow, threw
her body into the sea, and tried to leap after it.   In
this, however, he failed, for before he could take the
spring he was seized by his captors, who, baulked of
their proposed atrocities on his daughter, promised
him a death of intense agony.   Well they kept their
hideous promise !   On their arrival at Kapiti, at the
great feast at which they celebrated their successful
raid, the wretched man was brought before them and
tortured to death in a most hideous manner—by
having red-hot bars of iron thrust through his body.
Terrible indeed had been Rauparaha's revenge !

Billy Simpson's narrative had the effect of causing
a gentleman residing in Akaroa to write to the
Akaroa Mail the following letter, which will be found
very interesting :—

THE ONAWE MASSACRE.

Sir,—I have read with great interest Mr. Simpson's account of the massacre at Akaroa, but I think
there are several statements therein that require correc-
tion.   It is stated by him that Te Pahi was murdered
at Kaiapoi by a chief named Tangatihira.   This is
altogether wrong, as he was murdered at Akaroa by

T

a chief named Te Mairanui ; and that is why his
brother Rauparaha took revenge on the Maoris here.
The correct version of the affair, as far as I can learn,
is as follows :—About the year 1827 Te Pahi, or, as
he was sometimes called, Rakakura, went on a voyage
to Sydney, and from thence to England, where he
was presented to King George, who took a great
interest in the sable chief, and made him some hand ·
some presents when leaving for New Zealand.   Te
Pahi took great interest in all he saw when in
England, and on his return described the country in
glowing colours to the Natives ; also, the immense
bodies of troops he had seen, and how they were
dressed, armed, and drilled.

About a year after his return (this would be about
the end of the year 1829), he made up his mind to
make a friendly visit to the Natives of this island,
and for that purpose sailed in a large canoe, accompanied by Rauparaha and about fifty followers, all
armed with guns, some of which he had brought out,
and some he had purchased at Sydney.   They called
at most of the pas along the coast, and were everywhere kindly received.   They reached Akaroa about
three weeks after their departure from the North.   It
is said by some that they walked overland from'
Cloudy Bay to Canterbury, but, from the nature of
the country and the number of rivers which had to
be crossed, this I don't think at all probable.

The principal chief here at the time was named
Te Mairanui, but whether he lived at Onuku or at
Wainui, where there was a large pa, 1 am unable to
say.   However, it appears he had in his possession
a large block of splendid greenstone, which Te Pahi
happened to see, and, after admiring it, asked the
chief for permission to take it back with him to the
North.   This was indignantly refused by Te Mairanui,
who said, " It belongs to the tribe, and we are going
to make mere meres (greenstone clubs) out of it."

" Well," said Te Pahi, " If you don't give it to me
I will come and take it," and with that he left for
the other pa, at which he was staying. On telling
Rauparaha about the greenstone being refused to
him, he said, " Tell Te Mairanui that if he does not
give it to you we will make a prisoner of him instead,
and take him back with us." This message was
duly delivered the next day, and still the greenstone
was refused. Next morning, Te Pahi and six others
went across to the pa, and, as usual, sat down.
Each had a loaded musket in his hand. Te Mairanui
and his men had had a talk, and agreed amongst
themselves, if he came again to demand the greenstone, that they would kill him ; so when they saw
them come with the guns they formed a plan, and
they were rushed from behind, and all of them clubbed
to death, their own guns being used to finish them.
The Maoris then commenced to fire them off, the
sound of which was plainly heard by Rauparaha and
the others Shortly afterwards a canoe came down,
bringing word of the fate of Te Pahi and his men.

Rauparaha heard the news of the death of his
brother's party, and was very " pouri," but did not
attempt to be revenged at this time. He said to his
men, " Tenei a na kino mahi tau ka hoki ki te
kianga " (this is bad work ; we will return home) ;
so, having got his men all together, he departed, vow-
ing vengeance at some future time. On his way
back he called at most of the pas where he had been
well treated coming down, and laid them waste,
killing great numbers of the Natives, who were not
prepared for a mob of well-armed men like these.
The pa which offered the greatest resistance was at
the Kaikorai, where the Natives were well fortified
on a small hill close to the sea. Rauparaha and his
men attempted to take it, but were several times
repulsed. He agreed to wait and starve them out,
and, after doing this for a few days, he hit upon a

plan worthy of a better cause. He said to two of
his men, who were splendid swimmers, "I want you
to go in the sea and pretend to be kekenos (seals);
swim along the beach until you get opposite the pa,
then come in and flounder in the surf, and they will
rush out to kill you. We will watch them, and as
soon as they leave the pa we will rush in." The plan
succeeded only too well. The hungry Natives in the
early morning seeing, as they thought, two seals
sporting in the surf, ran out in a body to take them,
as their provisions had been exhausted for three days.
Rauparaha had his men scattered round, so that
possession was gained almost at once. And now the
guns began to tell, and these poor Natives, wasted
by hunger and continual watching, had not the
strength to resist, so, after numbers of them were
shot, the rest threw down their arms and surren-
dered. The men who were playing the seals paid
the penalty of death, as they were caught before
Rauparaha had time to relieve them. From this
place about forty prisoners and a lot of greenstone
were taken.

They then left for the Straits, and on their arrival
found the brig Elizabeth, Captain Stewart, loading
spars. A bargain was struck with him : that for
fifty tons of dressed flax he was to land Rauparaha
and fifty fighting men at Wangaloa, Banks Peninsula, and bring them back to the island of Te Manu,
in the Straits. The captain agreed to this, but it is
said, whilst he was down below with Rauparaha,
over one hundred Natives came on board, and concealed themselves below until after the vessel was
well outside. The Peninsula was made in two days,
and the brig beat up and anchored abreast of the pa.
All the Natives were out of sight under hatches, so
that she was supposed to be a whaler, and as a good
trade was generally to be done with them, some of
the Natives put off to her. It happened that in the

first canoe which boarded her were Te Mairanui, his wife, and a daughter, twelve years of age. Rauparaha was watching from the cabin windows, and came up on deck and seized him, and, with the assistance of some others, handcuffed him and put him, with his wife and child, below. A rush was then made for the ship's boats, and what canoes were alongside, and all made for the shore, where a terrible scene of carnage ensued. All the Natives that could be seen were butchered in cold blood. The account of the fight on Massacre Island (Banks Peninsula) is, I believe, correct, as several of the victims were cooked and eaten ashore. At dusk the Natives came back on board, most of them bringing kits of human flesh with them, which were afterwards cooked on board ; but I do not think it is true that any of the prisoners were killed on the brig and cooked, as stated by Mr. Simpson. Stewart, it appears, was in a terrible fright when he saw the way things were turning out, as he said he had no idea that there was going to be any blood shed over the affair ; but this is rather doubtful, as he must have known on what errand the Natives were bound.

On the passage up to the island of Mana, between the Straits and Kapiti, the prisoner, Te Mairanui, was tied by a rope to the main-mast, so that he could walk about a little. His daughter was allowed to run about on deck, so he called her to him and said, " They are going to kill me and make a ' taurereka ' (slave) of you, but that will never happen," and, picking her up, he knocked her brains out against the hatch combings. After the arrival of the brig, Te Mairanui and the other prisoners were taken ashore. He was given two days to cry, and was then to be killed. The story of red-hot ramrods being run through his body is, I believe, incorrect. He met his death in the following horrible manner : A straight tree about fifty feet high was chosen, and

to the head of this a block and haulyards were rigged
up.   One end was fastened to his heels, and, head
downwards, he was run up and let go with a run,
striking the ground with great force.   Three times
this was repeated ; he was then hauled up clear of
the ground and the veins of the neck opened, and
the first to drink his blood was the widow of the
murdered chief, Te Pahi.   He was afterwards taken
down, cooked, and eaten.

Shortly after this, Stewart interviewed Rauparaha
about his cargo of flax, which was promised to him,
but he was very insolent, and refused to give it to
him.   He was afterwards given one ton, and that
was all the payment he ever got for his share in the
bloody transaction.   He loaded up with spars and
sailed for Sydney.   The news of this horrible massacre had preceded him, and there was some talk of
his being tried for his complicity in the affair ; but,
owing to the lax state of the laws in New South
Wales in those days, it was allowed to blow over.
Not caring to go back to New Zealand, Stewart
cleared for a South American port, and was never
afterwards heard of.   It is supposed that the brig
and all hands were lost.   It is supposed by some
that the discoverer of Stewart's Island and the captain of the brig Elizabeth were one and the same
person, but this is not so.   The Captain Stewart,
after whom the island was named, was a man very
much respected, who gave up the sea and settled
down in Poverty Bay, where he died in the year
1844.—Yours, etc.,   G.J.B.

No. 12.—JIMMY ROBINSON.

The collector of these histories has been fortunate indeed in procuring the autobiography of one of the most celebrated Peninsula veterans, and begs to thank the kind friend who took such pains to secure it for him. The true history that follows was sent in an autobiographical form, but it has been thought better to alter certain portions into the narrative style.

The subject of this number, James Robinson Clough, was a native of Bristol. How he came to drop his surname one cannot say, but he was universally known as Jimmy Robinson, or Rapahina, as the Maoris called him. When a boy, he ran away from home and took to the sea, as is generally the case when a boy does run away. After several years in the East India trade, he found his way across to America, and there joined a new Bedford whaler called the Roslyn Castle, which was bound south. On board this vessel he stayed three years, and met with many an adventure. Whales were much more plentiful in those days than they are now, so that at the end of this time the Roslyn Castle was a full ship. She had some remarkably good takes off the Solanders, and for over three weeks her fires were never out. During one of these chases our hero very nearly lost the number of his mess. A large sperm whale, a cow with a calf, had been singled out, and the chief mate's boat, in which Robinson was pulling bow oar, was the first to make fast to her. As soon as she was struck, the whale sounded, and the line ran out fast, but she came up almost immediately, and went straight for the boat. Turning close to it, she gave one stroke with her flukes, cutting it clean in two, and killing the two midship oarsmen, tossing the others up in the air. They dropped close to the wreck, and managed to hold on to the oars and.

wreckage until picked up by the captain's boat. This same whale was taken two days afterwards. It was known by the iron in it, and turned out a large number of barrels. Calling in at Stewart's Island for wood and water, four fresh hands (Maoris) were engaged, who had been a trip before, and turned out good men at the oar.

After cruising about up the east coast of New Zealand, they ran into Akaroa, as their captain intended to recruit here for a month. It was blowing a gale of wind from the north-west when they made the Heads, and it was as much as they could do to work the ship up the harbor. Some of the squalls were terrific, and as they had her under pretty small canvas, it was no joke working her, where the tacks were so short. After getting about half way up, the wind was a good deal steadier and the harbor wider, and they dropped anchor abreast of the present town of Akaroa. This was in March, 1837. There were three other vessels lying there at that time, two being French, and one a Sydney whaler. The skipper laid in a good stock of pork and potatoes, the Maoris being very willing to trade, taking principally tobacco and slops for their produce. The crew were allowed to go ashore a good deal, and here it was that our hero fell in love with a young Native woman, who proved as good and fond a wife to him as any of his own countrywomen could have been. She was the daughter of a Native chief named Iwikau, a chief of the Ngatirangiamoa, and was about twenty years of age. To quote his own words : " I was twenty-three myself at this time, so that we were about a match. As money was of very little use here in those days, I took all I had to draw from the ship in trade, and as we had been very lucky, my share amounted to over six hundred dollars. Amongst my purchases was a five-oared whale-boat, which the skipper would not part with

until after a lot of persuasion. I had a good stock
of clothing, dungaree, coloured cotton, and tobacco,
so that I was looked upon as a Rangatira Pakeha.
There was another white man living here at the time,
known as " Holy Joe," but how he came to be called
that I cannot imagine, as he was anything but
what the name implied. I always looked upon him
as a runaway from Van Diemen's Land, and such he
afterwards told me he was. At this time there were
over a thousand Maoris living round Wangaroa
Harbour, for that was the Native name of it. There
were also settlements in all the Bays, round as far as
Port Cooper, so that there must have been about
three thousand Maoris on the Peninsula, including
those to the south of Akaroa.

Jimmy Robinson was present and helped to hoist
the English standard in Akaroa. His own version
of it, as told to our informant, was as follows :—" It
was in the year 1840, in August. I had been up to
the Head of the Bay getting a load of pipis, of
which the Maoris are very fond. I had in the boat
with me my wife and her youngster, who was about
a year old, and named Abner ; ' Holy Joe ' was also
with me, as I found him more useful in handling a
whale-boat than the Maoris. We were beating
down with a light south-west wind, when I noticed
a ship come round the point with a fair wind. I
said to Joe, ' We shall get some tobacco at last,' as
we had been out of it for some time. We then stood
towards her, but when we got a bit nearer we could
see her ports, and that therefore she was a man-of-
war. I said so to my mate, and he said, ' If she is,
for God's sake let me get ashore.' I suppose his
guilty conscience pricked him, or else he had not
finished his time, and thought he might be recognised. To satisfy him I said I would land him, and
paid her head off for the shore. I had not got far
when I heard a blank shot fired and saw some sig-

U

nals run up, so I thought I was wanted as a pilot
perhaps, so hauled on a wind again and ran alongside.   She had come to an anchor by this time a
little above Green's Point, as it is now called.   She
turned out to be the British man-of-war Britomart,
Captain Stanley, who came to the side and asked
me to step on board, which I did.   He asked me
who the female was, and I told him, so he said,
' Ask her to come on board.'   I could hardly per-
suade her, but she came at last, and squatted down
on deck with the young one in her arms.   The captain ordered the steward to bring her something to
eat, so she soon had a good spread of pies, cakes,
and fruit in front of her, but she seemed so nervous
that she could not eat them.   The captain asked me
to come below, so I went down, and he asked me all
about the place, how long I had been here, and how
many vessels had called, and their names, and how
many Maoris were living here   I gave him all the
information I could about the place, so he told me
that I must be sworn in as Her Majesty's inter-
preter, as he intended to take possession of the
islands in Her Majesty's name, and wanted me to
explain it to the Natives.   I was given a bell and a
small ensign to roll them up next morning, which I
promised to do.   We got what we wanted in the
shape of tobacco, and something to whet our whistles
as well, and went ashore.   I sent word all round to
the Natives, and next morning there was a great
muster on the sandy beach between the two town-
ships.   Three or four of the ship's boats were ashore,
and a party of them were sent with me to get a flagstaff.   We had not far to look, as we soon found
and cut down a kahikatea as straight as a die and
forty feet long.   A block and halyards were soon
rigged on and a hole dug, and it was very soon up.
After all the Natives were squatted down, and the
chiefs set out by themselves on an old ensign, the

captain commenced to read his errand here to the
Natives, all of which I had to interpret ; but there
was so much of it, I forget what it was all about. I
know, however, that it ended up with God save the
Queen, after which the British standaid was run up
and a discharge of musketry fired by the marines.
A salute was also fired with the big guns on board,
over which the Natives got in a great state of excitement. The captain invited myself and several of the
chiefs on board, where he gave us a grand spread,
and I was presented with a lieutenant's uniform,
and each of the chiefs had a marine's coat given to
him. Next morning the French vessel arrived, and
landed her colonists, as is already known. The
Maoris did not look upon their arrival with much
favor, and, if it had not been for the presence of the
ships, an attempt would have been made to drive
them away.

"After this several other white men took up their
abode round Akaroa, so I thought I would shift my
camp, and left for Ikeraki, taking all my possessions
in the whale-boat, including my three youngsters. I
stopped there for over four years, but part of that
time I spent in Peraki, where there were always one
or two whalers, from whom I got plenty of work, and
made a good bit of money in the way of supplying
them with vegetables and potatoes. On one occasion, during a drunken spree, while I was lying in
my bunk, I was stabbed in the breast with a knife no
less than sixteen times, and you can see the marks
of them yet. (On exposing his chest, the marks
could be distinctly traced.) I happened to have a
thick monkey jacket on at the time, or I should have
been killed. It was the whaler's cook who stabbed
me, and the captain put him in irons and gave him
bread and water for a month for it. I made a good
bit of money selling spars to the whalers. There
were some nice silver pines growing in Peraki then,

and I got as high as thirty dollars each for some of them. Drinking rum and working in wet clothes brought on a bad touch of low fever, and for three weeks I was in bed. As a last resource, my wife, who was a powerful big woman, carried me over the hills as far as Wairewa (Little River), where there was a Native doctor supposed to be very clever. Anyhow he cured me with native herbs, so as soon as I got better I left my wife and family for a bit, and went up as far as Kaiapoi, taking a couple of the Maoris with me as guides. There were several large pas in that district also, one up where Riccarton now is. I spent a month or two going about from one to the other, and then I returned and stayed a few years on the Peninsula again. During this period I lost my wife, so I made up my mind to go round and live on the Plains. I left my two girls with their friends, and took my three boys round in the boat, with the assistance of a couple of Maoris. I went right up the river Avon, and can say that my boat was the first ever taken up that river by a white man. We stopped at a small pa near the mouth of the river for a couple of days, and then proceeded right up as far as Riccarton, which took three days, as the boat was heavy and the river ran with great force. Shortly after this I met Mr. John Deans, who had come to settle on the Plains, and took him up the river to the place where he is now living, and afterwards conveyed his family and goods the same way.* I worked for him for a bit, helping him to put up his whâre, and afterwards engaged with him as shepherd."

But he found this sort of life too dull and solitary, so left, and went north, where he engaged with Mr. Darby Caverhill, and managed his run for a bit.

---

*It must be remembered this tale was related to my informant some years ago, when Mr. Deans was alive.

What is now known as Motanau was the place where they were living. He only stayed here about two years, and then went south again, and came across what is now known as the Alford Forest. Being struck with the fine timber here, he thought it would be a fine place to settle, so he purchased the section where his house now stands, and he did very well out of it. He lived all alone here, his eldest boy being married, and living on Mr. Acland's station, Mount Peel. He happened to save Mr. Acland's life one time when he was crossing the Rangitata, and has been there ever since. His second son, George, he had not seen for some years. He went back to live with the Maoris on the Peninsula ; and his youngest he lost the run of altogether. He sent him down to Christchurch about eight years ago, to get some tools and to get the horse shod, and he never heard a word from him since. He believed he got on the spree and sold the horse, and, being ashamed to come back, cleared off to sea.

Although living alone, Robinson's house was a picture of neatness. It was situated on the edge of the bush, about half way between McCrae's and Single Tree Point. There was a splendid garden of about two acres, filled with the choicest fruit trees, the sale of the produce of which brought him in a good bit of ready money. Living so close to a public-house, most of it found its way there. When on the spree he would do almost anything for grog, and on one occasion, not having anything to raise the wind, he was seen there endeavoring to sell a large family Bible for a couple of nobblers. When away from drink he was a capital worker and a good bushman, and as there was always a good demand for fencing material, he sometimes did very well. About 1872 his house was burnt down, and everything in it destroyed. What grieved him most was the loss of a little pet dog in the fire, and for days

he kept looking for it round the bush, thinking it
had escaped, but he saw nothing of it. Several of
the neighbors lent him a hand, and a fresh house
was put up and the garden renovated a bit, but most
of his best apple trees had got killed. He was persuaded to be a teetotaler for a bit, and tried it for a
time, but he went to see the Ashburton races in
1873, and being so well known in the district, his
acquaintances wished him to have a drink. He
explained that he was a teetotaler, but he would have
a drink with them, and put it away in a bottle, and
this he did until he had several bottles of mixed
spirits, which he took back with him, and then commenced to break bulk, and until all was finished
there was no work done. Drink and hard living
now commenced to tell on this once iron constitution,
and a paralytic stroke, from which he suffered,
seemed to hasten his end. He went down to see
Mrs. Deans, who kindly offered to get him into the
Old Men's Home, but he would not hear of it, so
after staying in the Christchurch Hospital for three
weeks, and feeling better, he set out home again to
the Alford Forest. But he seemed past work, and
lived, one may say, on the charity of the neighbors.
He left the public-house to proceed home one winter's
evening, and was found dead about half way, with a
half empty bottle of spirits beside him. It was
supposed that he sat down to have a drink, and,
falling asleep, was frozen to death. Thus died pen-
niless in 1874, James Robinson Clough, a man who,
with the opportunities he had, should have been a
second Rhodes. It may seem strange, but it is
nevertheless true, that the end of the subject of this
number and that of Walker, both men who were
almost the first Europeans on the Peninsula, should
have been so similar, both dying from the immediate
effects of drink on the Canterbury Plains.

When living with his two sons, Abner and Robinson, he used to make them read the Bible aloud to him every evening. He was working for a good while in the employ of Mr. Justin Aylmer at Malvern and other places, and bore the reputation of being an excellent bushman. His favorite book was a translation of Herodotus, which he was constantly reading. He told Mr. Aylmer that he had once resided in Sydney, where he had been employed in a store, fallen in love with his master's daughter, and married her. He was wild in those days, and having a dispute with his wife, cleared out one fine morning, and never saw or heard of her again.

No. 13.—JIMMY WALKER.

Amongst the " Old Identities " of the Peninsula, one of the most remarkable was Jimmy Walker, or " One-eyed Jimmy," as he was often called, from the fact that one of his eyes was gone. Our informant tells us that he believes his right name was Quinn, but no one ever called him anything else but Jimmy Walker, or One-eyed Jimmy. The way in which he first became known as Walker is rather curious. When he first came to New Zealand he was a very strong and powerfully built man, standing over six feet. Being not only a sailor, but a sailor accustomed to boats, he soon learnt to manage the canoes, when he went to live amongst the Maoris. After a short time he became so expert that none of the Natives could " hold a candle to him," as he used to . say. The result was that the Maoris christened him " Waka," the Maori for a canoe ; and as his Christian name was Jimmy, he gained the appellation of Jimmy Waka, or Walker, which stuck to him till the day of his death.

His first arrival in New Zealand was in the year 1839, when he landed in the Bay of Islands. He was then about eighteen years of age, and immediately after running away from his ship he went into the bush, where he followed the occupation of timber splitting for some time. He soon became very expert at this work, but as soon as he got a cheque he used to knock it down, as was the fashion in those days, in one of the neighboring grog shanties, which were common enough even at that early period, being established principally for the benefit (?) of the whalers who used to frequent the coast. After a time he got tired of this life, and went over to Auckland. When he got there he was employed by Sir George Grey as a gardener. The great Proconsul took quite a fancy to this stalwart, good-looking, good-natured young sailor, to whom work seemed only fun, but, alas ! those good looks, which stirred the Governor's sympathy, were the cause of Jimmy's speedy departure. Amongst Sir George's household was a very pretty Maori girl, whose susceptible heart softened at the sight of this handsome stranger, and she soon made known to Jimmy, in that unmistakeable way which is common to the sex, be they white, brown, or black, that she loved him. Nor was he slow to return her affection, and the result was that they neglected their work that they might be together. Sir George remonstrated with him, but in vain ; the greater the opposition the fiercer burned their love ; and, at last, finding all argument useless, he was dismissed. If they thought, however, that by dismissing Master Jimmy they were going to retain the girl, they were much mistaken, for he had no sooner left than his faithful dusky belle followed him. She persuaded him to leave the haunts of civilisation and come to live with her tribe, and the syren's voice prevailed, and Jimmy went with her, and spent some happy years amongst

her Maori relatives. He soon acquired the native
tongue, and became quite a " Rangitiera nui "
amongst them. Owing to his knowledge of the two
tongues, he used to conduct the barter between the
Sydney traders and the Natives. From them the
hapu used to get supplies of slops, stores, grog, etc.,
and payment for these used to be generally made in
kind.. Jimmy used always to have a number of
Natives in the bush employed at splitting posts and
rails and shingles for this purpose, and others were
employed in flax scraping for the same end. Jimmy
was very sharp at the trading, generally getting the
best of the bargain.

After living in this way for eight years, the chief
thought Jimmy was getting too bumptious, and
tried to take him down. A serious row ensued, and
Jimmy was very nearly shot by the enraged Rangitiera. However, he managed to escape with his life,
though he left one of his eyes behind him in the
scrimmage, and so gained another cognomen. All
his gear, however, was forfeited, and he left the pa
without anything but the much damaged clothes he
had on his back. It is not recorded what became of
her who had left Sir George Grey's household for his
sake; but Jimmy used to hint that the eight years of
connubial felicity had somewhat chilled the first glow
of their mutual passion, and that there were some
things that he left behind him that he regretted
even more than his dusky bride. However, as
Jimmy used to say, " he was not long on the broad
of his back," for a very short time after he engaged
with Captain Ford, of the American whaler Eliza,
with whom he remained two years. During this
time the vessel was coast whaling, and as they had
good luck, she was a full ship at the end of that
period, and sailed for New Bedford. Walker, however, had no fancy for leaving New Zealand, so he
was paid off at Russell, in the Bay of Islands, and

from thence he worked his way down the coast, stopping at Akaroa. He lived here with the Maoris for some time, and afterwards went to reside at Little River, where he took out a bush license for splitting shingles and posts and rails. He frequently employed a number of Maoris at this work, in the old style, paying them with slops and other articles of trade. At intervals he went to Christchurch, where he invariably got drunk.

Shortly after the Otago diggings broke out he found his way to them. He had excellent luck at first, but with his habits money was of little use to him, for the faster he made it the quicker he spent it. At the end of a few years the neighbourhood in which he was working was pretty well exhausted, so he started on a prospecting tour into the little-explored back country, accompanied by his mate. They travelled to places that no white man had previously visited, and it was then that Jimmy had the adventure of his life. This was no less than catching a glimpse of a living specimen of the great apteryx, the huge moa bird. One need hardly say that Jimmy's tale about his meeting with a live moa was much doubted, but to the day of his death he always swore that it was a fact, with such earnestness as left no room to doubt that he himself thoroughly believed that he had seen that great bird, that is supposed to be extinct. Whether he and his mate (who also affirmed the same thing) were suffering from some strange hallucination, or whether they really did see this wonderful creature, will probably ever remain a mystery; but there is still a wide stretch of unexplored country in the county known as the Fiords, and it is possible that in this almost inaccessible region a last specimen of the moa may yet be found. Our informant gives us the tale told to him by Jimmy in almost the same words that were used in relating it :—" We were camped,"

says he, " out in a deep gully a little above the creek
which we had been prospecting for the last three
days, getting the colour in most places. The hills all
round us were mostly covered with tussocks, with
here and there a little patch of bush in the gullies.
On this particular evening we had just knocked off
work, and were putting things a bit straight after
supper, when I was astonished to hear my mate sing
out, 'Good God, Jimmy ! what's that ?' On turning round I could scarcely believe my eyes, for there,
right in front of us, standing on the opposite side of
the gully, was the moa bird that I had so often
heard of from the Maoris. It was walking about,
and as the sides of the gully were pretty steep, I
should say the bird was not more than 150 yards
from us, and a bit above the level of our camp. As
soon as I saw it I knew at once what it was, so I
told Bill, my mate, it was the moa, and that the
Maoris were awfully frightened of it. At that he
got very nervous and began to shake. The moa, I
should say, was about eight feet six inches or nine
feet high, and from the knee downwards you would
think he had a pair of officer's boots on, quite shiny
and black. His feathers were a lightish grey colour,
and his head he seemed to be able to turn round any
way, as it would first look at us with one eye and
then turn round and look with the other. I must
confess I felt a little bit skeered myself, as we had
no gun or anything, only a tomahawk, to protect
ourselves with. However, after he had surveyed us
he cleared out, taking immense strides as he went,
and in the dusk of the evening he was soon lost to
sight. My mate got so excited over it that he
wanted me to break up the camp and make tracks
back. He could not sleep a wink the whole of the
night, and roused me up at daybreak next morning.
After some persuasion on my part I got him to
consent to follow the trail a bit. On getting over

to where it had been standing, we found a pile of its
dirt, and a little further on, where there was a small
spring in the side of the hill, we noticed quite distinctly the track of its feet in the soft earth. I have
a pretty big hand, and I spread it over the footmark,
but could not span within three inches of it, from
my thumb to my middle finger end ; and from the
depth it sunk in the soft earth, it must have been a
good weight. We followed on for about two miles,
but could see no sign of it, but coming to a small
flat, we noticed that the heart of several of the cabbage trees had been pulled out, and part of them
eaten, so that we were pretty sure it was done by the
moa, as there was no one else in the district but
ourselves. My mate was determined to leave the
place, and as our tucker was nearly run out, I was
compelled to go back with him. We had about
eight ounces apiece for a little over two months'
work, so we packed up and started back, arriving at
Queenstown in about a week. We told our tale
there, and were of course called liars, and several
other nice names. I got locked up over it, and this
is how it happened. I had described the whole
affair to three or four up-country hands, and when I
had finished one of them—I forget his name now—
called me a b——y liar. I hauled off and gave him
a plug in the eye ; then we had a regular set to, the
finish of it being that several of us got locked up,
and when called upon before the magistrate next
morning, I told him the provocation I had got, and
how the row commenced, so he let me off pretty
light. He seemed to have some faith in my story,
and got me and Bill to recount the whole of it to
him. Several of the storekeepers offered to fit out
an expedition to try and capture the moa   I offered
my services to lead them to the place, and they also
engaged an Arab, who was reckoned a dead shot to
go with us, but he got his neck broke while breaking

in a young horse, so that kept us for a bit. I had
now run through all my money, and having a bit of
a quarrel with those who were getting the thing
ready for a start, I ' chucked it up.' "

This is the story just as he told it to our informant, and on venturing to doubt the veracity of
his statement he flew into a most violent passion,
and wanted to know what good it would do him to
make up a bundle of lies. He seemed quite earnest
over it, and really we cannot but believe there was
some truth in it. He said he intended to have
another go for it some day, as he reckoned if he
could get it alive it would be as good as a pile to
him. Several times he tried to get the Little River
Maoris to go with him, but in vain. In one of the
bush fires at the River his whâre was consumed. It
stood on Mr White's ground, just after you commence the rise of the hill, about a quarter of a mile
from the corner. Like most of the old hands,
Jimmy came to an untimely end. After leaving the
River he struck south, and was found dead on the
banks of the Rangitata, close to Sir Cracroft Wilson's station. A bottle of Hennessy was his only
companion. It is needless to say it was empty.

Mr. and Mrs. Hahn, who used to live within a
short distance of Jimmy Walker at Waikouaiti, and
who knew him well, have forwarded us the following
further particulars regarding that veteran. It
appears that some nineteen years ago he was splitting posts and rails at Johnny Jones' bush at
Waikouaiti, having gone there from the Tuapeka
diggings. Jimmy here dropped across a widow who
was sister to a Mrs. Winsey. She had been married to an old skipper, who had given up "the
briny," as he called it, and died in the happy possession of an oyster saloon in the classic neighbourhood
of the Minories, in London. When this unfortunate
event occurred her sister wanted her to come out

here, and she complied. She was a decent woman
about forty, and, being fair, no doubt attracted
Jimmy from the force of contrast with his former
dusky companions. Her relatives being old and
feeble, she began to look out for a home, and, no
doubt influenced by her former relation with the
ocean, kept company with the Cyclopean Jimmy.
She accepted him when he told her he had lots of
money, in fact, had made his " pile." Of course she
only married him for a home and his money, and she
lived to bitterly repent her folly. They were married in Waikouaiti, and kept up the " spree " for
three days at Mrs. Winsey's house, which was
situated on the edge of the Hawksbury Bush. After
the great " spree " Jimmy's money was almost done.
They lived with the Winseys for about three weeks,
while Jimmy was building a hut in the Hawksbury
Bush. He got permission to do so from the late
John Jones, for whom he was working. The hut
was built of split slabs and covered with calico. He
soon began to ill-treat his wife, and the Winseys,
having got tired of Jimmy's company and the rows
occasioned by the quarrelling of the two, told him he
must take her away, so as soon as his hut was
finished he moved into it. It was built a little way
in the bush, on a small clearing a short distance
from Hawksbury House. When they got in the
hut Mrs. Walker soon displayed her ability at house-
keeping, for she arranged her half-tent, half-hut, in
such a tasteful manner that it was the talk of all the
people round that neighbourhood. When Mrs.
Walker was living with her sister, before she knew
Jimmy, she had some cattle which she bought when
she first came out. As soon as they were married
Jimmy sold these and spent the money. This was
the first of their quarrels, which led to his thrashing
her, the castigation no doubt reminding him of the
system used in correcting Maori ladies. He became

a perfect brute to his wife, thrashing her in the most
unmerciful manner. He always performed this
operation late at night, never striking her in the day-
time. All the men about there seemed to be afraid
of him, and consequently he was let alone, though
universally hated by his mates, Charlie Anderson,
Billy Caton, Jack Pope, and a Swede These four
men used formerly to work in Okain's Bay, but went
away from there to the Tuapeka diggings. Jimmy
was considered a good bushman in those days, so his
mates stuck to him. Mrs. Walker frequently
brought Jimmy up before the late Mr. Mellish, who
was Magistrate there, and who used to caution
Jimmy, who would promise to act better if he was
let off, but never did. The Resident Magistrate
eventually bound him over to keep the peace, but
this was too much for Jimmy, who no doubt thought
he could not trust himself, so cleared out again for
the diggings. Mrs. Walker still lived in the same
place, and used to take in needlework. After a time
Jimmy sent her a little money. Although frequent
enquiries were made about him, after this he was not
heard of. During this time Jimmy encountered the
moa. Poor Mrs. Walker was found dead a few
years after on the road through Hawksbury's paddock. She died of heart disease, brought on, it was
said, by the ill-treatment and frights she had received
from Walker. It was only after she was married
that she suffered from heart disease.

No. 14.—" CHIPS."

Amongst the remarkable inhabitants of Akaroa, our worthy friend " Chips" may fairly be enumerated. He is a true Pakeha Maori, a race now fast disappearing from amongst us. He has a great reputation amongst the Natives, for two reasons. One is his great skill in building and mending boats and other vessels, he being a ship's carpenter by trade ; and the other his no less ability, according to them, of patching up human craft. As a doctor he has gained great fame, and no doubt the faith with which his prescriptions are taken tends in no small measure to their success. " Chips " is not an old Peninsula resident, most of his life having been spent in the North Island. His whâre is on Mr Check‧ley's ground, near Green's Point. The road, after leaving the Cemetery gates, is very rough, part of it being a narrow track on the edge of a considerable precipice, and how " Chips " manages to get home safely in the dark nights of winter is a mystery. On one occasion he did slip over, and fell a considerable distance, but was saved by clinging to the long grasses. The boat-shed where " Chips " works is only a few yards from the whâre, but is on Government land, being within a chain of high water mark. It is a very primitive edifice, but is spacious, and well furnished with a great variety of the necessary tools. A visitor will generally find " Chips " at work here, and in no degree disinclined to enter into conversation. He is a very intelligent man, of fair education, and, as will be seen by his narrative, has seen a great deal of the world.

Adolph F. Henrici, known familiarly as " Chips," was born at Hamburg. His father, a respectable tradesman, wanted him to become a linen draper, but he had taken it into his head he would be a ship's carpenter, and, with the aid of a schoolfellow, he

secretly visited an old ship's carpenter on Sundays,
from whom he learnt the trade. His father was
still more displeased at an attachment he formed
with a young girl in the neighborhood, and there was
a separation, " Chips " going his first sea trip in the
year 1837, the ship being the Friendship, of Sunderland, and her destination New York. The trip
was uneventful, and he then went to India in the
Francis Smith. From there they went to China
with opium and other cargo, and got into great
trouble because the captain's wife was aboard, the
mardarins searching the vessel. The lady escaped
by being put into another vessel, which luckily
was not searched. The laws were strict against the
introduction of opium, but the authorities received
bribes and winked at the trade. After many adventures in this trade, " Chips " went to England.
From thence he paid a visit to his native town, but
he did not stop long, proceeding to Bordeaux in an
English vessel called the John and James. She
loaded for Mauritius, but calling in at the Cape of
Good Hope on her way, " Chips " left her to join
the Thomas Sparks, Captain Sharp, bound for Wellington and Nelson, New Zealand, with emigrants.
This was in 1843, and in January, 1844, the ship
arrived safely in Wellington. Here " Chips " left
the ship, and worked for a time in the Hutt Valley.
Getting tired of this, he went whaling at Table
Cape, on the East Coast. There were three boat
crews, no Maoris amongst them, a man named
Dawsey, a half-caste negro, being in command.
They only got one whale in the season, but she
yielded eight tons of oil. His great skill as a boat
builder now became known, and he was offered a
good sum to go to Poverty Bay to repair a little
vessel. He went there, and remained some time,
but a Native chief living at Ahuriri, known to the
English as Jacky Tighe, pursuaded him to go to
w

Hawke's Bay, where, he said, there were a number
of boats to build. He then went and lived at Paka-
whai, on the Ngararora River, where he resided with
the Natives at a big pa and built many large boats.
The Maoris thoroughly appreciated his skill, and a
Rangitiera named Tokamanu, who was afterwards
one of their representatives, wanted to give his sister
to " Chips " as a wife. The Rev. Colenzo, however,
opposed this, and so enraged Tokomanu that he
threatened to burn the church and return all the
Maori Testaments. " Chips," however, who was
not particularly enamoured of the lady, persuaded
the enraged chieftain to listen to reason, and his
sister was bestowed on another Maori.

About this time Bloody Jack came on a visit to
Te Hapuka, a great Maori warrior living in the
vicinity, who, though not of a high Maori lineage,
had raised himself to be a " Rangitiera nui " by his
bravery and skill in warfare. Bloody Jack came
across the straits from Akaroa in a big boat called
the Mary Ann, which was the identical vessel for
which he had sold the Peninsula to Hempleman.
On leaving Ahuriri he presented the boat to his
host, Te Hapuka Now, this gift was not such a
very great one after all, for the native vessel had
fallen into terrible disrepair, and was perfectly useless
without it was skilfully mended, an operation
involving special knowledge. But Te Hapuka had
seen what " Chips " could do, and in his difficulty
had turned to him. He had of course heard all
about Tokomanu's sister, and knew " Chips " had
no wife, and, being a wily savage of an economical
turn, he offered to provide " Chips " with a female
companion if he mended the boat. Three girls from
Mohaka happened to be visiting at the pa, and he
gave " Chips " his choice of the lot. Now this, to
say the least of it, was a trifle arbitrary, for he had
no right to either of them, and two were " tapu " to

Maori chiefs. The third, who was the one "Chips" fancied most, was only "tapu" to a Native of no pretensions as to blue blood, residing at Mohaka. However, Te Hapuka didn't care whether he had a right to them or not ; he wanted his boat mended, and "Chips" wanted some one to look after his whâre and cook for him, so the bargain was concluded, "Chips" selecting the young lady who was betrothed to the Maori of "low degree." It will thus be seen that "Chips" gained his bride (his present wife) by repairing the boat for which Banks Peninsula was sold to Hempleman !

Now, the Maori to whom "Chips'" wife had been betrothed was exceedingly wroth, and so were all the rest of the family ; but "Chips" did not care for this, being protected by the powerful Te Hapuka, and by and by these new relatives of his came to the conclusion that it was not a bad thing at all to have a Pakeha Maori for a near connection, and became reconciled to the match. A new trouble, however, soon arose. Te Hapuka, directly his boat was mended, got tired of "Chips," and formed the plan of taking the wife he had given him away, because, having learned something of European cooking and behaviour from "Chips," he thought she would be a good wife to his (Te Hapuka's) son. "Chips" was kept in strict ignorance of this, but the father of Ene Mari Ropini, for such was her name, was spoken to. Now, he was perfectly satisfied with "Chips," who, in his opinion, had given "utu" enough for his daughter ; and besides, he knew the girl was attached to "Chips," and would suffer from a separation. He did not, however, dare to express his thoughts openly while Te Hapuka was near, so he dissembled, and pretended that he would acquiesce in the arrangement in a short time. One day he went to "Chips," who was building a boat in the bush, and said to him, "If I were you I should build that

boat bigger ; you might have to go a voyage in it."
" Chips " thought something was up, and took the
hint, and built the boat fit for the sea instead of for
the river, as at first intended.   Te Hapuka didn't
like the evident friendship between " Chips " and
his father-in-law, and the latter was so frightened
that he used to go away and sleep in a fresh place
every night, with a tomahawk by his side, being
afraid Hapuka might take a fancy to destroy him.
An uncomfortable month or two passed in this way,
and at last one evening Hapuka announced his
intentions with regard to the girl to several of the
Maoris, and fixed the following evening for the
abduction.   A friend of " Chips' " worthy father-in-
law told him what Hapuka had resolved on, and he
at once went to " Chips " and said, " It is time for
you and my daughter to be at Mohaka."   Thoroughly versed by this time in Maori warnings, and
knowing the case was desperate, " Chips " got the
boat ready for sea, though the weather was very
bad.   This fact was probably his salvation, for Te
Hapuka never dreamt that the boat, which he looked
upon as only fit for the river, could live in such a
sea.   " Chips," his wife, and his faithful father-in-
law and friend, passed a dreadful night, tomahawk
in hand, fearing that every sound that they heard
was the dreaded Te Hapuka, or some of his myrmi-
dons, coming to tear them away from each other for
ever.   Great indeed was their relief when the grey
dawn enabled them to steal down to the boat.   The
sea was by this time moderating, and with hopeful
hearts they committed themselves to the Ngararora,
whose rapid current speedily carried them out to sea.
The passage was an uneventful one, and they arrived
at Mohaka in good spirits.   Te Hapuka was furious
at first, and said he would take his warriors and
burn down the Mohaka pa, and do all sorts of things,
but remembering on reflection that the defences there

were very strong, and that they were defended by a great many friends of the" Chips " party, he thought it better to extend his patriarchal forgiveness.

" Chips lived at Mohaka for many happy years. He had plenty of work, for the stations along the coast wanted whaleboats to ship off their wool to the small craft that used to come to fetch it, and the small vessels also wanted repairing. His family increased rapidly, and the pa as a whole was very prosperous. The Natives, however, had one fear— they were on bad terms with the Uriwera tribe, that lived further inland, in a wild and almost inaccessible country, and were afraid of being taken by surprise. Some of them used to sleep in a pass some distance from the pa every night, in order to give warning of their enemies' approach, and the pas were strongly fortified. A few white people were now living on the Mohaka, and when the news came of the Maori war in the North, and the Waikatos announced their intention of killing the Queen's Maories and whites along that part of the East Coast, Government put up a substantial block-house at the mouth of the Mohaka, and sent some ammunition there, and a few troopers to defend it. There were two pas, both well fortified. As is the Maori custom, they were perched on the highest ground in the neighborhood. One was on the edge of a cliff more than four hundred feet high, the other was on an eminence surrounded by comparatively level ground, and as they had plenty of guns, the Natives deemed themselves impregnable. The Waikatos, however, never came, the troops were withdrawn, and the block-house was left in charge of the Maoris, who buried most of the powder. The news of Te Kooti's return from the Chathams, and the massacre at Poverty Bay, reached them, but they never dreamed of his visiting their locality, and the fears of the Uriweras had died out, so that no precautions were

taken. In April, 1869, the Hero arrived with
stores from Napier. " Chips " fetched her into the
river, and she discharged her cargo (which consisted
of stores of all kinds, including grog) on to the bank.
Now, the name of the chief of Mohaka was Paul
Rurepu, who was a very great Rangitiera indeed.
A wife of his was ill at this time, so he determined to send her to Napier in the Hero for medical
advice. She agreed to go, but insisted on " Chips' "
wife (who was a great friend of hers) accompanying her. The Hero did not intend to sail till
the 12th of the month, but on the 8th " Chips "
had a dream to the effect that if she did not leave
the river the next day she never would. The pre-
sentiment left by this dream was so strong that he
persuaded the captain to go to sea the following day,
against his will, which turned out to be a lucky job
for him, and all the others aboard. The Natives
had a plantation about two and a half miles up the
river, and the great majority of the young men and
women were working there at the time. Whilst
working at this plantation they used to sleep in some
whâres there, only returning to the pa at intervals.
More than sixty of them went to rest in these whâres
on the night of the 9th April. They only woke to
die, for at the first break of day some two hundred
Hau Haus, led by the ferocious and pitiless Te
Kooti, surrounded the whâres and mercilessly shot
down and tomahawked all. Out of sixty-five only
two—a man and a young girl—escaped to tell the
tale. The sound of the firing was heard at the pas,
and they knew that the Hau Haus were on them.
" Chips' " brave old father-in-law came to him and
said, " You must go and take your youngest boy
with you, or his mother will go mad. It is better
for you to go at all hazards, for they are sure to kill
all the white men, but may spare the Maoris. I
will remain here with the other children." " Chips "

had considerable difficulty in persuading any one to
accompany him in the boat, for the sea was very
rough, and they were afraid of being drowned. At
last one of his daughters, a white man who had been
working for him, and two Natives, got into the boat
with him and his boy, and they got safe to sea.
The white man was half dead with fright, and pulled
so badly that " Chips' " daughter gave him the baby
boy to hold, and took the oar herself. After warning people on the coast, they reached Napier in
safety and gave the alarm.

After killing all the people on the plantation, the
Hau Haus divided into two parties, one going down
each side of the river. Their progress was one of
blood. A Mr. Leven, a white settler, and his wife
and three children, were first killed ; the next victims
were a Mr. Cooper and a lame shepherd. Seven
whites were thus added to the list of murders, but
the more they killed the more bloodthirsty they
seemed to be. Arriving at the smaller pa, the one
situated at the brink of the precipice, they assailed
it with the greatest fury. A number of men, by
cutting holes for their toes in the clay and soft rock,
scaled the height, the projecting palisading saving
them from the guns of their foes. Once at the
fence they soon made an impression on it, and the
defenders of the pa being called upon to open the
gates, and promised quarter, admitted the enemy.
They first demanded that all arms should be given
up, and killed several men. Hatea, a Native who
worked for Chips, on being called on to give up his
gun, refused, and Te Kooti immediately aimed at
him, Hatea returning the compliment ; both fired
together, but unluckily Te Kooti escaped with a ball
through his leg, while poor Hatea fell dead. The
Hau Haus next tried to fire the church, which was a
raupo building. Strange to say, on this occasion
this inflammable material would not burn, and, after

trying three times without avail, they called out that
the church was bewitched by an unfortunate woman
who was sitting near, and murdered her most bar-
barously with their tomahawks, literally chopping
her to atoms in their mad frenzy. The great
majority now went down to the block-house, and
burned and destroyed as they went. Finding the
stores that Captain Campbell had landed from the
Hero, they soon got at the grog, and before long
many were in a state of beastly intoxication. Night
now descended on the horrible scene. There were
four of " Chips' " children in the pa, the eldest, a
girl of fifteen, having recently married a Maori.
Their poor old grandfather, who had been such a
good friend to " Chips," had been murdered, and
they determined to endeavor to escape. Slowly and
cautiously they made a hole through the wall of the
pa on to the side of the precipice, across which ran a
narrow and difficult path. At length the work was
accomplished, and one by one three of " Chips' "
children and two others, who were their friends, crept
through the hole, and stood in safety outside the pa,
the watchfulness of the Hau Haus being relaxed
through their frequent potations. It was only then
that they discovered that the youngest one was not
amongst them. Her heroic elder sister did not hesitate a moment. Telling the others to proceed, she
returned to the scene of danger, and miraculously
passing unharmed amid the drunken Hau Haus
returned with the little one, and at last stood safe
outside on the ledge of the precipice. But her
second passage had aroused some of the Hau Hau
guards ; the alarm was given, and two of them discovering the hole through which the brave children
had escaped, rushed through in pursuit, after giving
the alarm by firing their guns. They met with a
speedy and terrible death Not knowing the ledge,
they stepped into the outer darkness, and falling

down the precipice, were shattered on the rocks below. Two other Hau Haus, either undeterred by, or unaware of their comrades' fate, gained the ledge in safety, and sped after the poor children. The spirits they had drunk, however, probably rendered their footing uncertain, and at a treacherous turn in the path they too slipped and fell, meeting the same well-deserved fate as their comrades. Guarded, as it would appear by a special Providence, the children reached the bottom of the cliff in safety, and stood on the banks of the Mohaka. On the other side was comparative safety, so they made up their minds to swim it. One was nearly drowned, but eventually all landed in safety ; some horses belonging to a neighbour were caught, and before dawn they were far on their way to Napier, and safe from the pursuit of the Hau Haus. The Hau Haus never discovered the place where the powder was buried, which was a great disappointment, as this was their principal object. They remained in the neighbourhood for some time, the Government having no force to cope with them, and they retired by the path they came.

"Chips" went to live at Pakowhai again, and after a time was persuaded to go to Lake Taupo to build some boats by Mr Ormond, who was then superintendant. His daughter Anua had run away from home and come to Akaroa, and on a visit to her father she spoke in such high terms of the place that he determined to come and live here, so some six years ago he came. Both he and his wife are much respected by the Maoris, and much loved by their children.

x

No. 15.—THOMAS RICHARD MOORE, M.D.

(CONTRIBUTED BY THE REV. R. R. BRADLEY)

Here is the name of another celebrated old identity. Dr. Moore arrived in this Colony by the Sir
George Pollock, about the year 1851, and bought
land in Charteris Bay, where he settled ; but, not
being up to the rough-and-tumble life of a colonist,
he was finally obliged to sell out to the present
owner, Mr. R. R. Bradley, the whole of his interest
in that Bay. He afterwards settled in Christchurch,
and devoted himself to his profession, where he
would undoubtedly have reached the height of his
ambition, but death stepped in, and he died suddenly
about twenty-two years since. He was a man of
bright intellect, with which he adorned his profession
to such a degree that if any case seemed hopeless,
the cry was always, "Send for Dr. Moore ; if he
cannot do you good, no one can."

On his arrival in this country, and with the intention, as noted above, of turning farmer, he brought
with him four celebrated cows, that have since left
their stamp on many of the herds of cattle on the
Peninsula. Mr. R. Rhodes, in particular, owes not
a little to the bull Brother Phil for the improvement
of his stock at Ahuriri and Kaituna. The names of
the imported cows were Flash, Duchess, Creamy,
and Old Dunny (an Alderney). Mr. Rhodes purchased Flash at the doctor's sale, and also Brother
Phil, and remnants of their stock could almost still
be traced in Mr. T. H. Parkinson's herd. About
ten or twelve years ago, when a person had a beast
to sell, and could only say that it had been bred
from Dr. Moore's stock, it was thought quite enough
to establish its quality. One person really did
obtain possession of a female calf, the doctor being
obliged to part with it instead of wages ; but on the
whole, like most wise breeders, he was very careful

about parting with his female stock. The doctor's
cattle eventually became a mixed lot, but such was
the celebrity of the above-named imported cattle,
that any cow that came from Charteris Bay must be
good. We have heard that the doctor, previous to
leaving England, had practised successfully in Salisbury, of which city he had been mayor. His widow
and family are still in the Colony.

No. 16.—FRENCH FARM AND THE
SURVEY.

About the years 1858 and 1859 a great many
new settlers came to New Zealand, and of these not
a few came to the Peninsula, more particularly the
passengers by the barque Indiana and the ship
Clontarf, most of whom settled in the various Bays
of the Peninsula. Amongst these we may mention
Messrs. G. J. Checkley, Joseph Bates, Kennedy,
and S. and J. Hunt. Some of these new settlers
went to dairy farming, others to bush work. Few
had much capital to start with, and most of them
are now comparatively prosperous men, thanks to
their energy, and the splendid timber, capital soil,
and good climate of our Peninsula. The timber was
then to be found everywhere in very large quantities,
and the climate was more humid in consequence.
Its removal has largely increased the droughts in
summer, and old settlers think that planting should
be largely carried on, to mitigate the extreme heat
of the sun, which now burns up the bare hills for
several months in the year.
One gentleman, Mr. F. Moore, left the barque
Indiana in Lyttelton, in the year 1858, with a very
small capital, which he, like a good many more,

speedily good rid of, not seeing at the moment what
he was to do in New Zealand.   He came down to
the Peninsula, and joined Mr. Tribe's gang in the
French Farm Bay, cutting blocks for the old Government buildings, piles for the Lyttelton jetty, firewood,
etc., at which employment he was occupied nearly
two years.   Very jolly was the life led by these bush
fellows in the old days.   Many of them had been
delicately nurtured and well brought up, but they
turned to with a will, and found that they could do
hard work as well as those to the manner born.
Their-hard-won earnings were, however, in most
cases speedily disposed of.   They used to work like
slaves for a month or two, and then go to Akaroa
and knock it down in a few days.   Mr. Gibbs kept
the principal hotel, which was the one now known as
Bruce's.   He was a decent fellow, with a large cor-
poration, and the boys all liked him, for he was of a
very genial character.

Mr. Tribe rented the Government bush in French
Farm, and employed a great many men.   He was
universally respected, but in spite of all his enterprise, he never (through a series of misfortunes) succeeded in making the fortune he thoroughly deserved.
At one time he was burnt out in Lyttelton, and afterwards took the Central Hotel in Christchurch   He
eventually found his way to the West Coast diggings, when he was returned as a member for the
General Assembly, and did much good for the community he represented, and was as generally beloved
by the diggers as he had been on the Peninsula.

When Mr. Tribe gave up French Farm, Messrs.
Keegan and Wilkin bought a spot of ground on the
south side of Akaroa Harbour, on which Mr. Keegan
is still living.   Mr. Moore went over with them, and
stopped for a year.   At this time Mr. Townsend
was traversing the Peninsula on the survey.   He
was joined by Mr. Moore, who stopped with him

six months, and afterwards went with him up north.

At the time the big works were going on in French Farm, Mr. Shadbolt took the Head of the Bay Hotel, and succeeded in it most admirably. His predecessor was a Mr John Anderson (a Russian Fin), and in his time there were high jinks at the Head of the Bay, for in those days timber was worth twenty-two shillings per hundred feet, and the sawyers made their money very easily, and spent it as freely as they got it.

A gentleman named Dickens resided in French Farm before Mr. Tribe came there. He was a dairy farmer, and a good deal of the land there belonged to him. One day, in the year 1857, he left the house without saying where he was going, taking his horse with him. When night came he did not return, but his dog came back, and a search was instituted, which lasted for many weeks. His horse was discovered tied up in the supplejacks, but no trace or tidings of the missing man himself have ever been discovered to the present day. The present proprietors of French Farm are relations of this gentleman, who was very much respected and regretted.

There were many narrow escapes in those days, particularly to those engaged in boating. On one occasion, at Christmas time, Mr. Townsend sent a boat's crew to Waikerakikari from Akaroa. It came on to blow fiercely from the south-west, and the crew had to put into Lucas' Bay, where they laid that night. There was a keg of rum in the boat, and before midnight they were drinking it out of the heel of an old boot. Next morning they resolved to start, though it was still blowing very hard from the south-west. Jack Miller was the steer-oarsman, and he kept the men in good heart. In spite of the heavy seas and furious wind, they managed all right till they got near a reef that runs out near Waikera-kikari shore.   Here the sea was breaking furiously over the reef, and they had to wait for over two hours before Miller gave the word to pull across. When he did he said " Pull, and pull like h—l, boys !" and so they did pull, and just as the boat cleared the reef the rowers saw the bare rocks staring up abaft.   It was a marvellous escape ; another moment and the boat must have been dashed to pieces, and all on board drowned, for no one could have swum in such a sea ; and had it not been for the iron nerve and quick eye of Miller, none would have lived to tell the tale.

No. 17.—JOHN HENRY CATON.

There is a very picturesque bay on Lake Forsyth named after the subject of this memoir, who was well known all over the Peninsula as a dealer in stock.   He was a man of a great variety of trades, up to anything, and was much liked by many in the early days.   He once kept the Canterbury Hotel, in Lyttelton, and afterwards (in conjunction with D. Taylor) purchased a run near Tamutu, at the head of Lake Ellesmere.   It is said he was born in Smith-field, close to the celebrated market, and he used to boast that he had been connected with stock since his birth, for that reason.   He went to Sydney in 1849, and came to Canterbury in '53.   It was about 1860 that he purchased the run previously mentioned, and entered extensively into cattle dealing, a pursuit which made him known in every corner of the Penin-sula, from which he drew no small portion of his supplies.

The great event in his life happened later.   He

arranged with Mr William Wilson, of Christchurch, familiarly known as "Cabbage Wilson," to enter into a speculation for buying a large number of cattle in Nelson and Marlborough, and taking them to Dunedin, where they were scarce. Mr. Wilson found the money, and the large drove was collected north and driven south, where they were disposed of at a large profit, the purchase money exceeding £2000. His instructions were to bank this money in Dunedin, where he received it, but this he did not do. He returned from Dunedin with the money in his pocket, in company with Mr. H. Prince, and when they arrived at the Waitaki, the boundary river between Otago and Canterbury, he tried to make an arrangement with one of the men that when they were crossing the river they should create a disturbance amongst the dogs, so that a stock whip might be used, and in the scuffle a carpet bag he carried, supposed to contain the money, might be lost overboard. The man in question agreed, and when they were crossing the river the plan was carried out, but, unluckily for Caton, a passenger rescued the carpet bag before it sank, so this plan failed. They rested that night on the north side of the Waitaki, and Caton made an excuse to leave the camp to look after some horses in the river bed. He went away, and during his absence night came on. On his return he asked the tent keeper where was his carpet bag, about which he evinced great anxiety. He afterwards called attention to the tent's being cut, and declared the carpet bag had been taken, and after a long search the carpet bag was found ripped open, and despoiled of its supposed contents of £2000. Prince, being afraid he might be accused, gave notice to the police, and when Caton reached Rolleston, Detective H. Feast, Sergeant-major Pardie, and our friend Sergeant Willis, of Akaroa, were waiting for him. They searched him without result, but at the bottom of a pair of long boots, hung over a chair to dry, the £2000 was found. The trial created great interest, and he was eventually sentenced to four years' imprisonment at Lyttelton Gaol. After his release he went to Sydney, where he was drowned some time after in the river McLachlan. He was a man of remarkable talents, and might have made quite a prominent figure in life had it not been for his unfortunate propensity. His name is quite a byword in the county. The latter event recorded took place about 1872.

No. 18.—THE CHIEF PAORA TAKI'S STORY.

(CONTRIBUTED BY THE REV. J. W. STACK.)

You want to know when Te Wherowhero came here. I will tell you, for I was one of the first to see him. Our interview came about in a strange manner. I was on my way from Port Levy to the Maori village at Pigeon Bay, which was situated close to where the steam wharf is now. I was accompanied by another Maori, named Hapakuku. On nearing Mr Hay's house we became aware that our movements were being attentively watched by several Europeans. My companion grew rather nervous when he found this out, and wished to turn back. He was too familiar with the dark doings of our own people in former times, not to suspect the white men of some evil design against us. I laughed at his fears, for I had mixed enough with white people to know that we had nothing to apprehend from them. As we drew nearer I recognised the Akaroa policeman, who was a friend of mine, and then was able to assure my companion of our perfect

safety under his protection. When we got up to the
Pakehas they all shook hands with us, and then the
policeman asked us whether we knew anything about
a boat that was then sailing up the harbour. We
told him it was not a Maori boat, and that we had
noticed it entering the Heads from the south as we
descended the hill. The white men then talked
together, when the policeman told us that one of his
companions was the mate of a whaling ship anchored
in Akaroa Harbour, that six of the crew had run off
during the night with one of the boats, that they
had come over in search of the deserters, and that if
we would help to capture them we should be liberally
rewarded. They believed that the approaching boat
contained the missing men. We consented to assist
them, and were told to keep about on the beach,
while they retired to a neighbouring settler's house,
where we saw them watching the boat with a spy-
glass through the half-open door. The boat made
at first for the Maori pa, but the crew seemed to
change their minds, and headed straight for where
we stood, at the mouth of the creek. On their
coming within hail, they asked if they could get any
food on shore. The settler who was with the policeman and mate when we first met came down, and
told them they could get what they wanted at his
house. Four of the men then jumped ashore, leaving
two in charge of the boat. We all walked up to the
house together. On entering the kitchen I did not
see the policeman or his mate ; they were hidden
away in an inner room. When the meal was prepared, the men sat round the table, and ate as if
they were very hungry. Presently I was told to go
to the beach and send up the other two, who were in
charge of the boat. We all walked up to the house
together. On my telling them my message, they
seemed very glad, and jumped ashore without delay.
I got into the boat and pushed off. As soon as I

got clear of the beach, I hurrahed and danced about, to the evident astonishment of the two men, who stood for a while staring at me, and then went on, evidently never suspecting the cause of my shouts, which were so loud as to attract the notice of the people of the village, who ran out to see what all the noise was about, wondering what crazy fellow could be larking in such an idiotic manner as I appeared to be doing with the white men's boat. They did not know that it was a preconcerted signal between the policeman and myself. I pulled the boat in to the village, where I got the Maoris to help me drag it up, and, after stowing away the oars and gear, I returned to the settler's house, where I found all the men still sitting round the table. As soon as I got in I stood with my back against the door, and a minute or two afterwards the bedroom door opened, and the policeman and mate walked into the kitchen. It would have made you laugh to have seen the crestfallen expression on the faces of those men, who, with their legs under the table, could not stand up quickly, and could have no chance of escaping or successfully resisting, seven men standing behind the seats, and ready to pounce upon them if they ventured to move. They exchanged looks while quietly submitting to have their wrists manacled. As soon as they were all fastened together, we started for Akaroa Harbour. It was a rough journey for the sailors, fastened as they were, for the path that led up the heavily timbered valley was very narrow, and continually crossed by a narrow stream. On reaching the Head of the Bay we lighted a signal fire, and soon after a boat came from the whaler and took us all to Akaroa, where the deserters appeared before Mr. Robinson, the Magistrate, and were ordered by him to return to their ship. The captain took Hapakuku and myself on board with him, where he gave us each a good suit of clothes as a reward for our services. We slept on board, and the next day after breakfast I went on deck, which was almost entirely covered with empty casks, as the mate was busy stowing the full ones at the bottom of the hold. Wanting to have a look round, I stood upon some casks near the bulwarks, and looked over the side. I had not been many minutes there before I saw something that quite startled me : I saw a large ship opposite Onuku, and coming up the harbour without any sails—coming so fast that the water spouted from its bows like a wave recoiling from a rock-bound coast. When I could get my breath I called out, " O, look year ! look year ! What dat ? Water break all er same stone on er beats !" Several persons sprang to my side, amongst them the captain, who, as soon as he looked, said, " Steamer !" That was the first steamer I ever saw. It was soon at the anchorage, and the whaler sent a boat on board, when I found that Sir George Grey, Te Wherowhero, and Te Horeta were on board. Sir George asked where all the Maoris were, and I told him at Port Levy. He said, " Go and tell them that I am here with Te Wherowhero." I went off at once and returned the following day with twenty companions. We had an interview with the Governor, and then I went to Onuku, where Te Wherowhero had gone to confer with our people. We stayed all together in William's large house. I woke in the night and found our guest smoking. There was a large oil lamp burning, which gave a bright light. I saw him go out once, and noticed that his body was beautifully tattooed. His stay was very short, for the next day he and the Governor went away in their steamer, and we saw no more of Te Wherowhero.

No. 19—STORY OF A SNAKE HUNT IN AKAROA HARBOUR BY MRS. TIKAO.

(CONTRIBUTED BY THE REV. J. W. STACK.)

The impression sure to be produced by the heading of this story will be, that it is simply a hoax which no amount of testimony can substantiate, for it must seem incredible, in a country where such reptiles are unknown, that a snake hunt ever took place in the immediate vicinity of Akaroa. But the story will not appear so improbable when it is known that several attempts were made in the "early days," by visitors to these shores, to acclimatize snakes; and the presence of the reptile found and killed in these parts was doubtless due to the ill-judged zeal of one of those insane naturalists, who, regardless of all consequences, seemed determined to solve the question whether snakes could exist in New Zealand. Mrs. Tikao's story is as follows :—" We had often listened with eager interest to the stories told by our countrymen of their narrow escapes from being bitten by serpents; and the accounts they gave of the deadly effect of snake bite only served to deepen our hereditary aversion to all reptiles. You can imagine the commotion and excitement caused by the reported discovery of a snake on the shores of the harbour. It was found by a coloured man named Jim, who lived a long time with the Maoris at Takapuneke, near the Red House. He was a sober, industrious man, and highly respected by us. Having gone for some reason to O Tipua—the promontory between Akaroa and German Bay—he was startled by the discovery of unmistakable signs of a snake's presence. The spot where the discovery occurred was close to the cliff used by the men-of-war frequenting the harbour as a target. He hurried back at once to warn every one against going near the place. He told the Maoris not to approach the place even for the shell-fish found only at low water. There was no need to repeat the warning, for we were all too much alarmed to venture anywhere near O Tipua, and already in imagination we saw the country swarming in venomous reptiles. Jim told us that he used to track and kill snakes in his own country, but that it was so long ago, that he almost forgot how to proceed, but he promised to do his best to rid us of the dreaded pest, which had appeared in such an unaccountable manner in our neighborhood. There were two French men-of-war at anchor in the harbour at the time, and Jim applied to the captain of one of them for help, who supplied him with a musket and ammunition, and sent in one of the ship's boats to the spot where the indications which he first saw awakened his alarm. Every one was very much interested in the success of Jim's efforts, and the Maoris, seated in boats and canoes, watched his movements from a safe distance. On landing, he proceeded cautiously along the hill side, picking his steps through the tussock grass and scrub. At last we lost sight of him altogether, and he was so long hidden from our view that we began to be alarmed for his safety, many exclaiming that he had fallen a victim to his zeal for the general safety. The report of his gun, however, assured us of his escape, and not long afterwards we saw him approaching the beach with something like an eel, about a yard long, fastened to the end of a rod. He brought it down to the beach, and showed it to us. It was spotted black and white. Jim told us that it was necessary to burn it, in order to prevent its young ones coming out of its body and stocking the place, so a bonfire was made and the snake consumed."

No. 20—THE MYSTERIOUS DISAPPEARANCE OF MR. DICKEN.

In the article entitled " French Farm and the
Survey," brief mention is made of the mysterious
disappearance of Mr Dicken, of French Farm, but
merely a few words were given, and it is therefore
with much pleasure that we are able to lay before
our friends a clear and detailed account, that was
furnished to our informant by Mr. Edwin Silk, who
was, at the time Mr. Dicken disappeared, renting
some land from him, in conjunction with Mr. Tribe.
It appears that in the summer of 1857 Mr. Dicken
and Mr. Silk went out one morning to look after
some stray cattle.   They went over a lot of country
in the neighborhood of French Farm, and got home
unsuccessful at about 4 p.m.   Mr. Dicken then
declared his intention of searching for the missing
stock on the Barry's Bay fern hills.   He accordingly
went away on his pony, refusing the company of Mr.
Silk, who offered to go with him.   He had a collie
slut following him.   When evening came, and Mr.
Dicken did not come back, Messrs Tribe and Silk
were both anxious, for the roads were very bad, and
they feared he might have had a fall.   They therefore got out the dingy, and pulled to the Head of
the Bay Hotel, which was then kept by Anderson,
in order to find out if anything had been seen of Mr.
Dicken there.   Finding on their arrival that he had
not gone in that direction, they went to Barry's
Bay.   Mr. Tribe had brought a cornet that he was
in the habit of playing with him, and when they got
to the Barry's Bay hills he made them ring again,
but to their mortification and dismay there was no
response, and they had to return home.
     Next morning they renewed their search in the
flax and scrub that were on the edge of the bush
that fringed the Barry's Bay fern hills.   At last, in

a pig track, they saw the marks of the pony's feet,
and following the trail they came to the pony himself. He was tied to a flax bush, but so lightly that
the least pull would have set him loose. There,
however, he had evidently stayed since the previous
night, and further observations showed Mr. Dicken's
own track leading into the bush. They followed it
for a few chains, but it then became imperceptible,
and though they again and again tried to see where
it led, and Mr. Silk knew the print of the boots so
thoroughly as to be able to identify their marks anywhere, they could find nothing to guide them.
Eventually they returned to French Farm and gave
the alarm to Mr. Dicken's family, and to the people
living at Akaroa   Search parties were organised,
and every hill and gully was searched for a week,
but without result.   The search was most thorough.
There was a big totara tree in the bush, and each
party on going in used to mark on this tree the
direction in which they were searching, so every
gully was scoured.   Miss Dicken offered a reward
of £500 for the body of her brother, alive or dead,
but the men could not have searched better than they
did for any reward.   The Maoris offered to come for
a certain sum down, but they did not fancy having
anything to do with a corpse, and rather shunned
the search, their superstition being awakened by the
whole matter.   What seemed most puzzling was
that the dog did not come back, as it would if anything had happened to Mr Dicken.   At last the search
was given up, and the Akaroa people went back, the
understanding being that if the dog came back, or
there were anything fresh happened, Messrs Tribe
and Silk should make a smoke at a certain point to
let the Akaroa people know.
    Just a fortnight after Mr. Dicken's disappearance,
Mr. Silk was at the back of the house at French
Farm, washing his clothes, when, looking round,

what was his astonishment to see Mr. Dicken's slut crawling up to him. She was a mass of skin and bone, and must have been fasting during the whole of her absence, and she crawled up to him in that guilty way, which dogs have when they know they have done wrong. Her hair was matted and stained with red clay, and this struck him as most remarkable, as there was no red clay to be found in the neighbourhood of Barry's Bay, the nearest being some miles away.

Mr. Silk gave the signal agreed on, and three boatloads of men came over from Akaroa, and they took the slut to the place where the horse was found, and tried to make her show them the road her master had taken. All was useless, however, for she would not go anywhere, and eventually the second search had to be abandoned without any result, and the mystery has never been solved to this day. Mr. Silk had a list of the things Mr. Dicken had with him, so that the body might be identified if it were ever found. One of these things was his pipe. It was a clay, and a triangular piece had been broken out of the bowl, so that it would hold very little tobacco. Only the day before his disappearance Mr. Silk had said to him, "I had better give you another pipe," but he was a small smoker, and replied, "No, the pipe holds enough for me." Mr. Silk could also identify his knife, and the pattern of the nails in his boots, which was peculiar. Some day perhaps this knowledge may help to solve the mystery. The slut became the property of Mr. Thomas Brough, and was eventually killed for biting one of his children.

No 21.—HARRY HEAD.

Among the more remarkable men who from time
to time have led isolated lives on the Peninsula, one
called Harry Head may be mentioned, who, some
fifteen years ago, took up his residence in Waikerakikari. Previous to his arrival this Bay had been
quite untenanted, as it was covered by dense bush,
and almost inaccessible both from land and sea. It
appears that it was for these very reasons that Head
selected it for his abiding place. He chose a Government section in the valley near the beach, and put up
a shanty, which he roofed with tree ferns. Here he
lived all by himself, and friends who visited him on
rare occasions used to find him industriously occupied in the bush or his garden, in a very primitive
garment, consisting of a sack in which holes had
been cut for his head and arms. At certain intervals he used to tire of this Robinson Crusoe kind of
existence, and visit the residents of the neighbouring
Bays in very scanty clothing. In his habits he was
almost a wild man, and it is said he had lived long
amongst the North American Indians. Instead of
riding with an ordinary bridle, he preferred the Indian
fashion of a string turned round the horse's lower
jaw. This string used to be composed of coloured
strands, Indian fashion. He was credited with the
power of long abstinence from food. He has been
known several times to start to walk from Akaroa to
Christchurch with nothing but a little sugar in his
pockets, his only clothing being some home-made
trousers and a blanket, which on grand occasions he
used to encircle at the waist with a gaudy parti-
coloured cord and tassels.

Harry Head was a great lover of music, and used
to play simple melodies by ear on the piano, when
occasion offered. Strange to say, however, the
instrument he loved most was the drum, which he

used to aver was capable of great expression, as well
as power. He was also an excellent performer on
the banjo. Once on a time he had almost resolved
to abjure his solitary and wandering existence for
domestic felicity, but the mother and friends of the
young lady on whom he had placed his affections
strongly objected to him, and he had to return to his
solitary wharê in Waikerakikari. He appeared to
be a man who had read and throught much, and was
considered of a genial temperament by those who
knew him intimately.

He was the first man who took stock into Waikerakikari. He purchased a number of calves, and
got a gentleman to assist him in driving them there,
a difficult task indeed in those times, when there was
no track and a dense bush all the way. A start was
effected at six one morning, and his companion had
to go about two miles out of the road to satisfy
Head, by seeing a group of Nikau palms. At last,
after a lot of trouble, they arrived at their destination, and it being most sultry weather, the dwelling-
house was found to be a very suitable one, and fit
for the Astronomer Royal, being open to the stars
of heaven. The wharê in which his visitors slept
was composed of weather-boards, was about eight
feet square, and was a regular old curiosity shop,
being filled with all sorts of nicknacks and curios he
used to pick up on his visits to Christchurch and
other places.

One of his strangest notions was, that with properly manufactured appliances human beings would
be able to fly. He gave much attention to this
hobby, and even ventilated the subject in public in
the old country, after leaving the Peninsula. He
once paid a visit to the West Coast, and on his
return walked back over the ranges at the rate of
some fifty miles a day. This, however, seemed to
entirely cure him of any desire for future rambles on

foot, for it was his last pedestrian feat. He eventually returned to England, and astonished his
friends there by his remarkable costume and strange
style, and no doubt they were heartily glad when he
announced his intention of proceeding to his old
home in America. He is now, to the best of our
informant's belief, located at Dacotah, where his
primitive habits appear to have enabled him to with-
stand the effects of the terrible seasons, which have
been so fatal to other Europeans. Before leaving he
sold his property to the Messrs. Masefield, and his
old clearing is now the site of the sawmills erected at
Waikerakikari by the energetic Mr. John Smith.

From Mr. W. Masefield we further learn that
Head's real name was Alexander, and that he was
the son of a bookseller, who had him well educated.
He was an excellent mathematician, and a fair Greek
scholar, besides understanding a good deal of botany.
The latter was much cultivated by him during his
sojourn on the Peninsula, and he was constantly in
correspondence with Dr. Haast. From his youth he
had strange fancies, and, when young, slept a night
at Stonehenge, on what is known as the vertical
monument, in the hope that mysterious dreams
would come to him from the forgotten past. The
dead Druids, however, made no sign, and a cold was
the only result.

He was born at Chippenham, in Wiltshire, and,
on leaving England, went to America, and joined a
party to the Rocky Mountains. He had a great
admiration for the North American Indians. He
afterwards went to Vancouver Island, and thence
worked his passage Home in a lumber ship, which
made the longest passage on record. After a brief
spell at Home he came out to Australia, and was at
the diggings for some time. He walked over a great
part of Australia, and applied to join the Burke and
Willis expedition, but was too late. He there formed

an acquaintance with Baron Von Muller, with whom
he used to correspond upon botanical subjects After
a time he came across to New Zealand, and walked
over the North Island, and then came across to Nelson, and from there continued his pedestrian expedition to Christchurch. He was one of the first men
to cross the range. He afterwards came to the
Peninsula, to Le Bon's Bay, and saw Mr. Cuff there,
and wanted to get some land ; but Mr. Cuff told
him it was all his. He then went Home again, and
after a short stay came again to New Zealand, and
was at the Otago diggings, being one of the first at
Gabriel's Gully, and did well there. He had, however, been so charmed with the Peninsula, that it
was not long before he came back to it to get some
land and settle.

He bought a piece of land where Mr. Lelievre's
house now stands, at Fisherman's Bay. He sold it
after some time to Mr. Lelievre, and bought a place
in Paua Bay. He had a wharê there, and locked it
up one day to go to Christchurch. When he got to
Christchurch, however, he made up his mind to go
to England, and when he came back to his wharê,
long after, he found the place was broken open, and
his things gone. He then sold the land to Mr.
Narbey, and went on to Mr. Townsend's survey
party, and helped to cut the present line from Barry's
Bay to Little River. He then bought land in Waikerakikari.

He was a splendid hand in the bush. Unlike an
ordinary mortal, it was his practice to go in a bee-
line from one place to another, utterly regardless of
tracks. He never lost his way, and used to accomplish long distances in a wonderfully brief period. He
once started to carry a tub from Barry's Bay to
Waikerakikari, through the bush. He had it on
his head, and it struck against the branches of a
tree, hitting him so smartly on the head that he

remained unconscious for many hours. When he left the Peninsula he had fully £500 in his possession, and when he reached England he increased his capital by lecturing on philosophical subjects. With a very powerful and acute mind, but of exceedingly erratic temperament, Harry Head narrowly missed being a great man,

---

No. 22.—THE LOSS OF THE CREST.

The well-known ketch Crest, Captain Ellis, left Akaroa one Sunday evening in October, 1868, loaded with telegraph poles, for a port to the north of Kaiapoi. She had on board Captain W. A. Ellis, master and part owner ; J. B. Barker, part owner ; Edward Cunningham, seaman ; and Mr. W. Belcher, of the firm of Belcher & Fairweather, Kaiapoi, who was passenger and charterer. The weather was fine when the vessel started, and no one dreamed that anything had gone wrong till the following day about noon, when Mr. J. B. Barker arrived in Akaroa, and stated that the vessel was wrecked, and that he was the only person who had escaped. He stated that he had managed to land in Flea Bay in the dingy, and that he had told the Messrs. Rhodes, who resided there, of the catastrophe.

This news was, of course, looked upon as final, every one thinking that the rest of the persons aboard the ill-fated Crest had come to an untimely end. Later in the day, however, the startling news was brought that two of the Rhodes had gone out in anything but a safe boat, to view the locality in which the vessel had been reported to be lost, and had rescued Cunningham from a rock to which he

had swum after Mr. Barker had left the vessel.
Cunningham informed the Messrs. Rhodes that Captain Ellis and Mr. Belcher were still alive and aboard
the craft, and several attempts were made by the
Messrs. Rhodes to rescue them, but they were totally
unavailing, as the wreck had drifted into a cave,
over a considerable distance of kelp-covered shallow
reefs, upon which even in the calmest weather the
sea broke fearfully. Cunningham stated that Ellis
cou'd have escaped as he did, by swimming, but
refused to leave Belcher, who could not swim.

As can be imagined, this news created a great
deal of excitement in Akaroa, and boats manned by
volunteers were at once despatched to the scene of
the wreck, in the hope of saving the unfortunate
castaways. The weather remained moderate, and for
three days every plan that could be thought of was
tried to rescue the unfortunates, but without avail.
The vessel in the meantime had broken up, and Ellis
and B lcher had got upon a ledge of rock within the
cave. It was thought that Ellis had received some
injury, and was incapable of swimming in consequence, but of course nothing certain on this point
can ever be known. Those who proceeded to the
locality in the hope of rescuing the unfortunate
sufferers cannnot reproach themselves with leaving
any means untried. Ropes were drifted over the
kelp into the cave, and Ellis upon one occasion
managed to get a hold, but the strands parted, and
the temporary communication was destroyed. A
colored man named Dominique, a celebrated swimmer, spared no pains in his endeavors, but he tried
his utmost unavailingly.

Captain Schenkel, of the Prince Alfred, was
unremitting in his attempts, and devised many
schemes to save the castaways, but they were all
frustrated by the unrelenting ocean, which appeared
determined to prevent either the entrance of the

rescuers, or the exit of the unwilling explorers from
the gloomy cavern.

The poor fellows were plainly to be seen, and their
cries could by heard by those who were risking their
own lives in the attempt to save them   They had
rigged two pieces of rope from the roof of the cave,
to which they fastened a board, and when the tide
began to flow, they had to sit on this board to prevent themselves being washed away. At high water
the mouth of the cave was covered with the surging
water, the scene being described by the eye-witnesses
as terrible in the extreme.

For three days this fearful suspense continued,
but on the boats going out on the fourth morning,
the cave was discovered to be vacant.   No doubt
weakened by continuous suffering, thoroughly exhausted, and unable to hold on any longer, they
must have been washed away during the night.

Words cannot pourtray, nor imagination conceive,
what these poor fellows must have suffered before
succumbing.   Without food or water, buffetted by
the waves, to see help so near and yet of no avail—
it is dreadful, even at this length of time, to contem-
plate their terrible sufferings.   The sympathies of
every one in Akaroa were strained to the utmost by
the fearful suspense, and never before or since has
Green's Point been watched with such intensity as for
the appearance of boats with news regarding the
calamity.   Our informant states that he hopes never
again to feel the fearful anxiety which he experienced during the time the attempts at rescue were
being made.

Captain Ellis was well known throughout the
district, and was universally respected.   A tablet to
his memory is to be seen in St. Peter's Church,
Akaroa.   It was placed there by the Oddfellows, of
which society he was a member.   Mr. Belcher, as
before stated, was a resident in Kaiapoi, where he

was much esteemed.   The calamity threw a gloom over the whole Peninsula.

The tablet erected in St. Peter's Church to the memory of Captain Ellis bears the following inscription :—"This tablet is erected by the Oddfellows, M.U., of this district, to the memory of Captain William Ellis, aged 43 years, who perished through the wreck of the ketch Crest, near the north head of this harbour, on October 29, 1868."

Stories of the Bays.

PART THE SECOND.

No. 1.—LE BON'S BAY.

THERE are different tales in explanation of the manner by which Le Bon's came in possession of its name. One is that the whalers in the very early days were accustomed to bring in the whales to the Bay and there try them out. In the course of time the beach was covered in whale bone, and the place was called the Bone Bay. Another story tells how Captain Le Bas came in his ship to Le Bon's, mistaking it for Akaroa. He sent a boat's crew ashore, and one of the crew was named Le Bon. The Bay was named after him. Captain Le Bas stayed in the Bay for some time. There were a great many whalers of all nations about in those days (during the fifties), but they seldom called into the Peninsula bays by all accounts, generally making Akaroa Harbour their head quarters. Le Bas' ship is supposed by some to be the first ship that was anchored in the Bay.

There was a Maori pah on the beach before white men came into the Bay, but they had all gone before the first settlers arrived. Skeletons are often found in the sand, and some curios, such as greenstone tomahawks, ear-rings, etc. Traces of the pah still remain, and lead to the conclusion that there was once a large number of Maori inhabitants. Abundance of stumps of totaras were found about the Heads. The trees had evidently been cut down for canoes. As in most bays where the Maoris lived, strata of bones of all kinds are found where they had been heaped up after a feast, mixed with fish bones and shells. A close examination proves also that the natives did not confine themselves to this food. Piles of human bones, which are all separated from one another, and piled up close to the kitchen middens, disclose the fact that cannibalism was a common practise amongst them.

Mr. Cuff, father of Mr. Cuff of Cuff and Graham, was the first settler in Le Bon's. He went there with his family, and lived in a tent for some time, and eventually built the house now on Mr. Henry Barnett's property. It has been added to, however, and so much improved that there is little of the old house left. When Mr. Cuff came, the Bay was covered in dense bush and heavy timber : that was in 1857, Le Bon's being much later settled than most of the Peninsula bays. Mr. Cuff saw that there was a great deal of valuable timber, and started a sawmill on the banks of the creek close to his house. Mr. Cuddon, now in Christchurch, brought the engine down, and the vessel was floated up the creek. There was a great difficulty in getting the engine ashore, as it sunk in the mud, and it was some time before the mill was got into working order. It came on to blow severely, and the vessel that brought the engine was detained a month in the Bay. When it did start the mill had plenty of work. The flat was covered with white and black pines as thick as they could stand, and the sides of the valley grew immense totaras and other timber. Mr. Cuff brought cattle with him, and improved the land about his house. The walnut trees still standing were planted by him, and are nearly as old as those on Muter's place in German Bay.

The Maria Ann and Gipsey, ketches, were the first vessels that carried the timber from the Bay to

Lyttelton. Messrs. Thos. Oldridge and Stephens owned them, being partners. They came to Le Bon's about 1860, and soon afterwards went to Laverick's, returning to Le Bon's some years afterwards. Mr. Stephens, it will be remembered, lost his life on the brigantine Lizzie Guy. The ketch Maria Ann was sold afterwards in Lyttelton, and the Gipsey, on her way from Lyttelton to Le Bon's, was run down by a steamer off Long Look-out. A man well known (a Dutchman), by name Charlie Smith, commanded her at the time. No lives were lost. These two vessels carried an immense amount of timber to Lyttelton. The vessels anchored in the Bay, and punts and rafts were floated down the creek laden with the timber from the mill, which was situated about a mile from the sea.

Some years afterwards, during a great storm, two vessels were wrecked—the Breeze and the Challenge. The Challenge was sunk while at anchor. The Breeze was driven into Nor'-west Bay and smashed up. Their crews managed to get ashore. At a quite recent date the Gipsey and Diligence, which replaced them, were also wrecked ; and the Hero, well-known from her several narrow escapes, met her fate also in Le Bon's.

Messrs. Saxton and Williams took the mill from Mr. Cuff about 1861, but only worked it for six months. Mr. John Cuff, son of the owner, then managed it. Messrs. Oldridge and Stephens ran the mill for some time, and after that Mr. Drummond McPherson, well known in Canterbury, bought it. A man named Rouse bought it from him. In 1865 Mr. John Smith took it over. He had a great many men working for him, who are now settlers in the Bay. He also introduced the Danes, who now own among them a good portion of the land in Le Bon's Bay. Mr. John Smith got the contract from the Provincial Council for building the old jetty and the tramway to it from the mill. About £1000 was thrown away on this work. The tramway could never be made to act, and a ship-load of timber never went down by it, punting and rafting being resorted to as of old. An attempt once to get a shipment of cheese away by sending it down the tramway to the jetty proved a failure. The tramway was never of any use whatever, and was left to decay. Some portions of it are still to be seen. About this time Mr. Hartstone, in company with a man named Savage, who acted as engineer for Mr. Smith for some time, started a mill on the headland above where the new jetty has been built. Mr. Dalglish, who previously to this had been working for Mr. Piper in Duvauchelle's Bay, soon afterwards took this mill, and still owns the property. Mr. Dalglish made the mill much larger, and exported a great deal of timber. Mr. Smith, when he had worked out the timber in the Bay, rented Mr. Dalglish's mill for some years.

The greatest event that ever occurred in Le Bon's was the tidal wave of 1868. It came at one o'clock, and caused much terror. Mr. Bailey's house was carried bodily up the Bay, and deposited on the tops of the trees on the flat. There was three feet of water in Mr. Smith's house on the flat, and all day the waves kept coming up. A whaleboat was carried out of the river and placed on a bridge. The bridge was loosened and carried out to sea, and again the boat and bridge were brought back.

Following on this was the renowned gold fever. It appears Miss Gladstone, the sister of Mrs. Smith, found a piece of quartz well impregnated with gold close to the house, which, it was supposed, had been washed up by the tidal wave. The news spread like wild fire, and became known in Christchurch. A company was formed there, and two men were sent down to examine the Bays. These men prospected

Waikerakikari and Le Bon's, and found no signs in
the latter, but there were traces of gold in the former.
The men belonging to the mills were all the time in
a great state of excitement, and shovels and dishes,
and all the articles appertaining to gold getting were
in great demand. It is generally supposed that
some man wished to play a lark, and placed the
quartz there. No result came at any rate from the
discovery of the one piece of quartz, and the men
gradually settled down to their work again at the
mills, after every gully and bank in the Bay had been
thoroughly examined.

As may be supposed, there were many strange
characters in the Bays in those days. Sailors were
continually deserting the vessels, and kept in hiding
in the bush until they had gone. Men of all classes
and description worked together, and some of them
were men of no mean ability.

The bush was so dense, that a trip to Akaroa was
quite an expedition. Very often parties lost themselves for days, which can hardly be credited now.
The first track was cut by Mr. Cuff, for which he got
£100. It can still be traced, running along the
ridge on the South side of the Bay across the ranges
to German Bay, where it ran almost in the same place
the present road lies. About 1864 the Okain's,
Little Akaloa, and Le Bon's Road Board came into
existence. Mr. Henry Barnett was the first representative for Le Bon's, and Mr. George Hall acted
as Clerk to the Board. In 1870-72 the present road
to the Akaroa side was formed. Harry Head fixed
the grading. He also laid out the road to Nor'-west
Bay. Harry Head never lived in Le Bon's for any
time, although he was passing through and staying
at the settlers' houses. Few were as well acquainted
with the bush as he. As most of our readers know,
he lived in Waikerakikari and Gough's, then almost
inaccessible.

Butcher's meat was a luxury little known to the early people in the Bay. Wild pigeons abounded, however, also ka kas. The creek swarmed with eels of great size, and monsters of 40lbs or 50lbs were quite common. The general plan was for the men to go out on Sunday, and in an hour or so shoot enough game to last the rest of the week. As the bush disappeared, the land was sown down, and cattle introduced. The destruction of the bush was also the destruction of the game.

Messrs. Piper, Duvauchelle and Howland came early to the Bay, and worked in the mill. Mr. Bailey arrived in 1861. The Barnetts came in '63, Mr. G. Hall in '60, and Mr. D. Wright, now in Okain's, in '62. There were, of course, heavy bush fires, but the inhabitants lived on the flat, which was first cleared, so little damage was done to property. Mr. Bailey was once burnt out, but he was the solitary exception.

The first dairy was started by the Messrs. Barnett. Mr. Thos. Oldridge soon followed suit, and is still carrying it on. Messrs. Hartstone, Leonardo and others soon afterwards began making cheese, but it is only during the last twelve or thirteen years that dairying has become general. Mr H. Barnett first introduced sheep into Le Bon's to stock his fine property.

The present church was built in 1869: before that the preacher delivered his address from a timber stack. Mr. Smith had a school for the children in the Bay. Miss Pauer was the first mistress. Mr. Tom Berry, a well known character on the Peninsula, was master afterwards. The present school was built about six years ago.

Some years ago a man named Norris started in a boat for Okain's. It came on to blow, the boat was capsized and Norris drowned. Another accident occurred not long ago. Mr. Dalglish shot his

timber down a shoot into the Bay, and still does.
A man named Nielson was at the bottom of the
shoot when timber was being let down, and kept in
check by a chain. The chain broke and came down.
on Nielson, killing him.

With the exception of a few occurrences of this
sort, the Bay has had a very quiet history. It is
the old story of men building up a settlement isolated
from the rest of the world. The Bay prospers from
year to year, and grass seed and cheese have become
its chief exports. The low price produce commands
at present causes depression, but those who have
property in Le Bon's are confident that it has a
prosperous future before it.

No. 2.—OKAIN'S BAY.

Most of the Bays have got their names from some
trifling incident. Okain's is no exception. Captain
Hamilton, well known in the early times, and who
used to trade between the Bays and Lyttelton, was
passing this Bay in his vessel one day, and happened
to be reading a book on deck. The book chanced to
be by Okain, the Irish naturalist. Capt. Hamilton
therefore called the Bay after the author, and it has
been Okain's ever since. Okain's is perhaps the
largest of the Bays round the Peninsula, being much
wider than any of the others. The creek which
flows down the valley and empties itself into the Bay,
can be dignified with the title of river without mis-
application. The flat rises so gradually from the
beach that the tide is felt for more than a mile from
the mouth of the creek, and fairly sized vessels can
navigate it The beach is a great stretch of sand,
and the constant work of reclamation is doing on.

There are two Okain's, Big Okain's and Little Okain's. Little Okain's lies towards the East Head. It is a small narrow Bay of a rugged nature, and is remarkable for the many giant karakas that thrive there still. It was here that Moki, the renowned chief of the Ngai Tahu, landed first on the Peninsula during his expedition against Tu-te-Kawa, the great Ngatimamoe of Waihora (Lake Ellesmere).

It is not exactly known whether the Maoris had a pah in Okain's itself. It is certain, however, that they visited it a great deal in their hunts for provisions. Their headquarters were Pah Island, a small islet lying round East Head. It contains about three acres, and its formation rendered it a splendid natural fortification for the natives. The Maoris inhabited it to the time when the first settlers came to Okain's, and traces of them are visible to the present day.

The population of the Bay at the commencement of its settlement consisted chiefly of runaway sailors, and people who had reason for leaving the busy world for a time. There, safe from discovery, they employed themselves in sawing timber, which was plentiful, dense bush covering the whole Bay, a large proportion of it consisting of immense trees. As many as twenty or thirty pairs of pit sawyers worked at a time. Their mode of living was a very reckless one. They would saw a quantity of timber, send it away, and with a portion of the money it fetched, buy a quantity of provisions to last them until they could get another lot of timber. The rest would be spent in grog. When they got over the spree, back they went to work again, and repeated the same process. These men, had they liked, could have become wealthy, as timber sawing was a very profitable employment in those days, but they preferred the wild mode of existence, and there is no single sample of a man who departed from the rule.

It was chiefly in Okain's that the whalers in the early days got their spars, and shiploads of them were continually cut and sent away, the Bay being famed for its fine timber.

Very dense was the bush. It was in fact difficult to travel far through it in any direction. When a track wanted cutting, all hands in the Bay set to work for the common good. About two years after the first real settlers came—that was about 1850— a track was cut over to Robinson's Bay for the purpose of communication with Akaroa. It was a very rough one, and those that are now in the Bay that travelled it think it would have far from satisfied the present inhabitants. It was better, however, than the untracked bush, and the hardy pioneers were too accustomed to difficulty to think much of the hardships a journey to Akaroa cost them. Before this track was cut it was nearly impossible to get to the harbour, and, as in the other bays, men continually lost themselves while attempting it.

The first people who really settled in Okain's were Messrs. Fleuty, Harley, Mason, and Webb. They were there before 1853. They bought up fifty acres among them. Mr. Thos. Ware, who soon afterwards arrived, bought one-fourth of it from them, and still owns it. Mr. Webb afterwards went to Laverick's, and died in that Bay. Mr. Mason remained in Okain's until his death, which has only recently occurred.

The tidal wave of 1863 is well remembered by the old settlers. It spread a long distance up the Bay, flooding the houses on the flat. It left behind a thick sandy deposit, covering all the herbage, and it was some time before the latter grew again. A vessel that was being built down close to the river was carried off the stocks and floated round the Bay. No harm, however, was done to her As may be supposed, the event caused great consternation.

2B

There have been few casualties in the Bay. In the very early days a boat belonging to Mr John Roberts was capsized, and two men drowned. A boat, also, coming from Le Bon's was lost, and two men met their fate. Those who have passed through Little Okain's in late years may have noticed the wreck of a small vessel lying half buried in the sand. She has now been completely broken up. Her name was the Sea-devil, and she once belonged to Mr. Thacker. Soon after he sold her she was driven ashore during a gale, and became a total wreck.

Messrs. Moore, Sefton, Gilbert, and others were also very early settlers in Okain's. . They took up land on the same principle as Messrs. Webb, Mason, Fleuty, and Harley, three or four of them buying up a fifty-acre section and going into partnership.

As the bush was cut down fires became frequent, and a great deal of damage was done at times. The great fire which started in Pigeon Bay about five and twenty years ago, spread to Okain's. The fire lasted for a long time, and for weeks the sky was scarcely seen through the thick volumes of smoke. There have been several bush fires started in Okain's, but none as bad as this one. The summer had been a dry one, and the wind was favorable to its spreading. The whole Peninsula was ablaze, and after it had died out many wild pigs were found burnt to death. The native birds, besides, were never so plentiful afterwards as they were before the fire.

As in Le Bon's, the creek swarmed with eels of a great size, and in the bush, pigeons and kakas were plentiful. It was no difficult thing for a man with a gun to live in the bush in those days.

About three years after they came, Messrs. Mason and Fleuty commenced dairying, their old partners, Messrs. Webb and Harley, having left them and sold out their interest in the property. Messrs. Ware and Thacker soon started other dairies, and year after year as the bush was cleared others went in for dairy farming. Mr Ware brought the first sheep into Okain's about seven and twenty years ago. Mr. J. E. Thacker came to Okain's about thirty-eight years ago from Christchurch, and gradually bought up land, the six thousand acres purchased in all, now forming a magnificent estate. He erected a sawmill about fifteen or seventeen years ago, and soon cut all the suitable timber in the Bay. · It was the largest sawmill ever at work on the Peninsula, and could cut 70,000ft in a week, so that it did not take long to clear the land, a large number of hands being employed. The building in which the engine and machinery were once located is still in good preservation, and is now used as a wool-shed. The tramway to fetch down the logs to the mill went away to the top of the valley, and parts of it are still to be seen. The Alert, Jeanette, and Elizabeth were the vessels employed to carry the timber to Lyttelton, and they had all they could do to clear it away as it was cut.

The Okain's Road Board was formed in 1864, and the present road to Akaroa was made in 1878.

Okain's has settled down to a quiet peaceful exis-tence, the inhabitants being chiefly dependant on the production of cheese, grass seed, and wool, and as long as these commodities command any price this fertile Bay is bound to give generous support to its healthy and happy sons and daughters,

No. 3—LITTLE AKALOA.

One would naturally think Akaloa was a corruption of Akaroa. Some of those who have been connected with the settlement of this Bay, state that it received its name from a resemblance to Akaroa, and also from its position, as it lies directly opposite the harbour. The oldest settlers declare, however, that Akaloa was the original Maori name

No Maoris have actually dwelt in the Bay since it has been settled. A great many of them, however, lived at the Long Look-out, and during the raid of the North Island Maoris on the Peninsula tribes, Maoris came from all the Bays round to Little Akaloa for shelter. They hid in the bush, and on the ridges between the Bays. There was a great slaughter on the Long Look-out, in which the local natives were almost annihilated. Traces of this event can be found on slopes of the cape.

The first settlers to arrive were Messrs. Bennetts and Rix, fathers of the settlers of these names now in and about the Bay. Before they came there were sawyers in Little Akaloa, which, like the other Bays, was a refuge for runaway sailors and men of all descriptions. Seventeen or eighteen pit sawyers were once at work on the timber in the Bay. Messrs. Bennetts and Rix came from Wellington with Capt. Thomas. The latter was a Government surveyor, and came to lay out Lyttelton and Christchurch. This was in 1850. Messrs Bennetts and Rix came to Little Akaloa to saw timber for Capt. Thomas. In September of the same year Mr. George Ashton arrived. Mr Jones came soon afterwards, and purchased the first section of land sold in the Bay from the Canterbury Association. Mr. G. Ashton now resides on part of it. Amos Green, commonly known as Toby Green, was an early settler. He was a cripple. It seems he escaped from a whaling ship, and fled to the Maoris, with whom he lived for some time. Two settlers came to the pah and engaged him for work on their land, and as he was stepping aboard their boat he stepped on to a loaded gun, which shot him through the leg. He was always a cripple afterwards, though he did a great deal towards settling Little Akaloa. Mr. George Boleyn, father of Mr. James Boleyn, of Stony Bay, Mr. McHale, of Raupo Bay, and the Waghorns were also very early settlers.

As everywhere else on the Peninsula, the bush was very dense in Little Akaloa ; indeed it was perhaps more thickly covered than any other Bay. Mr. G. Ashton possesses a photograph of the Bay in those early days. It is greatly different from the present appearance of the locality, showing the settlement on the beach, and the valley and hills covered with heavy timber. It was a hard day's work to penetrate a mile into the bush, and find your way back again. It came thick down to the water's edge. Akaloa abounded in very fine pines and totaras, and gave plenty of employment to the numbers of pit sawyers who flocked there. A saw-mill was built in about 1860 by Messrs. A. Waghorn, McIntosh and Turner. Mr. McIntosh afterwards became sole owner. A man named Fenly, who had had charge of the mill in Duvauchelle's, then managed it. Messrs. Brown and Fraser afterwards took the mill from them. They started the public house in a building which had been intended for a dwelling house. The firm is still in existence in Christchurch. The saw-mill found work for many years, as valuable timber covered the whole surface of the valley. A tramway ran afterwards right up to the head of the Bay on nearly the same site on which the road now runs.

Messrs. W. Pawson, H. McIntosh and J. McIntosh cut the first track over to Duvauchelle's Bay, commonly known as Shaw's line. It ran on the opposite side of the valley to that on which the present road lies. Messrs, George Boleyn and John Bennett cut the first track to Okain's. The manner in which a road was tested in those days, to judge whether the contractors had done their work in a proper manner, was by taking a bullock along it laden with clay. This was done to test the track to Okain's. The Rev. Mr. Torlesse, clergyman at Okain's and Little Akaloa, was judge, and his report was unfavorable, and he wouldn't pass it. This gentleman got the church built in Okain's, and was schoolmaster there also. He frequently came to Little Akaloa, and preached in the open air. Mr. Waghorn's barn was then used as a place for worship. Bishops Selwyn and Harper both preached in this barn. The former anchored off the Bay in his schooner, and put a boat ashore. The inhabitants all collected on the beach, eager to see who their visitors were. On the boat arriving, the Bishop called out, " Do you know who I am ? I am Bishop Selwyn, the travelling Bishop," and he jumped first out of the boat up to his middle, and helped drag her ashore. He then went up to the barn, and preached to them, and also christened several children who are now residents in the Bay. He did not stay long, but left behind him a great admiration for his abilities and plain speaking, Bishop Harper made periodical visits to the Bay. In 1862 the school-room was built, Mr. Bishop being the first master. In the following year the building was made the church, and still remains so.

In 1853 Toby Green started the first dairy on the place where the Messrs. Waghorn now live. Mr G. Ashton soon followed his example, and as the bush was cleared so were fresh dairies commenced. Mr. G. Ashton kept up regular communication with the outside world by sailing a whale boat between Little Akaloa and Lyttelton, and carrying the mails. He also carried the Okain's mail, which he conveyed by the track, and rough times he had now and then. The main road to Duvauchelle's was made about 1868, and was a great boon to the inhabitants.

Of course there were some heavy bush fires in Little Akaloa, but no harm is known to have been done, as the settlers were always on the alert expecting them. The historical fire which spread from Pigeon Bay about twenty-five years ago will not be soon forgotten by those who were in the Bay at the time. It was difficult for days to breathe in the smoky atmosphere. Like the rest of the Peninsula in the early times, provisions in the shape of wild pigs, birds, and fresh and salt water fish were plentiful, and we are assured they were needed, as it was difficult to get anything in the Bay at the time of its settlement. Whalers sometimes came into Little Akaloa, but they did not stay long, their principal places of stoppage being Port Levy and Akaroa.

Mr T. Duncan who lately died in Christchurch, was the first who settled in Decanter Bay, afterwards owned by Mr W. Ashton, but since sold by him. There was a Maori pah on Decanter beach, and it was these Maoris who acted as guides to the pioneers of the other bays, having an intuitive knowledge of the way to reach them through the trackless forest.

The tidal wave was felt here, as elsewhere on that side of the Peninsula, pretty severely. A vessel by name the Struggler had been wrecked just before this, and endeavours were being made to float her again. The wave took her away up the flat, then out to sea and back again, not doing the least damage to her. Mr McIntosh's house was battered about, and one end of it was lifted up bodily by the water, the piles being washed from underneath it. It is considered that if the water had risen half an inch more it would have wrecked the house completely, as the wave would have come through the front windows. A sandy deposit was left all over the flat, and the houses there had half an inch of mud on the floors. The real harm done, however, was very trivial to what might have been expected.

Very few casualties have occurred in Little Akaloa. The vessels Minnie, Rambler, Caledonia, and Mary Anne Christina, the latter a schooner built in the Bay, as also was the ketch Minnie, were at times driven ashore while employed in taking timber to Lyttelton. The wreck of the Clematis (brig) was off the Long Look-out, and is of comparatively recent date. It was a calm, clear day, and she ran close in to the Look-out to shorten her voyage to Lyttelton. She struck on a sunken rock, and stuck there. The crew left her, and she stayed in that position for a day or two, when a fresh sea came and broke her up. The place where she struck was very close under the headland, and it was peculiarly daring of the Captain to attempt so short a cut. The rock is a sunken one, about five or six feet under, and the sea breaks on it when there is any wind. It seems remarkable that she struck in the only place where there was no escape.

The old wharf was built about 16 or 17 years ago ; a Mr. Barnes was the contractor. It was in a position, however, where it was totally undefended from the sea. The new wharf is in a more secure place, and there is deeper water off it.

Perhaps the most exciting event in the Bay was the burning down of the public houses, and it is no doubt fresh in the memory of most of our readers. The first building was unoccupied when burnt. A bar was fitted at once in an out-house. This met the same fate. A stable was then used, and that was also burnt, and no more attempts to sell liquor were made. The daring incendiaries, whoever they were, must have been wide awake to escape detection.

The great floods were perhaps more severely felt in
Little Akaloa than anywhere, and were attended
with loss of life : a child of Mr. May's being
drowned, and another narrowly escaping. The creek
bed was so clogged with debris that it dammed itself
continually, and the water came down in great
waves. Mr. William Ashton lived on the flat, and
the creek made a bend round his dwelling. An out-
honse, which a day or two before had been filled with
provisions, was completely washed away to sea. Mr.
Ashton would not leave the house for some time,
but finding the creek was dammed above, and fearing
danger he shifted over to his father's house, the
bridge by which he made his escape going half-an-
hour afterwards. In the morning he found the
house completely undermined and unfit for habita·
tion, and he was indeed lucky to have taken his
family and himself out of danger. The roads even
now bear testimony of the havoc done, several
bridges being washed away.

Little Akaloa is a happy valley, and now the
bush is all cleared is the home of many settlers, who
do not regret their choice   Cheese, grass seed, and
wool are the chief exports, and a good quantity of
firewood even now finds its way out of the Bay.

No. 4—GERMAN BAY.

German Bay, lying close to Akaroa as it does, is closely associated with its history. It was settled as soon as any other Bay on the Peninsula, and when the whole place was a forest wild was considered as one of the most fertile and convenient spots for habitation by the pioneers. It is not exactly known when Akaroa, German, and the other Bays round the harbour were first chosen as places of settlement by white men. It must have been very early in the century, however, when runaway sailors sought a home in the bush in preference to cruising after whales. Several of these men lived with the Maoris and took Maori women for wives. Some stray sailors lived alone in the bush, and German Bay was one of their retreats, it being then easy to live on the natural products of the land. This Bay was of course no exception to the rest of the Peninsula as regards the bush, which was once very thick and heavy. The space, however, we are informed, which is on the seaward side of the present road, was fairly clear, and here the first settlers built their whâres. Wild pigs, besides pigeons, ka kas, and other birds abounded, and fish was plentiful, so it did not require much exertion to obtain a supply of provisions.

As we all know, Capt. l'Anglois is said to have purchased from the Maoris a great part of our Peninsula, a block consisting of many thousand acres. This block of land extended from Peraki to Pigeon Bay, and included all the land round the harbour with the exception of one or two small places. A boat, it is believed, and some articles of merchandise were the payment for the land. £240 was to be the value of the goods given in exchange for this great stretch of fertile country ; but it was

never proved that anything like that amount was
given to the Natives, and the Captain gave up his
rights on returning to France to a company by name
the Nanto-Bordelaise Co. Capt. l'Anglois brought
out the Comte-de-Paris for this Company with
immigrants. The vessel arrived in Akaroa Harbour
on 16th August, 1840, just seven months after the
New Zealand Co. brought out emigrants to Nelson
and Wellington. There were sixty emigrants by the
Comte-de-Paris, and the Company granted them
five acres of land on arrival, to be chosen where they
pleased, and eighteen-months' provisions and all
necessary tools. Mrs. Malmanche and Mr. Waeckerlie are the only residents remaining who came
here under this Company. Mr. Lelievre came about
the same time, but he arrived in a whaler.

There were six Germans who came out with the
French settlers : Messrs Waeckerlie, Breitmeyer,
and Peter Walter were among them. All the
Germans formed a settlement in what is now
German Bay, the place thus getting its name.
They chose their five acres apiece there. A track
was cut to Akaroa, and the timber in the bush being
so good, the settlers employed themselves in pit
sawing. The land was excellent for cultivation, but
growing vegetables on a large scale didn't pay, as
there were no people to whom to sell them, although
the Maoris would row and then buy potatoes.

Patches of ground in the clearing were sown down
in wheat, as flour was a rarity, and the settlers felt
the want of it very much, only being able to get a
little when a whaler anchored in the harbour. The
yield was very great.

Even when these early settlers came, the Maoris
round the harbour were not numerous The French
thought, however, that it was as well to take precautions, as their man-of-war could not always stay
in harbour to protect, so a guard house was built in

German Bay close to the beach, but luckily it was never required for the purpose intended.

Just after the arrival of the immigrants, the N.Z. Company sent down a Mr. Robinson to act as a Resident Magistrate, and a Constable   This was rather officious on the part of the British, as New Zealand was not declared a British Colony until 1841.   This gentleman afterwards bought land in German Bay.

By degrees, as the bush was cleared in German Bay, the English flocked there, and soon outnumbered the original settlers.   As may be supposed, there were some large bush fires, but little damage was done to the inhabitants, who tock precautions in time.

Captain Muter, afterwards Colonel Muter, arrived in 1851.   He was the first to purchase land theie under the Canterbury Association.   The property is that now occupied by Mr Phillips.   Capt. Muter built the house.   He planted out trees, which are about the oldest of their kind on the Peninsula, and have always been remarkable for their growth. With him came Mr. and Mrs. Funnell, sen., and Mr. and Mrs Hammond.   Capt. Muter had the misfortune of losing nearly all his implements and goods in Lyttelton.   They were put in a boat, which sank after leaving the ship.   Commodoie Lavaud also lived in German Bay.   Kuebler was the name of one of the original settlers who died in the early years.   Mr. Wool was the name of a man who has long since left.   Messrs. Hempleman and Whelch, father of Mr Thos. Whelch, of Akaroa, were among the first to take up land in German Bay. Mr Libeau, sen., was the first to start a dairy, and he found a good sale for his produce among the other settlers.

Mr. Waeckerlie lived in the Bay until 1842.   He then married and came to Akaroa, where he built a

flour-mill on the site of the Chinamen's house. Mr.
Breitmeyer was the only original settler who had a
family, but most of the others in time married and
settled down. Almost as soon as cattle were introduced from Sydney, dairying commenced ; on a very
small scale at first, each calf being of great value,
and beef an enormous price. As the land, however,
was cleared and sowed down, it became the settlers'
chief employment, and, with the production of grass
seed, has remained so to the present day.

German Bay was very beautiful when covered in
bush, and, unlike many other Bays, has kept its
beauty. This is chiefly owing to the early settlers
taking care to plant out English trees as the bush
was burnt. The willows, which are an important
part of the landscape, were grown from slips brought
by the emigrants from St. Helena, where they were
taken from the tree over Napoleon's grave.

No 5—ROBINSON'S BAY.

This Bay received its name from the man who
first bought land there. Mr. Robinson was sent
down to Akaroa to Act as a Magistrate by the New
Zealand Company, being accompanied by a constable to enforce his authority. This was in 1840.
Mr Robinson bought 100 acres, and the land is that
where Mr. Saxton now resides. He never lived in
the Bay for any length of time.

The Bay is a large one, and covered with heavy
timber as it was then, it was soon seen that a mill
would pay there. The early history of Robinson's

Bay is the same as that of the other Peninsula inlets. Runaway sailors here found a refuge, and lived by pit sawing. It was no difficult matter in those days for sawyers to make £5 or £6 a week, and then not exert themselves very much. The life they led, though lonely, was not an unhappy one. ·Building a whâre in a convenient place by a creek, they stored up a good supply of provisions and necessary tools. They varied their fare, and spun out the quantity by occasional raids on the wild pigs and birds, and they had not far to look for these. When they got a decent cheque they revisited the haunts of civilization, and after knocking it down, went back and repeated the same process.

The Pavitts put up the first saw-mill in the Bay. Mr. S. C. Farr built it on the same site as that on which the mill afterwards worked by Messrs. Saxton and Williams stood. Mr. Hughes also possessed a mill here about the same time. These mills, however, did not cut much timber. In 1865 Messrs. Saxton and Williams bought the land now occupied by Mr Saxton. The old mill was found to be in a rather dilapidated state, and not capable of doing much work. The new owners entirely renovated it, employed a great many men, and in a short time produced 1,000,000ft of timber yearly. The timber was punted out to vessels in the Bay. Messrs. Lardner and Sims carried a great deal of it away in their punt. Capt. Malcolmson, in the well-known Antelope, and Mr. E. Latter's vessels, among which were the Foam and the E. and U. Cameron, were kept busily employed. The s.s. Beautiful Star once took a cargo to Dunedin, and also the s.s. Wainui. There were a great many vessels employed at different times. Mr Hughes built the Isabella Jackson on the spot where Mr. Johnstone's house now is. The Pavitts built the Thetis on the beach.

Nearly all the old settlers now in the Bay, and many in different parts of the Peninsula worked for Messrs. Saxton and Williams, thirty hands being employed by the mill. About 50 bullocks were used in dragging the big logs down the hills. The flat, of course, was first cleared, and here forty acres of hay were annually grown for the bullocks. The house of the Pavitts was situated a few yards away from Mr. Saxton's present dwelling. During a bush fire it was burnt, and they had to build a whâre in the bush. The bush fires at times were very severe, and once the whole Bay was in a blaze, the inhabitants having to camp out in the open close to the beach.

Mr. Johnstone was one of the earliest settlers in Robinson's Bay, Mr. Barnett, of LeBon's, also lived there before going over the hills. Mr. Piper, of Duvauchelle's, was in the Bay in the first year of its settlement, and Mr E. S. Chappell was an early inhabitant. Messrs Whitfield, Duxbury, W. N. McDonald (deceased), Kingston and Tizzard came in a vessel called the Barracouta from the Otago gold fields. Mr Gundy owned the place now occupied by Dr. Fisher, and was one of the first settlers. Mr. B. DeMalmanche rented a large portion of Messrs. Saxton and Williams' land, that principally which was cleared. The Currys and many others came soon after the mill was started.

Mr. Johnstone, who was bullock driving for the mill owners, and Mr. L. LeValliant were the first to start dairies. Messrs Saxton and Williams commenced a dairy which they rented to Mr. B. DeMalmanche. On this dairy as many as eighty cows were milked, the buildings being where Mr. Saxton's house now stands. As the land was cleared, the men in employment in the mill bought it up and started dairying. The first sheep were brought into the Bay about twenty years ago.

Mr Saxton came out in the ship Westminister in 1858, in which ship also came Messrs A. Rodrigues, J. Wilkin, and others. Although in the Bay in that year he did not settle there until 1865, when he went into partnership with Mr. Williams, and they started the saw mill.

The only fatal accident which happened in the Bay was that by which a man named Tozer lost his life. He was cross-cutting with Mr. Kingston, and was on the lower side. On being sawn through, half of the log rolled on the unfortunate man, and crushed him to death. Mr Tolly, now living in Ashburton, once had his leg broken when turning a log drawn by bullocks.

The owners of the mill put up the jetty, which has gone to ruin. They bore all the expense of having it done, besides supplying all the timber. A tramway was laid up to the mill, and extended up the valley three miles. This saved a great amount of labour, as vessels came and loaded at the jetty, and the nuisance of punting was done away with, besides saving a lot of work with the bullocks.

The owners of the mill built a school for the children of the men at work, on the site of Mr. Morgan's house. Afterwards, when Mr. A. C. Knight was Minister of Education, the Government bought land and erected the present school.

It is not many years ago since all the valuable timber was cut. The old jetty and tramway have gone to ruin, but a new wharf has recently been put up. The mill property is now a sheep station occupied by Mr. Saxton. Dairying is the chief occupation of the settlers in the Bay.

No. 6.—DUVAUCHELLE'S BAY SOUTH.

Duvauchelle's Bay is not single like the others, but contains two distinct valleys, each having its own watershed, and separated by a distinct ridge. In this article we propose to treat of that portion nearest Robinson's Bay, all of which (with the exception of a few sections) is occupied by Messrs. Piper Bros. The name was derived from two brothers who held a couple of sections under the Nante Bordelaise Company. They never lived in the Bay, and yet it still bears their name. It was never a French settlement at all, and the first that is known of it is that Rauperabau had a big cannibal feast just where the tramway crosses the main road. When forming the tramway, Messrs. Piper and Hodgson disinterred many old bones and other relics of these terrible festivities. Messrs. Narbey, Jandroit and others were living in the valley later on, sawing timber. The first section disposed of by the Canterbury Association was one of 200 acres, which they gave on their collapse to Lord Lyttelton, Lord Cavendish, and Lord Charles Simeon in part payment of money advanced to the Association. These 200 acres were first held on a nominal lease from Mr. Harman, agent for the nobleman in question, by William Augustus Gordon, brother of the great "Chinese Gordon," whose death at Khartoum startled the civilized world. He resided in the Bay many years, working some time for Mr. Piper. He eventually went to Invercargill, where he died. The first land bought under the Canterbury Provincial Land Laws was bought by Messrs. Cooper, Hodgson and Wilson. It was purchased in 1857, and consisted of fifty acres. They were sawing there for some eighteen months, and then Mr Harry Piper made his first purchase in the Bay

2D

—a thirty-acre section where his house now stands. The history of the Bay, as all Peninsula men know, is intimately connected with the gentleman we have mentioned. He had arrived in Canterbury in July, 1852, having come out in the " Old Samarang " with Sir Jno. Hall, Mr A. C. Knight, Mr Wright (chief postmaster of Lyttelton), Mr Brown (brewer of Christchurch) and many other old settlers. Mr Piper came down to the Peninsula in November of that year to Mr T. S. Duncan, the late Crown Solicitor, who was then cockatooing in Decanter Bay. The following May (1853) he went to Mr John Hay in Pigeon Bay, and stayed till that gentleman left for Home, at the end of that year. All the Pavitt family were sawing in Pigeon Bay at that time There were seven of them, three pairs sawing and one man cooking. There was a great flood that autumn, and boats could float where the present road now runs. In those days Mr. E. Hay had pigs by the hundred, which were known by their tails being cut. They were fetched down to feed by blowing a cow horn Wild pigs were of course distinguished by their long appendages. They were very plentiful, and used to come and feed with the tame ones, and strange to say the pig dogs (a breed known as McIntosh's, half bull and half kangaroo) when let loose, never touched a short tailed pig, but always went straight for the wild ones. One day Capt. Thomas, of the Red Rover, and old " Skippy " (a whaler) saw a big wild boar running from the dogs up the road, and valiantly tried to stop him, but he quickly threw both over on their backs, strange to say without inflicting the slightest scratch. This pig was killed by Mr. Tom White ten minutes after. To show how bad these wild pigs were, Mr. Turner was stuck up for a long time on the fence at Hay's corner by a big boar, and a man named Joe Scott, coming round from Sin-

clair's to Hay's, was stuck up on top of an old saw
pit for several hours.

After leaving Hay's, Mr. Piper went sawing with
Mr. Hillier in Pigeon Bay, and after that went
boating with old "Skippy," and afterwards sawed
with Mr. Turner in Pigeon Bay. Mr. James
Pawson, of Little Akaloa, came over to Robinson's
Bay to flitch for the Pavitt's at the saw mill, and
Mr. Piper went mates with him, and then went to
Hendersons, at the Commercial Hotel, Akaroa,
where an immense business was then doing.
LeBon's was the next place visited, where he joined
Messrs Cuddon and Wilson in a small sawmill, tho
first erected there, but previously worked by the
Cuffs. He afterwards sawed for some months with
Eugene, the Frenchman, in Radcliffe's Gully, Ger-
man Bay. Mr. Piper afterwards sawed in Pawson's
Valley. In 1859, whilst residing in this place, Mr.
Piper was induced by Messrs Hodgson, Cooper,
Wilson and Henderson to join them in erecting a
saw mill in Duvauchelle's, near his 30-acre section.
At first the speculation was a total failure, owing in
a great measure to defective engineering. Mr. Henderson then failed, and his fifth was sold to the other
four proprietors, to whom the late Mr. Robert
Heaton Rhodes proved on that occasion a good
friend. The first two cargoes of timber were lost,
owing to demurrage charges caused by Mr. Henderson's failure. Some three years after that, Messrs.
Piper and Hodgson bought out Messrs. Cooper and
Wilson, and became sole proprietors. From this
time the mill progressed favorably, and in a few
years was improved and altered, the firm going to
the expense of over a thousand pounds. The
partners had sown down the logging roads and
where the fire had run through the tops, with
English grass, and the first cocksfoot Mr. Piper
bought was from Mr. George Armstrong, who had

purchased it at Wellington, and let a bag go as a
favor at a shilling a pound (alas there is no such
price now a-days !)   It flourished exceedingly, and
Mr. Piper sold many tons afterwards at from 6d to
6½d per lb.   Indeed Messrs. Hodgson and Piper
and the Messrs. Hay were the principal producers of
cocksfoot in the days of its introduction.   In 1874
Mr. Piper bought Mr. Hodgson out, but kept the
mill running about six years after.   Altogether
some 20,000,000ft of timber were sawn out of the
valley, nine tenths of it being totara, and grand
totara at that.   Mr. Piper purchased the rest of the
valley after Mr. Hodgson left, and has since
remained sole proprietor, but eighteen months ago
let the property to his sons, Messrs. Harry and
James Piper.   Mr. Piper married in June, 1859,
his wife coming out with Mr John Hay in the
old Caroline Agnes.   Mr. Piper was one of the
old Peninsula boat's crew who held an unbeaten
record of victory for seven years against all comers,
both in Akaroa and Lyttelton.   There were three
Pawsons and W. Cormick in the Lyttelton crew
besides Mr. Piper, and one of the McIntosh's pulled
in Akaroa.   Mr. John Barwick, the well-known and
esteemed Clerk of the Akaroa and Wainui Road
Board, is another resident in this part of Duvauchelle's, besides Messrs. Piper.   He lives upon one
of the original Duvauchelle sections, of which he has
been the occupier for many years past.   Mr. Libeau's
pretty home is in the corner of the Bay.   When the
mill was in full swing, forty men were always
employed.   Clearing was very expensive in those
days, the first lot of 70 acres being let to some
Maoris for £4 an acre, and a bag of sugar and a
pound of tobacco for every ten acres.   Mr. Piper has
been associated with the local Government bodies
since their start.   He helped before the Road Boards
were established, and has served well and faithfully

both in them and the County Council, holding the
position of Chairman in both bodies.

The Duvauchelle's of to-day is a very different
place from that of the old times, when the saw-mill
was first established. Where the mighty totaras
once proved a home for thousands of native birds,
good succulent grasses nourish stock which brings
wealth to their proprietors and revenue to the
Colonial Government. Many regret the passing
away of the old order of things, and sentimentalise
over the loss of those timbered solitudes where
supple-jacks were thick, and the wild pig luxuriated ;
but we cannot help fancying that to the thinking
person the present landscape is far more gratifying.
True gloomy Rembrandt-like shadows have disappeared, and the tui no longer plumes his jewelled
wings on the summit of some forest monarch ; but
in the stead of the past beauties are smiling slopes
of grass, which carry in thousands those gentle
friends of man, whose feet are truly said to make
golden the soil over which they pass. It must not
for a moment be thought that the settlers in Duvauchelle's have had no idea of preserving the original
loveliness of the valley. A large patch of bush
has been saved near the Summit, and endeavours
have been made to encourage all vegetation sheltering the water courses with most satisfactory results.
The konini, the tutu, the ribbon wood, and dozens of
other aboriginals spread a grateful shade over the
waters, and lessen evaporation, while giving intense
satisfaction to the artistic taste. Nor is this all,
for on all sides rise plantations of trees from other
countries. Of these the blue gums have best repaid
their growers. In one place on the flat they reach
an altitude of at least an hundred feet, rising side
by side straight and graceful. The pinus insignis
has also done well, and the macrocarpa fairly, but
the larch does not seem to thrive with that luxuri-

ance which might have been expected from the soil
that contains the remains of so many thousands of
its giant predecessors The creek is all protected
by willows on its banks, and many other forest
trees, including oak, silver poplar, sycamores,
and Scotch pines. There is a nice garden and
orchard, and a tennis court, which we think will
fairly challenge comparison with any on the Peninsula. In the future the Bay will be far lovelier than
it is now : the old stumps will gradually disappear,
and the many old buildings connected with the mill
be destroyed, and covered with the sheltering grass
whose silent march conquers so many scars on the
bosom of old mother earth. Smooth and smiling
with a peaceful English look will be the Duvauchelle's of our grandchildren. But to those of the
present generation, by whom the wilderness was
reclaimed, these very stumps have all an interest.
'· From this tree," your guide will say, "Came all the
fluming for the mill ; from that we cut 2100 feet of
8 by 1 boards from a single length." To them each
old stump is a reminiscence of a victory of industry,
a symbol of honest profit for hard toil, a part of the
old Peninsula life which has, with its many toils
and troubles and pleasures, passed away for ever
amongst the things that were. This is a valley
which formerly supported a few hundred pigeons and
a score or two of wild pigs, most of which were
unfit for human consumption unless under very
trying circumstances.

The great floods of 1886 did much damage in
Duvauchelle's A tremendous slip from the Okain's
road covered the rich alluvial flat with clay, and the
creek brought down boulders and rubbish till the
woolshed was threatened, fences covered to the top
rail, and much good pasture ruined for the time.
Many of the young gum trees died from the lower
portion of their trunks being covered, and it will be

many years before traces of the disastrous event will be obliterated.

No. 7.—PIGEON BAY.

Messrs. Hay and Sinclair were the first settlers in this Bay. It was in the year 1844 in the month of April that these gentlemen, leaving their families in Wellington, sailed in a schooner from that port to seek land in the south, where they had heard of fine plains. They had originally left Scotland in 1839, and were going first of all to settle in the north, but the tales they had heard of the Canterbury and Taieri Plains made them very anxious to explore them. On arrival at Lyttelton, their first port of call, they did not know the exact locality of the Plains, but seeing the hills low at the head of Governor's Bay, they thought that must be the road. Accordingly they climbed to the saddle of what is now Gebbie's Pass, but on arrival found to their disappointment only what they thought was sea on the other side, which was of course the waters of Lake Ellesmere. They then determined to try for the Taieri and accordingly sailed for Port Chalmers, and landed up by Anderson's Bay; but they were again unsuccessful, not going far enough to find the level land. They then determined to return north again, and sailed for Pigeon Bay, whither they had been driven by stress of weather on the way down. Here Mr. Sinclair announced his intention of making his home, as he was tired of wandering, and Mr. Hay decided to do the same. It was then agreed that Mr Sinclair should occupy that part of the bay now known as Holmes' Bay, but then as Sinclair's, Mr. Hay taking the main bay itself. They then returned to Wellington, and brought down their families and some four head of cattle, and farming and other implements, amongst which were a plough and harness. At the time of the landing Mr. and Mrs. Sinclair had three sons and three daughters, and Mr. and Mrs. Hay two sons (Messrs James and Thomas Hay, then three and two years old respectively. The two families lived together for nearly two years, first in a tent, and then in a thatched whâre.

We may here say that the inducement to settle in Pigeon Bay was that there was a settlement in Akaroa considered likely at that time to become one of the principal in the South Island. Finding they had not enough cattle, Messrs. Hay and Sinclair purchased some from Messrs. B. and G. Rhodes, for whom Mr Geo. Rhodes was then managing a run consisting of the land since occupied by Messrs. Armstrong, Rhodes, and Haylock. We must not forget to mention that the schooner that brought the Messrs. Hay and Sinclair and their families to Pigeon Bay, also brought the Messrs. Deans, Gebbies, Mansons and their families, all these old settlers so well known to our readers arriving at the same date. The cattle did wonderfully well in the bush, there being little clear land except at the points. As may be supposed, the living at those times was very primitive. There was no store nearer than Wellington, and consequently our settlers were sometimes out of flour, sugar, tea, and other things we consider necessary. Their principal meat food was pigeons and wild pork, and occasional ducks and teal. The pigeons were numberless, the old whalers having given the bay the name it bears from that circumstance. There used to be a good deal of exchange, too, with the whalers, who used to give slops and stores in exchange for vegetables and the beef, which was killed as the cattle increased. About three or four years after the landing, Mr. Sinclair built a cutter of about eight or ten tons, with the intention of taking the produce of the Bay to Wellington. When she was completed she was loaded with all the produce in the Bay—the result of a year's labour—and sailed for Wellington. The crew consisted of Mr. Sinclair, his eldest son George, Alfred Wallace, and another young man. Terrible to relate, the cutter never reached Wellington, and nothing was ever heard of her again. It was indeed a severe blow to the new settlers thus to lose the heads of one family and the whole result of so many months of arduous labour. Mrs. Sinclair was inconsolable, and let the place to Mr McIntosh, and went to Wellington. She returned after a time, however, and resided in Akaroa, and then again came to Pigeon Bay, Mr McIntosh taking up the Bay now known by his name Eventually in 1862 she sold out to Mr George Holmes and went to the Sandwich Islands, where she recently died at the advanced age of over ninety years. About the beginning of 1851, Messrs Sinclair and Hay built new houses, the former in Holmes' Bay, and the latter where Annandale used to stand. Mr. Sinclair's house was burnt, it will be remembered, only a few years ago, and Mr. Hay's house formed the kitchen at Annandale, and was of course destroyed by the ship. Immediately after the Wairoa massacre, the Maoris agreed to murder all the whites in the South Island. They arranged to make fire signals, known as the old Maori telegraph, and begin with killing the Deans at Riccarton, then the people at Port Levy, Pigeon Bay, Akaroa, and elsewhere. The massacres were all to take place on the same day, and the Natives were afterwards all to meet at

2E

Akaroa to destroy the whaling settlements. It was a time of great terror, and Mr. Hay hardly knew what to do. However, he determined to remain with his family in the Bay, and sell his life as dearly as possible. He loaded all his guns and pistols ready, and, strange to say, the pistols remained loaded for no less than twenty-one years ! Luckily the plot was frustrated. First of all there were among the whalers and settlers men who had Maori wives, and these told their husbands. A chief named Bloody Jack, too, wrote to the chief at Port Levy, telling him that he would be his enemy for life if he touched the whites.   There was some hesitation and delay, and eventually the plot was abandoned. The next great event was the arrival of the first four ships on the 16th December, 1851.   Need we say our settlers were delighted.   Now there was no need to fear the Maoris, and there was a probable near market for produce and the advantages of society.   It was indeed a red-letter day, and was duly celebrated. After the founding of the settlement, Mr Hay had considerable trouble in getting his land secured to him.   His original grant was for the North Island, where he had been unable to settle.   However, his claims were at last allowed.   At this time Messrs. Cuff, Stewart, Tom White, and a host of other settlers came to the Bay, and Messrs. Hunt, McKay, and others followed.   There was a fortnightly mail at that time, and the want of a school began to be keenly felt. Mr. Hay had some private teachers, not, however, of much ability, and then came Mr. Knowles and established the first school. Mr. Gillespie followed, and immensely increased the reputation of the school, and then came Mr. Fitz-gerald, and to him came many pupils from Christ-church, and in fact all Canterbury.   It was then, indeed, a most successful enterprise. The gold dis-coveries of Australia began to have a very beneficial influence at this time. Besides clearing out a great many of the old dissolute sawyers and whalers, it increased the price of produce enormously. Oats went up to 8s. a bushel, and potatoes to £8 and £10 per ton, and the settlers thrived. Afterwards the Dunedin diggings broke out, and so prices never got very low for years after. The cocksfoot industry on the Peninsula was started by Mr Hay. He gave at the rate of 2s. 6d. per lb for the first seed, which he found did wonderfully well in the Bay. Soon it spread, and a demand set in, and in one year Messrs. Hay Bros. sold no less than 70 tons at 8d per lb. Mr. Hay was never covetous of land. He always wished to see neighbours around him, and encouraged them to settle When he died in 1863 he had only really acquired between 900 and 1000 acres, but he had the pre-emptive right over 2000 more. During the subsequent trusteeship the estate enormously increased in value and acreage. It was eventually purchased by Messrs. James and Thos. Hay, the eldest sons, from the rest of the family, and is now, as all Canterbury settlers know, one of the finest estates in the colony. Some years ago, however, a great misfortune occurred. On the 18th August, 1886, a terrible slip came from the hills above the Annandale Homestead, and utterly overwhelmed it, burying the gatherings—the relics of forty years—in a sea of mud. Luckily it happened in the day time, and there was no loss of life. The bay is one of the best on the Peninsula. Its well managed Road Board has secured good roads for it. ¯ It has been well and thoroughly cleared and grassed, and its future is fully assured, as all can see who visit its many smiling homesteads.

The following is an interesting account of an attempt amongst Maoris to break the " Tapu " in Pigeon Bay in 1853 :—It appears that late in the year two sealing boats, carrying about twenty-five

Maoris and half-castes, amongst which were some
very pretty girls, arrived in Pigeon Bay from
Dunedin. Most of these settled in the Bay, and as
a good proportion of the men had been whaling,
they were superior in their ideas to the old Maori
superstitions, and laughed at the idea of the
"Tapu." A well-known Maori, named Toby, who
had been a headsman in whaling boats for many
years, took the lead in the movement, and after
many and many a "korero," he and those who
doubted the virtue of the "Tapu," resolved to test
it by attempting to seize two large sealing boats over
which the sacred Maori halo had been thrown, viz.,
the one from which Bloody Jack had been knocked
overboard and drowned whilst trying to land at
Timaru, and another owned by the young chief
Hapukuku. These two boats were each under a
bark whāre upon the small flat near the present
wharf, and the reason for wishing to utilise them
was that the natives at that time nearly supplied
Lyttelton with firewood and potatoes, which they
hawked round from house to house upon their backs,
and that these two boats would carry quite as much
as five whale-boats. At this time there were two
Kaiks in the bay. Thiah's occupied the flat near
the wharf, with a population of about seventy-five.
The other (Kingston's) was at the head of the bay,
with some 150, besides a few at Sinclair's, and four
whāres in the gully below the wharf, called
Hapukukas. The old natives were quite alive to the
proposed sacrilege, and had taken steps to prevent
it, and this too in such a manner that the break-
down was an utter surprise. Runners were sent to
Kaikoura (north), and to Temuka (south), taking
in the intermediate Kaiks, with instructions to go to
Pigeon Bay at a certain date. In the meantime the
breakers of the "Tapu" had hauled the boats to
Gilbert's shed to be repaired and painted. Gilbert

did not commence at once, which possibly saved
some trouble, but the day of meeting saw some 400
to 500 strangers arrive in hot blood ready to fight
for the old custom, and it nearly came to a contest,
only the renegades were too few ; so that after three
days' feasting, koreroing, and blazing away powder,
it was decided to cremate the boats. The boats
were hauled to low water, covered with dry scrub,
and burned, the natives, during the conflagration,
doing a cry. Thus ended the largest native gathering on the Peninsula since the white man's time.

No. 8—HEAD OF THE BAY.

Although the bays called Duvauchelle's and Head
of the Bay are often called by each others name, the
bay in which- Messrs. Piper, Barwick, and Libeau
live is strictly Duvauchelle's. That in which the
County Council Office and Post Office is, is really
the Head of the Bay. They are in reality one bay,
though two distinct valleys run back. Mr. Libeau
was the first white man who lived in Duvauchelle's
or Head of the Bay. He came ashore from a whaler
and built a whâre on the spot where his son's house
now stands. He arrived a year after the French
immigrants came out to Akaroa, and, was the father
of the present resident. For many years the only
inhabitants of the Head of the Bay were a number
of sawyers. Many of them afterwards became
settlers. Among them were Peter Connelly, Joseph
Bruneau, Cortner Nicholas, Louis LeValliant, Ber-
nard and his nephew, and Jas. Piper, The timber

in the valley was nearly all totara and black pine,
white pine growing on the flats close to the sea-
shore. Like the rest of the Peninsula, the Head of
the Bay was covered in dense bush, which ran down
to the water's edge. Even in those times, when
pigs were plentiful all over the country, the Head of
the Bay was famous as literally swarming with them.
Many and exciting are the tales told of pig hunts in
this locality, in the old days, by the early settlers.

· The Pawsons arrived in the Bay in 1850, and
cut the timber for the public house about to be built.
Mr Pawson, sen., came out to Port Nicholson in
1840, at the same time as Mr. Jas. Wright, of
Wainui, in the Coromandel, after a very stormy
passage of nine months, six weeks of which were
spent in the cove of Cork repairing the damage
caused by a terrific gale the vessel experienced
shortly after commencing the voyage. The family
remained in the Wellington Province for nine years,
and then left for Lyttelton in the Queen   From
Lyttelton they came to Little Akaloa in a ketch
commanded by Captain Bruce, of Bruce Hotel
notoriety. The boat belonged to the Maoris, and
was probably the same that Hempleman bought the
Peninsula from Bloody Jack for, The Pawsons did
not live in the Head of the Bay until 1857. They
came over occasionally for a time to cut timber.
They saw the fine timber the bay possessed in these
visits, and bought a mill from Mr Bryant in Barry's
Bay. The three brothers, Messrs. Jonas, John,
and William Pawson, worked it together for a number of years, erecting it a good way up the valley—
close to the house in which the latter now lives. Mr.
John finally bought his two brothers out, and worked
it himself for a time, afterwards building the big mill
at the bottom of the Bay. Messrs. Saxton and
Williams afterwards bought the mill, and worked it
very profitably. Mr. Shadbolt, who arrived about

the year 1855, was the last owner of the mill, taking
it and cutting out all the timber in the bay. Nearly
all the old settlers about the Head of the Bay were
employed in those times at this mill, and a great
quantity of timber was cut annually. The vessels
that took away this timber were all built in the bay.
Mr. Robert Close first started a boat-building yard,
close to where the jetty has been built. He built the
vessels Sylph, Sea-devil, and others. The latter is
very likely the boat afterwards owned by Mr.
Thacker, which came to grief in Little Okain's.
Messrs. Barwick and Wilson afterwards opened a
yard in Duvauchelle's. They had come to the Colony
from Tasmania. Mr. Barwick is by trade a ship-
builder, spending nine years at it, the earlier portion
at Sunderland and afterwards at London. The
partners, before coming to the Head of the Bay, had
built the vessel Foam at Red-House Bay. At Duvauchelle's they built the vessels Vixen, Breeze,
Spray, Dart, and the Wainui, afterwards converted
into a steamer. They also built the first three boats
for Timaru lighterage. The Spray is the only one
of these vessels that is now heard of. Messrs. Barwick and Wilson dissolved partnership when they
had built these vessels for Mr E. C. Latter, and Mr.
Barwick worked the yard himself for two years.
During that time he built a large punt, which was
afterwards turned into the ketch Alice Jane, that
is so well known all over the Peninsula. Mr. Wilson
was a very peculiar character, being very mean in
scraping together all he possibly could, and very
generous in distributing it, " giving the shirt off his
back," as one who knew him well puts it, " to the
first man who asked him." He was the first man to
open a store in the bay ; but it did not prove very
profitable to him, as he gave away most of his goods.
While Messrs. Barwick and Wilson worked the
ship-yard, they employed over thirty men. After

working the yard by himself for two years, Mr. Barwick gave it up as there was no work to be done, nearly all the timber in the bay being cut. Bush fires were pretty common in those early days. At the time the whole Peninsula was on fire, starting from Pigeon Bay, the whole of the bush in the Head of the Bay was killed, and the fire, bursting out afresh at intervals, was burning from January to May. The settlers in the Bay have been very fortunate, as there has never been a fatal accident there, the only serious one remembered being that by which a man lost his legs through having them crushed under a tree when he was bushfalling.

The public house was first owned by Messrs. Tribe and Selig. Afterwards Mr. Pawson, sen., became owner, and Mr. John Anderson took it from him. Mr. Shadbolt then bought it. Messrs. Vanstone, Barker and Brookes each managed the hotel after this, Mr. Shadbolt taking charge of it again when they had left it. Mr. Cooper had it after it was re-built, after being burnt down during the ever memorable hotel burning period. Mr and Mrs. Wilson now rule there most worthily.

During the early years in the history of the bay, the want of a school was much felt, for there were many children in the bay, belonging to the men working at the mill, and a place of worship was also much needed. Lord Lyttelton therefore gave half an acre for the purpose, and the men clubbed together and gave timber and work until they had erected a suitable building. The half-acre is that on which the church now stands, though it has been re-built.

The Akaroa and Wainui Road Board was shifted from Akaroa to the Head of the Bay in 1878. The office stood where the Courthouse now is. The permanent road to Little Akaloa from the Bay was made about 1864. At the same time the road from Akaroa to Christchurch was made up Red John's

Gully. The evidence of the Board's usefulness is
visible everywhere, and the bay is perhaps the most
central position where its headquarters could be
situated. The County Council offices were built in
1879, and the Post and Telegraph Office in the
same year.

Messrs Barker (father of Mr Beilby Barker) and
Fry established the line of coaches running from
Christchurch and Pigeon Bay to Akaroa. Mr S.
Lee has owned the business for some considerable
time. During the last few years communication
with Christchurch has been considerably facilitated,
and until the railway touches on Akaroa Harbour it
is unlikely we shall be able to reach the capital of
the province in a shorter time than we can at
present.

No. 9.—ISLAND BAY.

There are interesting associations of the past in
this bay, lying, as it does, over that rugged coast,
between Peraki and Land's End, as the West Head
of the harbour is called. It receives its name from
a towering rock guarding the entrance, and rising
up out of the troubled waters like an old castle.
The bay is lonely and deserted, and the traces of
those who lived there long ago are fast disappearing.
It is open to the sou'-west, and heavy seas roll in
there at times, as the cave-worn sides and the heaps
of smooth boulders on the beach testify well. Island
Bay was inhabited by whalers in the early days :
those brave men who lived hard lives and thought
danger a pleasure. Since the whales left the coast
the bay has been deserted and lonely.

The Maoris had a pah here. Traces of their stone walls and huts are still to be seen, and greenstone to be found. The writer picked up a small chisel of this substance, and many handsome implements formed of it have been discovered from time to time. These Maoris, in fact all of them along this coast, were a wild race. Horrible stories are told of their cannabilism, and some of the white men earliest in the bays have witnessed their ungodly feasts. When the Maoris wanted to settle a quarrel they went about it in a quite business-like manner. Over they went to Wakamoa, the next bay towards the Heads, and after they had had enough and buried their dead, came home. The ridges, graves of many a stalwart warrior, are conspicuous yet. The natives living in Island Bay had a fine natural fortress, for it was almost impregnable. Thick heavy bush behind, steep walls on either side (for it is quite a stiff climb into the bay), and a beach on which it is comfortable to land only when the weather is fine. A slip while climbing the rocky sides would be dangerous. A story is told of a Maori woman who was collecting firewood on the spur. She tied a bundle to her back and commenced to descend ; slipping, she rolled from the top to the bottom, and little life was left in her when she stopped rolling. The cheese from Mr. McPhail's dairy, before the road was made, was carried down on men's backs to the beach. However they did it is a puzzle, and a very few trips up and down would satisfy an ordinary Hercules. When climbing the side, and thinking of it, one fancies that it would have been a great temptation to let them roll in spite of all consequences. The bay, however, is little visited except by the cattle on the runs. There is a fine creek running down the valley, though on the tops of the spurs the land is very parched in summer.

About 1840 whaling stations were established all

along the coast, at Ikeraki, Peraki, Oauhau, and
Island Bay. Whales were plentiful at that time,
and there was always plenty of employment for the
boats of the whalers. Two large boilers, set in
stone, are still in the bay, and there were others,
which have disappeared. There is also an arrangement for hauling the whales on shore, fixed on the
same principle as the capstan of a ship. Heaps of
whalebone litter the beach and the sides of the creek.
A great quantity of it has, it is said, been carried
away to bone-dust factories. Staves of innumerable
casks are piled up around the boilers One can
imagine the wild scene the bay presented on some
dark night, from the sea, when the whalers were
busy boiling down ; the fires blazing up, and
showing their forms distinctly against the back-
ground of heavy bush. The stormy seas which
frequently roll into the bay show signs of having
been far up the creek, where lie embedded great
pieces of whalebone.

Messrs. W. Green (after whom Green's Point is
named), C. Brown and Hall were the first owners of
the Island Bay fishery. After leaving the station,
Charlie Brown went away in a whaling vessel never
afterwards heard of, and supposed to have been
wrecked on the coast. Hall left Akaroa one day in
a whale boat with a quantity of provisions for the
bay. The boat and its crew were never seen again.
It is supposed that they got fast to a whale and
were capsized, as the last time the boat was seen, it
was close to one that was spouting about the head
of the harbour. The next owner of the fishery was
Mr. George Rhodes, brother of Mr. Robt. Rhodes.
Sam. Williams, commonly known as Yankee Sam,
whaled for him. When the gold diggings broke out
in Melbourne, he went there. Mr. James Wright,
the hearty old Baron of Wakamoa, got the tripots
from him, and whaled there until the persecuted

whales left these waters to seek some quieter home.
At times when a school of whales appeared the whole
coast was very busy.   About thirty boats were often
out.   Casks were bought at Lyttelton, and when
filled at the bay were sent back again in small vessels.
The Maoris were employed on the stations, and
some of them were expert whalers.

No wrecks have actually occurred in Island Bay
itself.   A brig was lost between it and Land's End
some years ago, and all hands drowned.   She was
laden with timber, great quantities of it floating up
Akaroa Harbour.   Snufflenose, where the ill-fated
Clyde was lost, is a little way round the coast
towards Peraki.   It is believed that other vessels
have met their fate on this point, as wreckage has
been found from time to time.   There would be little
hope for mariners whose vessel dashed on the rocks
under those cliffs on a wild night, for the wind blows
with terrific force into the bight, and it has been
supposed that a current sets into it from the open
ocean, so that the danger was fearful indeed before
the lighthouse was erected.

The spurs slope gently down from the tragic
Bossu, connected with so many weird disappearances
and mysterious horrors.   The extent of the country
on that side of the hills surprises one who has just
come up the steep side that rises from the harbour.
There is much ploughable land there—thousands of
acres,—and all of the settlers in those parts grow
their fields of oats and vegetables in ploughed land.
The residents in Island Bay are : Messrs. James
Wright, McPhail, Niblett, and Randall.   The property formerly occupied by Mr. A, O. Knight is now
farmed by Mr. Randall.   The Baron of Wakamoa
was the first to settle in the bay.   After him came
Mr. J. McKinnon, who lived on the property now
owned by Mr. McPhail.   Mr. H. Niblett was next,
and Mr. Randall arrived recently.   The land is very

valuable for dairying purposes, and for pasturing sheep and cattle. The settlers now have a road as good as any on the Peninsula, and the difficult labour of shipping from the bay is done away with, as they can easily cart their produce to Wainui. It was to Mr. McPhail's house the survivor of the Clyde came, that being the nearest to the scene of the catastrophe.

The view from Mt. Bossu is a grand one—on one side the harbour, on the other the bight, across which are seen the snow-clad Alps, and, terminating the coast, the waters of Ellesmere. There are many picturesque spots in the bay, and the bracing winds from the open ocean make it a healthy place. There is a waterfall close to Island Bay two hundred feet high, which is a grand sight.

No. 10—LITTLE RIVER.

Little River was one of the latest settled portions of the Peninsula, although it is one of the most important places now. It is the outlet from the harbour to the Plains, and all of the Bay roads converge towards it. The settlement, consisting as it does of large valleys and fertile flats, well watered, was, it is not difficult to perceive even now, covered in dense bush. Since the mills have been at work, it has been a lively go-ahead place. There is still a large quantity of timber to be cut, but year by year the bush is disappearing. When it is gone, the chief export from the place ceasing, Little River will have to depend on its grazing and its cocksfooting ; and as there is such a large area suitable for dairying purposes, the export of cheese from the Peninsula will be largely increased when the bush land is cut up into dairy farms.

The Maoris in the early times had a pah at the mouth of the Little River. Tikawilla, or a person of some such name, was the chief. These Maoris obtained their food supplies from where Little River now is, hunting the wild pigs, and killing the wild birds. Little River was famous for its birds. The traveller through it in former years was always enchanted by the songs, scarcely ever ceasing, of the denizens of the bush. It was also a most beautiful place—prettier than it is now,—and some of the largest trees on the Peninsula grew there. The Maoris were rich in provisions, for the river and lake swarmed with tunas and other native fish. When Rauparaha came down with his warriors, he sent some of his men over to Little River, but hearing of their approach, the Natives did not await their arrival, but left their home for a time. It has always been, however, the district where the Maoris were in the largest number. A great many still live there, are on terms of equality with the European settlers, and own much of the best land about there. The Maoris annually grew large patches of kumaras on the hills above Harman's bush.

Mr. Price was in Kaiapoi as early as 1831. Shortly afterwards he was whaling along the Peninsula Bays, and while at Ikeraki came over to Little River. Seeing the excellent timber there, he set two pairs of sawyers at work in 1840. The whalers at the stations in the Bays about Peraki often came over to the River, either walking over the hills, or sailing round to the outlet of Lake Forsyth into the sea. Messrs. Smith and Robinson (the latter of whom was the first Magistrate in Akaroa) owned that property now belonging to Mr. H. D. Buchanan. Mr. Buchanan's father came over from Ikeraki and bought them out, Smith going to Australia. This was about 1850.

Mr. Birdling also came from the fisheries, and

bought up land about the River, forming that grand
property now possessed by him, and from which some
of the best stock in New Zealand is sent to the
Addington market. There was a good deal of sawing
done in Little River in the old times, a great many
runaway sailors from the whaling vessels around the
coast congregating there. The lower flats were covered
with tutu, Maori cabbage and other vegetation, and
it was difficult travelling to reach the valley. Wm.
Wood, commonly known as Paddy Wood, who
started Oauhau whaling station, was in Little River
early, and had land there. Messrs. White and
Coop were the first to start the saw-mill. The old
building is still to be seen just opposite the Railway
Station. To start a saw-mill there was a much
more difficult matter then than could be considered
possible now. The engine was dragged from
Christchurch by bullocks, and a great undertaking
it was. When the mill was fixed up, there was no
lack of material for it to work on. A tramway was
made to Lake Forsyth. This carried the timber,
which was punted over the small lake to Birdling's
Flat. Here it was put on another tramway, and
conveyed to Lake Ellesmere, over which it was
taken in punts and crafts to Hart's Creek, Leeston.
At one time there were several vessels employed on
the lake for this purpose. A steamer also was built
at Stony Point. There is very little left now to
remind one of these doings. A jetty is still standing,
which runs into Lake Forsyth, where the Christchurch Regatta is now held. The tramway has
disappeared. The timber had to undergo a lot of
handling, but its scarcity, and the good price then
ruling, justified the labor. As may be supposed, a
great many men were at work in connection with
this mill, and these with their families settled the
place. A school was built for their children close to
where the Forsyth Arms Hotel now is. There was

another school built at Stony Point, of which Mr. Dowling was master. The house now belongs to Mr. Birdling. About thirty years ago the road from Christchurch to Little River was made by Messrs. Radford, Buckingham and Edmonds. Before this travelling was guess work, and those who wished to go to Little River, travelled round the points and over the lake flats, making the journey much longer than it is now.

The first dairies started in Little River were those of Messrs. Stanbury and G. W. Joblin. These dairies supplied the men working at the timber, and were very profitable then. As the bush was cleared the land was sown down and cocksfoot cut. As soon as the railway line was made to Birdling's Flat the Terawera saw-mill was started, and is still doing a lot of work. The Western Valley mill was started some years ago, but has now completed its work. Mr. Stanbury made the road over the hill into the harbour. Little River has a Road Board of its own, and it has charge of a large district.

The new school was built about 1880, and the English Church before that, also the Maori Church on the Maori reserve. Both of these churches are prettily situated on the top of small hills, and are very picturesque. The Maori Hall, a commodious building, was erected in 1885, and is a great boon to the settlement, for here public amusements can take place. Formerly the inhabitants were badly off in this respect. The Forsyth Arms Hotel was built many years ago, and it was unfortunate for travellers that it was not built nearer the spot where the railway ends. The horrible murder which took place at this hotel will be long remembered. The settlement of Little River has been a quiet one, and unfruitful of startling events It has been a history of quiet prosperity. Some day perhaps the railway will be extended to the foot of the hill, and the

tunnel bored to the harbour, tapping the Peninsula.
Little River has a prosperous future before it, and
in time it will be like the rest of the Peninsula—a
collection of fine farms,—whose export will be cocksfoot, butter and cheese.

No, 11.—CHARTERIS BAY.

Perhaps the most picturesque of the bays on
Lyttelton Harbour is that known as Charteris. It is
so called from the surveyor who originally measured
its area, and is of very considerable extent, Separated
by a spur from the head of Lyttelton Harbour, it is
in reality the valley of Mt. Herbert, the highest peak
of our Peninsula, whose giant summits are far loftier
than those famed heights of which Macaulay sang
in his glorious verses that tell of the fiery warning
that flashed through England when the Armada was
seen approaching. As seen from the bay, Mt.
Herbert has two great peaks, The one of greatest
altitude is smooth to the summit, and towers in calm
serenity over a frowning rocky peak, which at the
first glance appears the real monarch, but in reality
is some 200ft lower. The saddle between these two
is really the commencement of Charteris Bay ; and
from the very topmost tier of the hard rocks that
crown the latter, gushes the spring that is the source
of the large creek which finds its way into the
harbour in the centre of the bay. It is said this
spring is so near the peak that a very little work
would cause it to flow in the opposite direction.
However, after a somewhat precipitous course it
reaches the head of a beautiful valley some three
miles in length, along which it runs to the sea, form-

ing many a cool pool and miniature waterfall in its
fertilising progress. Half way down the valley its
course is confined within rather narrow limits by a
great barrier of volcanic rock that almost closes the
upper flats from those below. Very little labour
indeed would make this a stronghold such as Black-
more tells us of in "Lorna Doone," a place where,
in the days gone by, a stately dame could in perfect
safety dish up those storied spurs which warned her
husband and sons that it was time to proceed on
another cattle stealing expedition. From this point
the valley rapidly extends in width, and is excep-
tionally fertile and well grassed.

The floods of a few years ago did considerable
damage, bringing down great masses of shingle, and
widening the bed of the creek very greatly; but
year by year the soil is gathering over the stones,
and the grass is creeping over their grey sides, so
that before long the emerald carpet will be as wide
as ever. The creek is not untenanted : besides the
eels, the trout that have been placed there have
thriven, and in cool pools at the end of rapids can
be seen gliding in the clear water. At the end of
one spur that embraces the bay (that on the Purau
side) is a magnificent pinnacle of rock. It is fitly
denominated Castle Peak, and so strong is the
resemblance of ruined towers, that were it on the
Rhine it would doubtless furnish many a tale to an
imaginative guide. These hill sides show no traces
of having ever been entirely clothed with the " forest
primeval," but in nooks of the mountain are many
patches of kowhai, ngaio, matapo, and other beautiful
native trees that flourish exceedingly in these sheltered
recesses. No part of the Peninsula can be more
beautiful than Charteris Bay when we saw it last, in
an autumn sunset, the great rocks that cast no
shadow here in a thirsty land, but hoard their liquid
treasures to their summits, frowned in the deep

purple of imperial majesty, and a thousand various
shades flickered and faded over brown hill side and
bright green valley, till a sombre haze shrouded all
in the soft greys of approaching night.

It was Dr. Moore to whom fate allotted Charteris
Bay when the sections were drawn for in England,
and he came out to Lyttelton in the Sir James
Pollock in 1851. He had neighbours on both sides,
for the late Mr. Manson, Mr. Gebbie, and their
families had settled at the Head of the Bay in 1845,
and Mr. Fleming was located at Port Levy, and Mr.
Rhodes at Purau. Dr. Moore brought some good
cattle out with him, and it was in Charteris Bay
that the nucleus of those Peninsula herds which
afterwards became so famous for their production of
butter, cheese and beef, were first reared. Brother
Phil, Cranberry, His Honor, and General Wolfe
amongst the bulls, and Flash, Duchess, Creamy,
and an Alderney named Dunny amongst the cows
were household words amongst the Peninsula
pioneers, and for a long time no female scion of the
famous herd found its way into other hands ; but
has not this been already recorded in the " Stories
of the Peninsula " by the Rev. R. R. Bradley ?
There was another owner of property in the Bay, a
Mr. Rowe. He had a section in the early days, but
went away, and was heard of no more. Five or six
years ago, however, news came he had been living in
Victoria, where he had prospered, and Mr. Helmore,
a Christchurch lawyer, took possession of the
property as his attorney. Dr. Moore did not make
a permanent home in Charteris Bay, and sold his
property to the Rev. R. R. Bradley in 1858. Mr.
Bradley was clergyman at Papanui before this, and
after he became a farmer, he preached at Purau on
alternate Sundays for seven consecutive years. Dr.
Moore, after the sale, returned to England, where
he had many connections, his father having been the

Mayor of Salisbury.   From October, 1858, to his
death. a period of more than thirty-three years, the
Rev. R. R. Bradley resided at Charteris Bay with his
family, and the principal part of it, some 2000 acres,
was in his possession.   A great part was once owned
by the late Mr. Manson, but he disposed of it
finding he had too large an area to manage.   There
are a few small settlers in the Bay, the Simpsons
and Hays, and very comfortable little homesteads
they have, and lead happy and contented lives.

The old buildings erected by Dr. Moore are still
standing : in fact he built the house in which the
Bradleys now reside, though of course it has been
repaired and altered.   He had also a stone dairy
and stalls, but these are fast falling into decay.   The
house is pleasantly situated on rising land about
half a mile from the beach.   In front is a fine view
of the bay, Rabbit Island, and the long peninsula.
which nearly joins it, and so much reminds one of
Onawe in Akaroa Harbour.   In the foreground are
newly grassed paddocks, a few stately trees, the
pretty homestead of Mr. Hay, and the school buildings, which are very neat   At the back of the house
is a splendid plantation of gums, with here and there
a pinus insignis and a macrocarpa.   In the bank at
the back a cellar has been dug out, and very cool it
is in the hottest weather.   A neat macrocarpa fence
bounds the flower garden, which is rich in many
flowers.   The roses look particularly nice, and
amongst the native shrubs and trees are specially to
be noticed some grand specimens of the mountain
palm, the giant cabbage tree, which here flourishes
most luxuriantly.   Winding down the path to the left,
past the garden, we come to the stockyard, which is
very massively fenced and paved with stones.   The
stables are most spacious and excellent, as might be
supposed, from their being under the management of
Mr. Orton Bradley, the present owner of the estate.

No. 12—GOUGH'S BAY.

The lower part of this beautiful Bay was the property of the Messrs. Masefield Bros. when the first edition of " Stories of Banks Peninsula " was published, but it now belongs to Mr. V. V. Masefield, Mr. Wm. Masefield having gone to the Sounds. The Native name of the Bay is Okururu, and the Messrs. Masefield quite agreed with the writer that it is a great pity the Maori appellation was ever altered. It appears that the present designation was given to it from a man named Gough, who lived there for many years among the Natives. These north-east Bays were amongst the last settled on the Peninsula, owing to the difficulty of access, and of getting away stock or shipping produce. This was so particularly the case with Okoruru, that during the great Kai-huanga or eat relation feud, many Maoris fled there in hopes of escaping the visits of their enemies by seeking a locality, the paths to which were almost inaccessible, and known to but few. Enterprising Europeans, however, soon ascertained the exceeding richness of the soil, and a French settler, named M. Guin, purchased a section on the flat, and sent M. Peter Malmanche there to occupy it, and took some cattle over. The difficulty of landing, however, on the Gough's Bay beach was proved in this case, for the boat conveying M. Malmanche and his things was capsized in the surf, and although all hands landed safely, a large box, containing his wife's clothes and some other things, went to sea. M. Malmanche was in despair, but next morning, on visiting the shore, he was delighted to see the box high and dry on the sand. His spirits immediately revived, and he ran towards it ; but what was his horror to find it was merely a

shell, for the treacherous ocean had dashed out the
bottom, and the valuable contents were, alas ! " full
fathom five." Peter Malmanche lived there some
time, but a mysterious accident occurred, which for
a period gave the bay an evil reputation. One night
he retired to rest as usual, but when his wife awoke
in the morning he was missing, and after a long
search he was found by her in the bush, some distance from the house, in an insensible condition.
There was a fearful wound on his head, and by his
side was an axe covered with blood and hair.   It
was with great difficulty his life was saved, but when
he recovered he could throw no light on the matter,
always declaring he remembered nothing from the
time he retired to rest till he recovered consciousness
after the accident. Investigations were attempted, but
the matter remains a mystery to this day.   He returned to the bay after the accident, and the whâre got
the reputation of being bewitched.   The most mysterious and appalling noises were heard in the night,
and are testified to by many persons above suspicion.
On one occasion Peter Malmanche nearly met with
another accident, that would probably have proved
more disastrous than its predecessor, for one night,
after being terribly annoyed by a succession of
these mysterious and unaccountable noises, Mr.
Wm. Masefield took down a gun, and vowed he
would shoot anything he saw in the neighbourhood
of the house.   Opening the door, he observed a dim
figure near the whâre, and, taking aim, had his
finger on the trigger, when a loud coo-ee caused him
to stop, and he found it was Peter Malmanche, who
had walked over from Akaroa.   It is thought that
these strange sounds must have been the work of
persons who were anxious to prevent the Messrs.
Masefield settling, but if so the fraud was very
skilfully devised and carried out, for to this day there
is no clue to the mystery.   It was in company with

Harry Head that Mr V. V. Masefield first explored the valley. Harry Head then lived at Waikeri-kikeri, and at that place the Messrs. Masefield bought some sections. Harry Head's wonderful powers of finding his way through the bush made him a splendid companion, and on exploring Gough's Bay Valley, and finding how fertile it was, Mr. Masefield determined to have it, and the brothers then commenced purchasing it. They exchanged the sections at Waikerikikeri with Mr. John Smith, for some land he had purchased in Gough's Bay, and the owners of the sections bought by M. Guin and Boirreau disposed of them, so that gradually an estate of 1200 acres was formed, containing some of the best land on the Peninsula. This land is divided into four paddocks of about 300 acres each, and there are several smaller enclosures for working the sheep easily.

Besides an excellent dwelling house, there is a large woolshed, excellent yards, and all the other usual appliances of successful sheep farming. Of course there is a dairy ; and speaking of this, when the Messrs Masefield first went to the bay they had cattle on the place, and a nice job they used to have with them, for the Bay was then of course all bush, and it was a terrible worry to get the cattle out, for horses could not be used in such country. To hear the marvellous adventures of one snail-horned bullock that would persist in preferring Gough's Bay to the West Coast, is enough to make one's hair stand on end ; but it is satisfactory to know that after all his extraordinary capers he eventually gladdened the hearts and stomachs of the Hokitika miners. The house is a comparatively new one, the former erection, in which the mysterious noises used to be so prevalent, having been burnt down. This fire had very nearly a fatal termination. The origin was unknown, but Mr. Valentine Masefield, awaking one night, discovered the place was burning. He made for the outer door and got it open, and then called to Mr. W. Masefield, who was sleeping in another room. The door was fastened on the inside, and no doubt was jammed, and Mr. W. Masefield, after trying it, was obliged by the smoke to retreat to his bed, where he threw himself down, expecting to be suffocated. Mr. V. Masefield, however, never lost his presence of mind, but running to the outside window, he broke the panes of glass, and tore out part of the sash by main strength. The fresh air rushing in revived his brother, and he came to the window, and somehow was dragged through, badly burned, but safe. It was only just in time, for five minutes later the house fell in, one great mass of flame. There is a clump of ngaios and other native scrub at the back of the house, and a few gums planted amongst them have grown wonderfully well. Going to the beach, which is half a mile from the house, one skirts a beautiful piece of bush that the Messrs. Masefield have left for ornamental purposes. These gentlemen deserve the thanks of all lovers of nature for the care they have exercised in this respect. Every here and there groups of the finest trees have been left, which add to the beauty of the scene, afford shelter to the stock, and a thousand times repay the grazing value of the land they cover. Barbarous vandalism and a desperate greed for every blade of grass has spoiled the beauty of many a Peninsula home, and the efforts that are now being made to raise plantations of pinus insignis and other trees, show what a wise thing it would have been to have spared a few patches of that unrivalled native bush that, once destroyed, no art can replace. The creek is crossed by a bridge of a very long single span, the great kowhai stringers of which show their elasticity, as well as their strength, as one passes over. The road is that by which the wool

and grass seed is taken to the shipping place, and
winds round the base of the hills. There is sand on
the borders of the creek. It is a black sand, like
that of Taranaki, and is full of metal, which can
easily be separated from it by washing. A little out
of the road is an interesting ngaio tree, on which a
disappointed Maori ended his troubles not many
years ago. It appears that he swung grimly in the
air, like an old highwayman on a heath, for many a
day, but that at last his friends scooped a deep hole
in the ground beneath the tree, and, severing the
rope by which he was suspended, let him fall into it.
These bones, however, were not destined to rest for
long, for a medical gentleman of Akaroa wanted a
good skeleton, and hearing of this, disinterred it and
carried it away in triumph. Maori bones are
common in Gough's, and the sitting-room was once
decorated with the bleached skulls, and huge femurs
of two grim old warriors, the desecration of whose
remains in " Kai Huanga " times might doubtless
have caused a thousand deaths. The tapu surrounding them, however, has now lost its power, and the
little hands of children have turned into playthings
these mouldering frames of mouths and eyes, from
which many an order for death and many a glance
of hatred may have issued. After passing this
" dule.tree " one comes to where a wooded valley
gives birth to a creek, which here joins the main
one. At the junction of the creeks grow a number
of wild potatoes. Year after year they spring up
with great luxuriance, and when I saw them were in
full flower, and doubtless had large tubers underneath. It must be the site of an old Maori garden,
and the sandy soil be peculiarly favourable for the
growth of the tuber.

Here is a saw mill, which has now been busy for
some years cutting the totara, matai, and kahikatea,
which abound on the table-land above, known as

2H

Crown Island Gully. It originally belonged to M. B. Malmanche, but is now in the hands of a company. Past the mill we come to a pathway hewn out of the rock, and leading to the shipping place. It cost some £150 to form this short rocky track, and put down the tramway and erect the crane. It was hard work, but it has answered well, for a steamer can now come in to within a few chains of the place where the produce is lowered into the boat ; and besides that, shipping can always go on except in southerly weather. The scene here is very grand : a great flat rock partially protects the haven where the boats are loaded, and against this the sea breaks in most imposing waves. There are some curious caves in these rocks, and one goes right through the cliff. It was through this that Mr. W. Masefield once came after a rather dangerous swim. Mr. Pilliett had said no man could swim through the surf, and one day, when a nasty sea was rolling in, and Mr. Adams was present, he resolved to prove to the contrary. He got through the surf all right, but the drawback was too strong for him to return ; and, finding he was getting exhausted, he made for some flat rocks outside the Heads, and thence by climbing and swimming he reached the other side of the cavern, and, watching his chance, came through. Those who have seen the place can alone realise the difficulty of the feat. On another occasion he swam off to the Red Rover, which was coming in to take away cheese and bacon. It was blowing hard from the south-east, and he remained on board all night. The Red Rover was then undecked, and they had to lay all night in the cold, covered over with what they could get. Next day, in spite of the gale, he swam ashore, and in a lull in the wind some produce was got aboard and some stores landed. Crossing the creek, one can visit the site of the old Maori pah. It is of large extent, and it is said some seven hundred Natives once lived there. The sea must have encroached a good deal on the land here, for the waves reach where some of the whâres formerly stood ; but a peculiar grass, sown and cared for by Mr. V. Masefield, has checked the encroachment of the sea. The earthworks surrounding the pa are still easily traced. They enclose a space fully two acres in extent, and this is again sub-divided. An immense amount of work must have been done, and the side of the hill on the south shows traces of having been cultivated from base to summit. Heaps of the bones of fish, dogs, seals and other animals testify to the enormous feasts once held here, and when the Messrs. Masefield first went there, the poles on which fish were stretched to dry were still standing. At every step sharpening stones, pieces of greenstone, stones ground into implements, and other curiosities can be found in the sand. A great cedar log was washed ashore here, and is inscribed with many initials from visitors. The stern of the Crest was dashed on these sands, and parts of the vessels wrecked at Timaru. The limb of the ngaio tree on which the Maori hung himself is a part of the boat used for shipping, and the piece of the Crest is a part of the dairy.

A few Maoris were living here to within twenty years ago. Some ten years before this the Natives then residing there purchased a boat of a man named Howland, living in Okain's. The boat was principally putty and paint, and proved a terrible bargain to the unfortunate purchasers. One day all the resident Maoris, with the exception of three women, went out in this boat to fish on the bank, which is some two or three miles out to sea. They caught a great number of huge hapuka, and these flapping about in the boat, soon opened a number of leaks, and she sunk, and not a soul was saved. The unfortunate women, whose husbands were aboard, saw

the catastrophe from the cliffs, but were powerless to
aid.   They refused to quit the spot, however, and go
to Onuku, though repeatedly urged, saying that they
would remain to bury the bones of their husbands
when they came ashore.   Many a weary year they
waited, but the bones never came, and at last one of
the faithful creatures died, and the others were then
removed by force by the other natives.   When their
friends were drowned these women took all their
valuables, placed them in two canoes, and buried
them in the creek.   They never divulged the secret
of the hiding place, and though the Maoris from
Akaroa have spent many a day in endeavouring to
discover them, their efforts have been unsuccessful.
Some day perhaps the wind in its freaks will lay
them bare, and then what a host of Maori relics
will reward the finder ! Speaking of canoes, this was
once a great place for them, and the best totaras all
through the bush have been felled to construct them.
One just finished is still to be seen on the top of a
lofty ridge in the middle of the dense bush, and
there is another commenced on the Waikerikikeri
side.   Think of the immense labour it must have
cost to get these vessels down, after the tedious work
of making them with fire and stones ! No white
man would have dreamed of such an undertaking.

The old landing place was under the south head.
Here it was only possible to ship in very calm
southerly weather, and even then was very dangerous.
There is a great cave here under the cliff, and at the
time of our visit a grand king penguin occupied a
ledge in it, and blinked at us as we lay watching the
waves roll in.   There is a curious cleft in the cliff
here, about 15ft above the level, and one day, curious
to find what it contained, the Messrs. Masefield took
down a ladder and inspected it.   Inside, within the
once warm folds of a cloak of pigeon's feathers, lay
the mouldering bones of a little child.   How many

years had passed since tender hands had reverently
placed it in this remote situation? The view from
this place is remarkably fine. The bold cliffs of the
northern head, which rise 600ft sheer from the sea,
the many rocks in the Bay against which the waves
dash sheets of foam, the southern head with its
400 feet of overhanging rock, and inland the peaceful
valley and gentle spurs, with patches of bush here
and there, and above all, the great peaks of the
main range—form together a most imposing
picture, and it was with regret I turned my steps
towards the house. Going back on the south bank
of the creek, through the flat, no one can help
noticing the extraordinary growth of grass. All the
posts in the 60-acre paddock you go through, came
from one great totara tree, and there were some left
over. The walk up the valley is very delightful, the
trees being of exceptional beauty. There are a
great number of nikau palms, and a curious kind of
broadleaf growing here, which I have never seen
before. It takes root in the forks of the big pines,
and gradually grows down till it reaches the earth,
where it roots, and gaining fresh strength, gradually
embraces and strangles the tree like the rata. It is
very beautiful, its leaves being larger and brighter
than those of the common broadleaf. The Messrs.
Masefield turned out turkeys and geese in the valley.
Three of each were turned out. The turkeys
increased so fast that in a few years there were
hundreds ; but of late they seem to be declining in
numbers. We saw several healthy broods. The
geese have always done wonderfully well, and there
is a great flock of them. The native birds are still
numerous, but the kakas and pigeons have disappeared. Mr. V. Masefield does not believe that
these birds have been shot out, but that they have
migrated to the West Coast. He says that the
kakas disappeared in a very short time : that one

month there were thousands, and the next none ; so that they cannot have been destroyed, but must have sought some other locality. Gough's Bay was once the home of innumerable wekas. For some years every tussock and every piece of bush was thick with them, and the dogs used to kill as many as twenty a day. A few years ago these also took their departure. From making enquiries, Mr. Masefield traced the arrival of these birds. They came in one immense line from the west, round Lake Ellesmere, and their course to the east must have been stopped by the sea at Gough's Bay. The red-headed paraquets also suddenly disappeared. There were some of the native rats nine or ten years ago. They were fond of living in the trees, and one was caught in the fork of a tree as it was being felled. The Norwegians, however, have since appeared, and the natives seem to be extinct.

The other residents in the Bay are Messrs. Geo. Kearney and Jule Lelievre. Both have fine properties, stretching from the end of the flat to the summit of the range. In the years to come, we have little doubt that all these gentlemen will have many tenants, and that this beautiful Bay—as in the days of old—will support a large population.

No. 13—PERAKI.

Very beautiful is the head of the Peraki Valley. Thick bush spreads out just below the Summit, and here were still to be found, a very few years ago, the wild pigs in considerable numbers. Here also is one of the last haunts of the native pigeon, and the moko mokos, tuis and other birds swarm in thou-

sands. The track winds on the left-hand side of the
gully going down, and crosses the first tongue of
bush running out on to the tussocked peaks pretty
near the Summit. In making this road a strange
thing occurred. Though the track was cut through
the virgin bush, where none had been known to go
before, the largest tree at the creek crossing, a large
broadleaf, was found to have been carved with the
letters L, y, A, r. The gully was thereupon called
after the lady who was then Miss Lucy Aylmer, and
it bears her name on the Government maps to this
day. The hills on the right hand side of the valley
are very steep in places, and there is one great beet-
ling crag that overlooks the valley, out of which
springs a marvellous stone steeple, a splinter formed
by some convulsion of nature into an exceptional
shape. Above this again towers the Devil's Gap, a
great double rock, between the pinnacles of which
the road to Little River passes. Grey and stern as
they are at the summit, near the base these rocks are
clad in the loveliest foliage, and wherever a fissure in
their sides gives room for a root to penetrate, there
is a curtain of emerald leaves. For a long way the
beauty of the scene is unmarred by the so-called
improvements, and we feel we are really travelling
under the shadow of " the forest primeval ;" but, on
a corner being turned, the usual hideous array of
trunk-covered ground and bare sticks, which look
what they really are—the naked skeletons of burnt
trees tortured in the fire,—spring up around us.

On reaching the burnt ground, we come to a
creek that has had its rocky bed torn into strange
shapes by a great slip from the top of the overlooking spurs. Mr. Worsley was camped near when the
slip came down, and woke and listened to the terrible
thunder of the descending rocks ; but they spared
him, stopping their mad course, however, only a few
yards from his tent. It must be remembered that

the writer fully recognises the absolute necessity of clearing the bush away, but he cannot help regretting it.   The reason that the upper part of the Peraki Valley is certainly more beautiful than any other place on the Peninsula, is that it is so completely in a state of nature—one great mass of varied foliage, " musical with birds."   It will go soon, and with it will vanish the wild pigeons, and the majority of the other birds.   Messrs. Snow and Anson did their very best to save some of the handsomer trees in the valley.   A few groves left here and there will, at any rate, remind one in a year or two, of a beauty that will then have passed away for ever.   But, to resume.   On and on we go down the long valley, the beautiful harbour being full in sight, its sheltered water smooth as a mill pond, while white crests ornament the waves outside.   There is a calm beauty in this scene too, different of course from the mighty grandeur of the peaks, and the wondrous variety of the forest tints, but yet of exceeding merit.   The centre of the valley is still here and there dotted with scrub, and wherever water has seamed the side of the spurs a line of green bushes marks its course.   Here and there the picturesque tents and huts of the bush and grass seed cutters relieve the eye ; and beyond all, the two long low spurs clasp in a loving shelter that historical sheet of water, on whose beach landed the first white settlers of this island.   Crossing numerous small creeks we at last reach the station, which is sheltered from the nor'-west by a row of great gum trees.   The house is surrounded by a pleasant orchard, which was planted and tended with great care by one of those Carews who were its former proprietors.   It is said that when he left he cut down two pear trees, saying that the fruit was so delicious he could not bear to think of strangers eating it.   There are convenient buildings all round, and good paddocks for the cattle.   The yards and

woolshed are some little distance down the flat
towards the sea. There are some five thousand acres
on the Peraki run, which is now the property of Mr.
F. A. Anson, Mr. Snow, who was formerly in
partnership, having gone to the North.

The great historical interest in Peraki centres in
the old whaling settlement that once existed on the
beach. From Mr. Anson's house to the sea, one
cannot take a step without being reminded of the
incidents recorded in Hempleman's famous diary.
It will be remembered that it was at that place the
brig Bee landed Hemplemen and his men to prose-
cute the whale fishery in the year 1835. There are
still thousands of the bones of whales to testify the
success of the party. Great heaps of them are all
around one, standing at high water mark, and there
are more sad memorials also in the mounds that
mark the spot where some of these adventurous
men, who met their death by drowning, lie buried.
On the left hand side, looking seaward, is a rock
called " Simpson's rock," where that veteran whaler
used to look out for whales, and nearly underneath it
is the point where the unfortunate steamer Westport
received the injuries that eventually caused her total
loss. The site of the " Long House," the principal
building in the old whaling times, is still visible, and
so are the places where the caldrons were fixed, in
which the oil was tried out. It was here that
" Bloody Jack " came with his followers to demand
the lives of those North Island Maori boys that were
working there ; the safety of one of whom was purchased by Hempleman and his men by the present of
a boat. By the by, we have all heard that Hempleman saved the life of one of these boys by heading
him up in a cask, and so hiding him from his
enemies ; but an altogether new version of this story
is now current. It appears it was not one of the
boys at all, who was headed up in a cask, but a young

fellow who came from Wairewa to Peraki, and who, knowing that Bloody Jack and his party were coming to Peraki, kept it a secret from Hempleman. When the party did come, and the boy Jacky was killed, and the other lad ransomed for the boat, Hempleman was so angry at not having received warning from this man of their danger, that he headed him up in a cask as a punishment, and kept him there for weeks, feeding him through the bung-hole. It was only at the intercession of some other Maoris he at last consented to his release ; and when the cask was broken open, and he was liberated, he was nearly dead with the frightful stench and the cramped position in which he had been kept so long. Mr. Simpson told me that a Maori girl was also killed here, and that the flesh was distributed ; so that it has been the scene of more than one dark tragedy.   It must indeed have been a lonely place in those days, and the brave fellows who lived there showed great courage.   The bush then came down to the water's edge, and rude and toilsome was the path leading to the Harbour of Akaroa.   Even when they got there, it was a great chance if they could have had any aid, as for many months in the year there were no vessels there, so that it may be said they carried their lives in their hands.   Hempleman must not only have been a courageous, but a very politic man, to save his little settlement in safety, when the fierce Natives could have murdered them whenever it suited their will.   Many a weary night he must have spent, fearing the worst, and he certainly had a just claim on the Government for a good grant of land after surmounting so many perils. His first claim was, I believe, the whole of the Peraki valley, bounded by the crest of the two spurs and the summit of the main range ; but, as we know, he afterwards grew more ambitious, and claimed a huge slice of the Peninsula.   Simpson tells me that the

men had very hard times when they first landed
at Peraki, Hempleman brought some boards for his
house, but the others had to sleep in casks for some
time, and afterwards they put up such very temporary
erections, being entirely unused to whâre building,
that they had to be stayed by lines, which had to be
shifted when the wind changed, so that they should
not be blown over. Hempleman's first wife was
buried there, but I do not know the exact spot;
in fact, the sand has drifted in patches over what
seems to have been the principal part of the settlement, which was not far above high water mark.
One large mound is said to denote the grave of a
Maori chief, but Peraki has never been a great
Maori burying place. In the adjoining bay, on
Mr. Buchanan's property, known as Tumble-down
Bay, there are great numbers of human bones, which
are sometimes laid bare by the action of the sea, and
then again covered by the friendly sand. Peraki
beach is a beautiful smooth and sandy one, without
rocks, and shelving so gradually, that we had to
walk out a very long distance at low water before we
could get far enough to bathe. The Bay abounds
with fish, and Mr. Thomas Brough and others often
used to go there to catch moki, kawhaia, and butter
and cray-fish, with which latter the rocky ledges
absolutely swarm,

· MORE STORIES OF OLD SETTLERS.

MR. PHILLIP RYAN.

In the long gully that runs up to the reserve for half-castes, from the back of the former site of Joblin's mill, now a part of Mr. Montgomery's estate, in the Western Valley, Little River, there is a comfortable whâre of the old type in a very snug corner by the creek side, which the winds pass by and the morning sun shines on. Here with his son dwells Mr. Phillip Ryan, one of those Peninsula pioneers whose life has been one long struggle in the van of colonisation. He is a man of fine presence, and must have possessed great strength in his time. Even now, after a long and toilsome life that has nearly reached ninety years, he is full of intelligence, and by no means wanting in bodily as well as mental vigour. He lives up here in the hills with his son, who is a half-caste, Mr. Ryan having married a Maori many years ago, who was his good and faithful wife till death came. He was born in Ireland in 1802, and his father was in the Commissariat Department of the British army during the Peninsula war. To Lisbon he went with his mother very early in the nineteenth century, and his early years were passed in following the movements of the gallant men whom Wellesley eventually led to victory. It was only a month before Waterloo that he returned with his family to England.

His early life had given him a taste for wandering and adventure, and when peace came, he sought the sea, and made five voyages out of London. He was at the North Sea fishery, and there served in a vessel of which our well-known Hempleman was mate. He was for a time in the navy, and then he turned his attention to the South Seas. Here he was cast away on his first voyage on one of the Society Islands. After this he made his way to Sydney, and from thence came to Otago in the schooner Return in 1838. Here he stopped for a time, but afterwards went in the same vessel to Timaru, where he was engaged during the whaling season of 1839. From thence he and two other men went to Oashore. They were fitted out with all requisites for whaling by Mr Waller, of Sydney, and got plenty of hands to help them from the runaway sailors who left ships in Otago and Akaroa, for at that time there were a great many ships coming in. Mr. Price was at Ikeraki at that time, and there were whaling stations at Peraki and Akaroa also.

On August 9th, 1840, which was a glorious day, Mr. Ryan saw a man-of-war's boat pulling into the Bay at Oashore, and a lieutenant soon landed, and, coming up to the house, asked him if he could give any information regarding the Comte de Paris. The Lieutenant told him he belonged to a British vessel of war named the Britomart. Ryan told the Lieutenant that a man named " Holy Joe " (the same mentioned by James Robinson Clough) had come over the hill that morning and could give all the news. " Holy Joe " told the Lieutenant that the Comte de Paris had been in Pigeon Bay, and that some of her people had landed, and had cut their names in the trees in that locality—now known as Holmes' Bay,—but that no French flag had been hoisted, and there seemed to be no intention to land anything from the ship. This was all the news Joe could give ; and as it was late the Lieutenant and his crew stopped at Ryan's house that night, and left at 4 a.m. so as to be back in Akaroa at the ship by 8 a.m. There were boats ready to intercept the Comte de Paris if she had attempted to enter Akaroa

Harbour, and a party went over the hills to Pigeon Bay, led by some Maori guides, to see no landing was effected there, and no French flag hoisted. At noon on the 10th the flag was formally hoisted by Capt. Stanley, who was in command of the Brito-mart, and a formal proclamation made by Mr. Robinson, the Government agent on board, taking possession of the South Island in the name of Her Majesty the Queen. It was Mr. Robinson who conducted all the subsequent transactions with the French, and Mr. Ryan speaks of him as a most able and kindly man. The guns fired to salute the newly hoisted standard were distinctly heard at Peraki, Oashore and Ikoraki, the wind being light, and the day exceedingly fine. After that season Ryan went to Port Levy, Mr. Waller, having failed. Thence he started a fishery at Motonau on his own account; but that was a failure, and so he came back to Port Levy, where he lived many years, being sawing most of the time with Tom White, who is still alive and hearty. He went two trips to America during this period, and one to Napier as mate of a brig, and in this latter excursion had the misfortune to break his leg. He used to carry the mail to Akaroa through the bush, and says he thought the trees on the way would not be cleared for a hundred years; but they are all gone now. The mail then used to go once every two or three months, when a ship came in. The steamers then began coming about, and the whalers deserted the coast. Besides, whale oil fell in price, and so from all these causes the whale fishery was, in a great measure, discontinued. Ryan remembers Mr. Fleming's first arrival in Port Levy. He came out in the Sir George Seymour, one of the first four ships, and he and Mr Arthur Waghorn, now of Little Akaloa, walked over the hills. Ryan says they had had good clothes on when they started, but in their passage through the bush these had been torn all to pieces, and they were in tatters on arrival. Tom White came to Ryan, and asked him to entertain them, as his whâre was so very untidy, because he had so many youngsters about ; and so Ryan did. Byan was the first man who sawed timber in Little River. He worked with an Australian native, named Green. Ryan was a cooper by trade, and it was that which made him so important at the whale fisheries. Mr. Ryan is very anxious to correct an error in the first edition of the " Banks Peninsula Stories, which states that James Robinson Clough was an American. He says he knew him well, and all about his family, and he was a native of Lincoln, England. Mr Ryan declares that the Maoris of the Peninsula were an amicable and honest lot of people, who never harmed anyone materially. He declares that the greatest violence ever offered was to take the tobacco, and perhaps part of the clothing of a runaway sailor, but says that, even then, they never allowed their victim to go hungry.

The old gentleman was cooking whilst the writer was there, and a very good cook he is ; but he is exceedingly reticent, as most are who have lived much in the bush. His greatest trouble is the gradual failing of his sight, which prevents him from reading. His son is one of the finest men it has been the writer's lot to see, and would make a model for the Farnese Hercules. He and his father are much attached, and lead a very pleasant and homely life in this lonely whâre, hidden in the spurs of the great ranges.

MR. THOMAS WHITE.

Mr. Thomas White, though he must be over 80 years of age, is very hale and hearty, and lives with his son, Mr. George Wright, in their pleasant home at the head of Holmes' Bay. Like many of our pioneers, he is an old sailor, and also a whaler, and in his long acquaintance with the Peninsula has seen it advance from a Maori populated resort of occasional whalers, to the pleasant home of 5000 Europeans. Mr. White is an American, having been born at Rhode Island He became an orphan at a very early age, his father being killed in one of the Mexican wars, and his mother dying, and his youthful days were spent under the roof of a friend of his dead parents. Rhode Island, as many people know, is a great place for shipping, and at 14 Mr. White went to sea. He learnt the ropes in several uneventful voyages, the only part of which he seems to care to dwell upon being a quarrel with the mate of a whaler at Rio Janeiro, which ended in his being left at that port, whence he shipped to England, arriving on the Thames on the very day of King William the Fourth's coronation. He shipped in a London whaler called the Timour, and in her he spent three years, one of his shipmates being our own Billy Simpson, formerly living in the Akaroa hospital. The first part of New Zealand he visited was the Bay of Islands, to which place he came from England in a whaler called the Achilles. He left her at this place, and went to Sydney in the Sir William Wallace. In Sydney he joined another whaling brig, called the Genii, and spent thirteen months in her on the New Zealand coast. His next vessel was the Caroline, belonging to Johnny Jones, of Otago, and on her being sold in Sydney he came to Wakaouiti in a brig commanded by Captain James Bruce, as a passenger. This vessel landed

twenty-three horses, which were amongst the first
brought to this colony.   From Wakaouiti he went
to Otago, and was there engaged by Paddy Wood to
go fishing at Oashore, and lived at that place some
years, working for Price some part of his time.

During this time Bloody Jack's men killed a
North Island boy, but otherwise all was quiet : the
whaling being very profitable sometimes, and an
exceedingly poor game at others.   Went to Port
Levy, and from there made a journey to Riccarton
for food, getting fifteen bushels of wheat from a store
deposited by Gilbert and Harridge.   At this time
there were only two Maoris at Port Levy and none
in Pigeon Bay, but they kept coming in their sea-
going canoes, many being from the North Island,
and soon there were quite strong settlements at both
places.

An old man named Jack Duff sold some bone and
had money in his possession about this time, and
mysteriously disappeared.   His wife last saw him in
the company of a Spaniard and a man known as
" Flash Harry."   Provisions were very dear at
times, twenty-five dollars being sometimes given for
a barrel of flour.   The Maoris as a whole were very
good to the whites, and Bloody Jack himself was a
very good fellow indeed.   Once he came to White's
house and demanded food.   It was given him of
course, and a short time after a hog was sent as a
present in return.

At Port Levy Mr. White married, and soon began
to have a family around him.   A tragedy took place
when his son Harry was a baby.   A Dutch whaling
ship put into Port Levy, and the carpenter and
several others deserted.   The third mate made himself very active in arresting the men ; and caught
two, and got them back to the ship.   The carpenter
came to White's house, and the mate after him.
White was on the verandah with Harry, the baby,

in his arms, and the carpenter and two runaways
were sitting at a table inside the house.   The mate
ordered the carpenter aboard, but, instead of obey-
ing, he shot him through the heart with a pistol that
was in his possession.   Word was sent to Wellington, but the ship was away before any steps were
taken, and so nothing was done.   Had the doctor of
the ship remained behind, no doubt the man would
have been hung.

The natives used to travel over the hills easily in
those days of no roads.   White has known a party
to take two tons of dog fish to Little River, the
Maoris there bringing in exchange two tons of eels.
An old Maori bearing the pleasant name of Rakika-
kinoki was specially celebrated for the way in which
he travelled the hills.   White was at Port Levy
when the Flemings came out, in 1855, but a few
years later went to Pigeon Bay   The Bay was full
of sawyers at that time, and a man named Billy
Webb, who kept a shanty at a place called the Pillar,
on the road between Pigeon Bay and Holmes' Bay,
had sometimes as many as forty boarders.   One of
these boarders fell over on the rocks and smashed
his head, and the question of foul play was raised,
but it is probable it was a pure accident.

Several vessels were built at Port Levy and Pigeon
Bay.   White himself assisted in building one 18-ton
craft, and Damon built several.   A vessel was built
for the natives at Nelson, and on her arrival Damon
offered them twelve cows for her, and cows were cows
in those days, but they would not sell.   The Maoris
grew many vegetables, and kept many pigs at that
time, and as a whole dealt fairly with the whites.
There was a big plantation of kumeras near where
Mr. Menzies' house now stands, and it appears to be
the only place where these roots have ever been
successfully grown on the Peninsula.   Mr White's
life has been uneventful in Pigeon Bay.   He has

reared a large family, who have lived happily together till, in the ordinary course of things, they
married, and went to houses of their own.   After
the whaling, White took to sawing and other work
like the rest, and eventually settled on a small farm.
A hardy and enterprising pioneer, he has done his
share in reclaiming the wilderness and peopling it,
and in spite of his advanced age, is still hearty. Let
us hope that he has still many years of quiet happi-
ness before him, amongst his children and grandchildren.

MR. WILLIAM ISAAC HABERFIELD.

This old identity has a most interesting history,
for particulars of which we are indebted to the
Dunedin *Evening Star.*   His narrative is as
follows :—

"I was born in Bristol on the 3rd June, 1815,
about a fortnight before Waterloo was fought.
There is the entry, in the Bible, in my father's hand-
writing.   He was a Captain in the navy—this is his
portrait in his uniform—and owing to his position, I
was placed as a youngster in the upper school at
Greenwich, a school for the sons of naval officers. As
soon as I was old enough I went to sea, joining a brigantine that was trading to the Mediterranean for fruit,
and the first work I ever did was to handle a ballast
shovel.   In this ship we made trips not only to the
Mediterranean, but also to Portugal and Spain, and
we were for some time running to Newfoundland.
I next joined His Majesty's brig, the Snake, as a
middy, and went away in her to the Brazilian coast,
where she was employed by Admiral Seymour in

chasing pirates and slavers. The Admiral was there in the Spartiate, his headquarters being Rio. My next experience was a voyage to the Colonies. I joined a ship that was bringing out a batch of male convicts, shipped at Sheerness, and bound for Tasmania, or Van Dieman's Land, as it was then called. Since then I have never left the Colonies. I got clear of the vessel in Sydney, and came from that port to New Zealand. This is as much as you need to know of my early life, which was a lively one, as you may guess; but of course what you want to know is what took place after I came to New Zealand. Well! I'll tell you.

"I came to Otago in a brig named the Micmac, and landed at Otago on the 17th March, 1836 (St. Patrick's Day). The very day after we landed, we killed a couple of fair-sized whales right up in the harbour. They were the first whales I ever saw killed. The boats were not away more than twenty minutes before they had them both, and they were killed in a twinkling. And I want to say here that we had two white women on board. Make mention of that, please. I'll tell you why. I had a regular laugh to myself when I read in one of the papers a little while ago that Mrs. Tom Jones was the first white woman to come to Otago. It shows what a precious lot they knew about it. Why, there was Mrs Brinn. She came down from Sydney with her husband in the Bee brig long before Mrs. Jones, and was here in Otago for some three years, eventually going back to Sydney with her husband, who was whaling at Waikouaiti and Otago. Brinn Point was named after her, from the circumstance that she frequented the spot to look out for the boats, when they were after whales. And the women we brought in the Micmac were here before Mrs. Brinn was. One of them was Mrs. Flood, and the other was Mrs. Garrett. They came with their husbands.

Garrett was a sawyer to trade, and went away in the brig the same trip, taking his wife with him. Flood was the storekeeper of the vessel, and left New Zealand again in the October or the November following our arrival. He had been a sergeant in the army, and a nice fellow he was. Neither the Garretts nor the Floods had any children. The owners wouldn't bring anyone that had any children, or incumberances as they were called.

"But I am getting off my course. I was going to tell you how I came here. This brig that I came in, her captain was a Welshman—I forget his name. I think he owned the vessel: he did so far as we knew. A whaler? No, she wasn't a whaler; she was a merchant vessel, loaded up with a general cargo for the Wellers' place. No, I don't suppose you do know much about the Wellers; but they were big people in those days, as you may believe when I tell you that they had then twelve vessels whaling for them. There were two brothers: one was George, and the other was named Edward, or it may have been Edwin, I am not sure which. They had the only store in the place anywhere about these parts, and a pretty big store it was. It was in the harbour—Otago Harbour it was called: what you call the Lower Harbour now. No! the store was not exactly on the Heads. It was on the point next to what is now known as Harrington Point, close to what you know as the Kaik. Edward, or Edwin, Weller was there himself. He and his brother were among the oldest colonists in New South Wales. The Mr. Weller I am speaking of had been a prisoner among the Maoris at Hokianga in his young days, and while there had got to understand the Maoris and speak their language He never owned any land, either in the North Island or the South, though he might have had as much as he could see almost for the asking. He was just a trader, and

he stuck to his business.   He is, I believe, alive now
in New South Wales—a very old man he must be.
The store that he had was always well stocked with
all kinds of slops and other things, and they used to
sell as cheap, or cheaper, than you can get things
now.   You could buy a splendid blanket for ten
shillings, and I don't suppose you'd get it for much
less now.

" No, that was not the only whaling station on
this part of the coast.   Afterwards there were
stations at Waikouaiti and at the mouth of the
Taieri, and to the north there were stations at
Timaru and Banks Peninsula, which used to be a
famous place for whales in those days.   But those
stations were all planted after my time.   If you want
to know which was the first whaling station in this
part of the country, I should say it was the one at
Preservation Inlet.   I have heard so.   That was a
very old one.   The next was the one at Otago,
where I came to.   Then came our place at Moeraki,
and the season after we started they set up a station
at Waikouaiti.   Johnny Jones?   No.   No one had even
heard of Johnny Jones then.   The people that
started whaling at Waikouaiti were Long, Wright,
and Richards.   They were Sydney merchants.   They
whaled one season and then they pitched it up—
failed, I believe—and it was then that Johnny Jones
came on the scene ; he bought them out in Sydney,
taking their boats, huts, slops, other stores, gear,
try-pots, and everything they had.   Jones sent
down the barque Magnet, under Captain James
Bruce, to take possession.   Bruce dropped his
anchor in Waikouaiti Bay in the middle of the
night, and before daylight had padlocked the storehouse and taken charge of everything movable.
The men, who at this time had not been paid, were
inclined to rebel, and John Miller, who was away in
charge of a boat at the time of the seizure, refused

on his return to give up the boat.   Eventually, I believe, the men got a passage to Sydney, and obtained the money due to them from Messrs Long, Wright, and Richards.

" But we must hold on.   I am going on a bit too fast.   I came down, as I was going to say, under engagement to the Wellers.   I and the others were under agreement to the firm for the whaling season, which, for bay whaling, reckoned from the middle of March to the middle of October.   They kept me for shore work mostly, giving us all sorts of jobs in summer time, when, as I have said there was no whaling.   One of the things we did was to go to Purakanui to blast stones and put up a fishing station there.   One of our head men was a Sydney native named Hughes, a real smart fellow either at shore work or in the boats, especially about whales. He had a fancy to leave the Wellers, and did so in the June or July after we arrived.   Two American vessels called in, and he went with them.   One of these was named the Merrimac, and the other was the Martha.   Captain Potter was master of the Martha.   They were bound for Banks Peninsula after fish, and a rare good time of it they had.   As I was told afterwards, they filled up in Peraki Bay just about as fast as the men could work.   Well, when they were full they came our way again, bringing Hughes with them.   He was all a-go to have a try on his own hook.   He had brought two boats with him and a complete fit out for starting a station, these things having been got from the Yankee ships, and he at once set about getting together a party from those of us who were willing to join.   Our time with Mr Weller was up in October as I have told you, and six of us agreed to go in with Hughes.   We went round in boats to have a look at the place which he had selected, Moeraki Point, as the site for the station, and everyone could see at once that a better spot could not be wished for. There was good shelter, sound anchorage, a nobby landing, and plenty of wood, besides which Moeraki was a very pretty place, and above all there were plenty of fish about. So we thought it a good spec to join Hughes.

"There were three partners in the affair : Hughes and a man named Thompson, and Sivatt, a cooper. The cooper was a very important man in all whaling parties, for d'ye see, we always get the staves down in ' shooks ' You know what shooks are? Yes, bundles of staves, and he had to rattle them together, and this took him all his time. I've seen any amount of those chaps that would put together their twenty tuns a day single-handed. Well, as I was going to say, we were all on a ' lay.' You know what a lay is, I suppose ? If you are on a 100th, when a 100 tons are got you get one, and when you are on a lay they find you : that's the difference between a lay and going shares. If you are on shares you find yourself, but of course you get a bigger chance than in a lay. The men get different interests according to agreement. A pulling hand will get, say, one share, a steerer one and a-half, and a headsman two shares—just as is agreed on. As I said, there were three partners in the spec, and the rest of us were on a lay—six of us white men and six Maoris that we brought with us from Otago. They were fine strapping fellows. We had our eyes open in getting them to join the party. You see, we got on very well with the Maoris, but there was just a chance that that state of things wouldn't last for ever, and it seemed to us that we had a double chance of securing a peaceful and quiet time by having these chaps with us. They were sons of chiefs, and if the worst did come to the worst we had them with us, don't you see ?

" Hughes was the head man of our party. We

sailed from Otago in the Magnet brig, Captain
Bruce—the man I referred to a while ago ; you
must have heard of him ; he died at Akaroa some
time ago,—and we cast anchor just inside of the
point where the lighthouse now is on the day after
Christmas, 1836.   And a beautiful place it was !
The bush was growing right down to the edge of the
water.

" Everything was quiet and untouched by anyone ;
and I doubt whether men had ever landed, for the
pigeons would come and light on your heads, and the
kakas weren't frightened when they saw us.   The
only thing that was short was water.   There was
but one pool on the peninsula ; and there is only
one now, strange to say.   You can't get water anywhere else, and all we get now is from the roofs
of the houses.   The water in the pool isn't fit to use
excepting for cattle.   It took us two days to land
our things from the brig.   There were a good many
things to get ashore, and the try-pots were heavy.
At last we got everything out of the Magnet, and
she went away.

" There were very few Maoris here in Moeraki.
A small party (some nine, all told), under Tongatahara, lived at the point, but none of the present
tribe were here.   Tongatahara's people went to
Akaroa soon after we came, and during our second
season the tribe now living at Moeraki came from
Kaiapoi : I mean, of course, the fathers and grand-
fathers of these Natives ; only two or three of the
old ones are left.   Rauparaha had driven them from
their original holdings.   It is scarcely correct to call
them a tribe, either ; they were the remnants of five
tribes or *hapus*—all that were left after Rauparaha's
repeated massacres—and came down here to keep
out of his road ; since, although he had been badly
beaten in Cloudy Bay, they lived in constant dread
of his reappearance.   It was about 1838 that the

2K

Maoris first came to Moeraki. They made the trip
in canoes and one whaleboat, which they had picked
up somewhere—a worn-out old thing that some of
the whalers had very likely cast off or given to them.
When we saw the fleet coming we hadn't the least
idea what the purpose of the expedition was, and you
may guess that we were pleased to find out later on
that the uninvited settlers were peaceably inclined.
Of course we soon got to see a good deal of the
Maoris, and we always got on very well with them.

" We started the first season with two boats, six
oars in each, and our venture turned out very well.
Whales were plentiful and not hard to take. They
used to come right into the bay, and there were so
many of them that we could most always pick the
ones we wanted. As I said, we landed at Moeraki
the day after Christmas, and commenced in March,
and by the end of the season for bay whaling (the
middle of August) we had taken twenty-three whales.
That was not at all bad. They came to somewhere
about eighty or ninety tons of oil. We had no difficulty in getting rid of it. There were any number
of traders ready to make a deal and go anywhere for
it. The first vessel that came to our station was a
brigantine about ninety tons, called the Sydney
Packet. She came in July, bringing us provisions and shooks to carry on with, and prepared to
trade for our oil and bone. While she was laying
to an anchor in the bay there a gale got up and she
came ashore. There was no life lost ; indeed, there
was no one hurt. First the stock of her anchor gave
way, and then she got another one down, and the
chain parted, and away she came, quiet and comfortable like, on to the beach. They took care to
put her on a soft place, and all hands got ashore
without any flurry. We tried to get her off, but
could not do so, and we gradually broke her up.
We got our oil out of her—she had six or seven

tons in her hold at the time ; and we also got her
boats and cut away the rigging, and in fact all the
movable things about her. The beach was a steep
one then, and she lay pretty close in. All the things
that we saved were taken away by the Magnet when
she next called.

"The life we led there was a jolly one. There
was plenty of work, and fair pay for it, though we
thought it rather hard that the vessels would give us
no more than £14 a ton for the oil and 1s. a pound
for the whalebone. These were carefully measured
and weighed out on the beach before any of the stuff
left us, and I can tell you we looked sharply after
our own interests. The only thing that bothered us
was that we hadn't got too much of a change in
tucker. We had a bit of beef at first—all salt, mind
you—but that soon ran out, and then we lived on
fish and kakas and pigeons, and for vegetables we
had to fall back on fern root, with a few potatoes
now and then, which we had to go down to Otago
for. We also brought some pigs up, and they were
the first ever seen in Moeraki. We built styes for
them, and kept them as long as we could ; but we
couldn't go on finding food for them, as we wanted
all our tucker for ourselves, so we had to let them
go, and they were the first of the pigs that afterwards spread all over this part of the country. As
soon as we could spare the time we made gardens,
and then we were all right. We had heaps of fish
and spuds, and if that kind of food will make a man
a Maori, I must be as much a Maori as anyone in
the country.

"After the first season Hughes went over to
Sydney for a trip. If I haven't told you before, you
may as well write down here that Hughes died in
Hampden somewhere about seven years ago, upwards
of eighty years of age, and he was buried there. He
was just the sort of man for early colonial life. He

could do anything, and had seen everything there
was to see this side of the world.   His father had
been a soldier, and came out as one of the guard
over a batch of prisoners in one of the first convict
ships that sailed for Sydney.   Well, as I was saying,
Hughes went for a trip to Sydney, and he brought
back a couple of new boats with him, so that we had
four to commence our second season with.   That
was a lively season.   Whales were numerous again,
and we got on very well.   In the middle of our
busiest time we had the bad luck to have one of our
new boats smashed—knocked to pieces without ever
being fast to a whale   We were out one day, and
hard at it, the boat in which I was being fast to a
big fellow.   He was properly handled, and was nigh
about done, when another boat came up to put an
iron into him.   We could see that the whale was
just dying—he was all of a tremble, and shooting
about here and there—and we sang out to the other
fellows to stand off ; but I suppose they didn't hear
us ; at any rate they came up in a round-about way,
and were pretty close, when he suddenly made a rush
right in their direction, and went clean over her,
turning her over by sheer weight, and in a minute or
two our bran new boat was floating about the bay in
shingles.   We cut our line sharp, and the whale
sank dead after his last effort ; but we picked him
up two days afterwards and got him in all right.
He was a good one too, though not the largest I
have seen.   The best one for oil I ever helped to try
out was a cow in calf, that yielded about eleven
tons

    " There was nobody hurt.   We picked up the men
in the water, and they didn't think anything of the
affair.   We didn't make such a precious fuss about
a thing of that sort as people would nowadays.   If
they get a wet shirt now they must see the doctor,
or else they die of a fright.   We had no doctors,

and if we had we shouldn't have bothered them.   I
suppose you won't believe, but I give you my word
that I've never tasted physic all my life, and never
wanted it.   But I must say that we were pretty
lucky.   We didn't have any serious accidents ;
losing our boat was the worst one ; and none of our
party were ever hurt.   No, sir, we did not fall out
and knock each other about.   We had no rows at
all.   Do you know what kept things so quiet with
us ? We had no drink.   It was an agreement with
us that there should be none.   Vessels that came
here for oil had it with them, but we never allowed a
drop to be put ashore.   Now and again some of the
boys had a nip when they went down to Weller's
place at Otago ; but that was a long way to go for
a drink, and, besides, the men were a steady lot, and
didn't care much about grog.

"The third season we increased our party, and
worked five boats.   One was a seven-oared boat, but
she was no use ; she was too long.   That was a
good season too ; but whales were getting to be not
quite so plentiful, and, to cut the yarn short, they
got scarcer and scarcer, until, after we had stuck
together for five seasons, the game was hardly
paying us.   There was not enough to buy a suit of
slops after a season's work ; so I went out.   The
others kept on for some time, but I had had enough
of it.   Another man and me then started to run a
whaleboat to Waikouaiti and Moeraki, bringing pigs,
potatoes and other things from Otago.   Weller's
was still the only settlement there.   There was no
such place as Dunedin ; the name even was unknown.
All round where Dunedin was afterwards built, there
was nothing but scrub, and it was a great place for
pigs   Port Chalmers was then called Koputai.

" You were asking just now about the Maoris,
and I may as well at this stage tell you something
about them.   In those early days there were, as I

have said, none about the hills where Dunedin now stands, and not very many at Weller's place. But there was an important settlement at the Heads, where the Natives had a fortified pah, and another at Purakanui. Did I know Taiaroa? Yes sir! I did; very well. Not the present Taiaroa, but his father, a regular thorough going Maori, who couldn't speak a word of English. He was much shorter than this Taiaroa, but a man of enormous strength. But he wasn't the head man among the Heads Maoris then—not by a long chalk. The principal men among them died soon after I got to Otago; it must have been the first season I was there. They called him Tattoo. That wouldn't be his proper name, but it was what we all called him. He was a man whose history ought to be written by some one. He was a noble fellow, a real natural chief. Though he had been to Sydney several times, he was in all respects a pure Maori in his ways, as well as in his appearance; but he was a superior stamp of a man, liked by everyone, and respected by all. He was always strangely quiet and dignified, and he had the manners of a gentleman. One could see that as he went about, he was always eager to understand everything he saw among the white men; but he would seldom ask—he seemed to be anxious to avoid bothering anyone with his questions; and he was never known to ask for anything. Besides, he never touched spirits, and he had a way of his own of enforcing obedience without arguing the point, and without using bad language. Poor fellow! He did not live to see an old age. He was still almost a young man when he sickened and died of consumption. I went to see him when he was sick, and just as I would have done for any decent man, I tried to find out what he wanted, and it struck me that a comfortable pillow would help him to lie a bit easier, so I fetched him a feather

pillow that I had brought with me from England—
my mother gave it me when I was coming away.
The Maoris looked on this act as one of extraordinary kindness on my part. and they never forgot it.
They would do anything for me.   I must say that
I have always found them mindful of any good turn,
and anxious to show their gratitude ; but their
kindness to me for lending that pillow was far
beyond what might have been expected.

" When Tattoo died, the next best man was
Jacky White—Karitai was his proper name.   He
was a more important man than old Taiaroa, who,
as I have said, or intended to say, was only of third-
rate importance then.   What sort of people the
Maoris were ?   Well ! you may safely say that they
were an industrious, decent-living lot.   They used
to be great hands at fishing.   I have seen a dozen,
and sometimes as many as twenty canoes, go out of
a morning fishing for barracouta ; and they would
take their double canoes outside the Heads without
fear of being blown off.   Sometimes, too, they used
to go in boats, when they could get them.   As to
drink, they did not often take it.   It is a lie to say
that they were a drinking crowd.   Those engaged
at Weller's were entitled, as well as the whites, to a
gill of rum in the morning before going out ; and
d'ye know what the Maoris did ?   They carefully
bottled it off as they got it, and afterwards sold it to
the white people at a little less than the price at the
store.   That's a fact, and I should like you to print
it.   They never drank the rum themselves, but they
were always ready to make a bargain with the white
men for it.   Yes, they were naturally business men
rather than drinkers: You folk who get your ideas
of what the Marois are like from the poor specimens
you see about towns have a wrong notion altogether
of what they are like when left to themselves without
contact with the white man.

" Another good thing about the Maoris as I knew them was that they were very particular about their women. Infidelity on the part of either husband or wife was punishable with death ; and among un-married people the relationships were as decent, to say the least of it, as you would find in communities of Europeans. The women had to work, but only at what were looked on as their proper tasks. But it was considered the right thing for a chief to have several wives. I am bound to admit that because it's a fact. Jacky White had four or five, and most of them had two or three : they were supposed to have as many as they could keep, or they were allowed to, which comes to about the same thing. These wives, however, no matter how many there were, were always properly treated, and not regarded as concubines, nor could they be put away at the will of their chief. Perhaps you don't know it, but it's quite true that the Maoris in those days had slaves. Each chief had some. I never could quite make out how they got these slaves, nor what their position was, but we always concluded that they had been prisoners taken in war. They did all the dirty work, and might be bought or sold, and it was no offence if a master killed one of them. I don't know any-thing about cannibalism among them. I never saw any, and they never would confess to having been given to that ungodly practice. Still I know that a slave's life was at his master's mercy, and goodness only knows whether, in the olden days, they always buried one that they knocked on the head. I once knew one of these slaves very well. Hughes, who was here before me, owned one. He was a big fellow, that we used to call Rogers. The Maoris were going to kill him, so the yarn went, and Hughes took pity on him and tried to save his life. The Maoris wouldn't listen to what he had to say, so Hughes thought he would buy the man ; and he went to the store, drew a lot of slops against his credit, and gave them to the Maoris for Rogers. The Natives did not touch Rogers after that, but looked on him as Hughes' property. The poor fellow came with us afterwards, and died while in our service.

" While I was going in and out among the Maoris an incident occurred, which will give you an idea of life among these people. Three American whalers were lying off Weller's place, having put in to refresh with wood and water before going further with their cruise. The carpenter belonging to one of these ships was on shore, staying at the house of a man named James Brown. There were a good many fellows about, and they had been making too free with the grog. One of the chaps there was a Maori, son of one of the petty chiefs, and he too had been drinking, just for once in a way—at any rate, what he had taken had got into his head. Well, this chief's son he fell out with Brown, the master of the house, because Brown would not give him any more grog ; upon which the Maori went away, loaded his gun, and came and stood outside Brown's window, waiting to get a chance to shoot Brown. While he was waiting there the carpenter happened to go to the door, and the Maori seized the chance to fire. I don't know whether he knew who it was at the door, but any way it was the carpenter who got the benefit of it, and he fell dead on the spot. The Maori at once made a bolt of it, and could not be found for two or three days. He was stowed away in the bush. At last old Taiaroa went and hunted him out and brought him to the store. " Here," he said, " is the man who shot the white man ; do as you like to him." The Maoris seemed to look on it as a matter of honor to find him. Mr. Weller put the man in irons, and sent word all round to muster as many whites as possible. He thought that this outrage

2L

would start the Maoris into a general rising, and that would have been a serious matter, as they were pretty well armed. I went up among the others, and I can tell you there was a regular to do. They clapped the murderer into a little room, and planted men to go sentry—go, watch and watch, until we came to a decision as to what to do with him. Mr. Weller's idea was to send him to Sydney to be tried. The Yankees wanted us to let them take him off to one of their ships and hang him at the yard-arm. We would not agree to that—it wouldn't be regular; and there we were—didn't know how to get out of the fix. The situation was a pretty serious one, or would have been if the Maoris had been nasty, for there were about a couple of thousand of them about the Kaik at that time, and about 400 or 500 more at Purakanui, who could have come across pretty quick, but they did not seem dangerous. They said they would not trouble what we did with the man. Their idea was that, as he had tried to kill Brown, Brown should be allowed to shoot him, and they would have been satisfied if the matter had ended that way. But we wouldn't have that. Well, I was standing outside the house where the Maori was locked up, and while talking with others who were there, we saw Tom Brown come out. This Tom Brown was one of our men—the one whose turn it was to watch inside. He came out just for a necessary purpose, leaving his gun behind. Before he could get back we heard a report, and then I knew what had happened. I knew the Maori was cooked. We rushed in, and there was the Maori and his woman—both shot. We could see how it was done. She had raised him up to a sitting position, and then hugged him from behind, while he had got the gun and pointed it towards his chest. The ball went right through him and lodged in the woman, and they were both dead. Then we saw how foolish we had been to let the

woman be in the room with him, and of course everybody blamed Tom Brown for going out without
taking his gun with him.   But perhaps it all ended
in the best way.   The Maoris made no fuss ; they
said they were glad he had made away with himself.
The last act in the tragedy was played by old
Taiaroa, who rolled up the man's body in a bundle
and humped it away by himself, saying that he was
going to bury it. What he did with it I can't tell
you.   No one ever saw the grave.   Pitched the
body overboard, perhaps.   The woman was buried
by her own people.   And that was the finish of a
very anxious time for all of us.

  " As I have said, all the settlers that I know of
who were in Otago before me are either away or
dead.   The two eldest that I know of are Dick
Driver, who was the first pilot in Otago, and now
lives in Purakanui, and Mr Apes, of Wakouaiti.
The latter is coming down to see me, and have a
chat about old times.   I had a visit from Captain
Jackson Barry some time ago, and he wanted to
make out that he knew all about these parts in the
earliest days, but I soon settled him.   He began by
asking me if I remembered the first whaling man
here, Johnny Jones.   I replied that I knew the first
whaler here, and that it wasn't Johnny Jones, and
that I was here myself long before Johnny Jones saw
a flax bush ; and that was enough for Mr. Barry, or
whatever you call him.   I can't abide those men who
let on to know what they don't know anything
about.

  " Mr. Haberfield's subsequent history has been
full of adventures. As modestly told by himself, he
altogether settled at Moeraki after he had been
running a whaleboat for some time ; and then,
feeling rather restless, he shipped with Captain Cole
on the schooner Rory O'More, which called at
Moeraki on her way to Akaroa for a stock of pigs, to

take up with other provisions to some American whalers that were lying there. This was a somewhat eventful trip. On arrival at Akaroa, she was engaged to convey to Wellington a prisoner who had been arrested for breaking into a store. The prisoner and the policeman (named Barry) and the witnesses were all to be taken up together. The schooner was owned by the well known Paddy Hood, and she had first to make a trip to his settlement at the northern end of the Ninety-mile beach, where the Little River empties itself, so as to get some provisions. On getting these aboard, she returned to Akaroa and picked up her party, which included an officer from a French man-of-war, who wanted to go to Wellington to make arrangements for victualling the vessel. There were altogether twenty-three souls on board when the Rory O'More sailed for Wellington—a port she was not destined to reach, as she overran her reckoning in a fog, and got jammed in Palliser Bay, where she was beached to save life, it being found that she could not help going ashore. The men stopped behind long enough to save the cargo, and then set out to walk to Wellington, which they reached in three days. Captain Cole was not in charge of the schooner when she was wrecked, another master having been shipped in his place.

" Mr. Haberfield was three months in Wellington, unable to get work, and scarcely able to obtain sufficient food ; from which difficulty he was released by the opportune arrival of one of Johnny Jones' vessels (the Magnet, then under the charge of Capt. M'Farlane) the mate of which (Mr. Lewis) took him on board and provided for him until he got a passage by her to Akaroa, from which place he was taken home by the schooner Mana (Capt. Sweeney)—a vessel that was to take a shipment of pigs from Moeraki to Mr. Fraser's station on Mana Island.

He then stayed at home for some years, afterwards
shipping in the cutter Levien (Capt. Arnett) for
Port Levy on the Banks Peninsula, where lived a
wealthy old bachelor named Greenwood, who gave
him a freight of wool, cheese and butter, with thirty-
two sheep on deck, for Wellington. This small
vessel, much overloaded, left Port Levy on Saturday
afternoon, and the next (Sunday) afternoon dropped
anchor in Wellington, opposite the Custom House—
a feat that was, in those days, considered wonderful.
A week later they left Wellington for Pigeon Bay,
having on board a complete fit-out for a schooner
then building there; thence to Akaroa, where they
took on board Mr. Watson, the magistrate there,
and brought him to Otago; thence she went to
Ruapuke and on to Stewart Island, where Mr.
Haberfield left her, coming back to Otago in a
schooner called The Sisters, belonging to the Akaroa
Maoris. About this time the survey of the Otago
Block was going on, and some six months afterwards, the survey being then finished, Capt. Arnett
brought the Levien into Otago harbour under contract to take the men (chainmen, bushmen, &c.)
engaged on the survey party to Wellington. Capt.
Arnett, who was no scholar, was very anxious to
get Mr. Haberfield to ship with him this trip, as the
latter on previous occasions had done all the ship's
business for him. Haberfield, however, obstinately
refused to go, not being pleased either with the
vessel, which was crank, or the captain, who was
reckless, and, besides, a bad paymaster. Haberfield
then went to Moeraki in his boat, and Arnett, who
left soon after him, dropped anchor in Moeraki Bay,
and made another attempt to get Haberfield on
board The latter was not to be persuaded, and the
cutter had to leave without him. She was never
heard of again; but a vessel which came into Akaroa
reported having seen a cutter answering to her des-

cription founder in a squall off the Kaikouras. She had eleven men on board, amongst them the Brown mentioned previously as being concerned in the shooting affair at Weller's. The Levien, it may be noted, was bought by Bloody Jack (Tuawak) and Toby, of Ruapuke, from an Auckland man. Bloody Jack was drowned at Timaru while in charge of an expedition got up amongst the Southern Maoris to go North and fight Rauparaha, which expedition got no further than Banks Peninsula, and was then abandoned. The Levien then became the property of Toby and Kehu (a son of Bloody Jack). This Kehu (who was remarkable for having six toes on each foot) sailed with Haberfield, and left the cutter with him, having no confidence in Arnett. Kehau was afterwards drowned in endeavouring to cross Foveaux Strait in a whaleboat during a gale of wind."

These are only some of the many adventures which Mr. Haberfield can relate. He was engaged in seafaring for several years, and at last settled, down to enjoy a peaceful old age, which we trust will last for many years to come.

PENINSULA STORIES IN VERSE.

AKAROA.

I.

Where do sunbeams brightest glisten,
  'Mid intricacies of shade ;
Where does love-lorn tui* listen
  To its mate in leafy glade ;
Where, when earliest spring is waking
  From its sleep each leaflet's fold,
Do the zephyrs, gently shaking,
  Pave the kowhai's† roots with gold ;
Where, with melody surprising,
  Does the bell-bird‡ welcome day,
Ere the golden sun, arising,
  Makes the night-mists pass away ;
Where do great koninis,‖ laden
  With their million berries store,
Purple lips of many a maiden ?
  'Tis in lovely Akaroa.

II.

Where do mighty tree-clad mountains
  Solemn guard the vales below,
Giving birth to many a fountain,
  Where in winter lies the snow ;
Where do great totaras,§ flinging
  Bronzéd foliage to the sky,

---

  *The tui, or parson-bird, one of the honey-suckers peculiar to New Zealand.

  †The kowhai is a native acacia, that in spring is covered with a profusion of golden blossoms.

  ‡The bell-bird, or moko moko, another New Zealand honey-sucker, that always welcomes the dawn with a strangely clear and deep note, like a bell.

  ‖The konini is the giant fuchsia of New Zealand, whose numberless purple berries are the delight of birds and children.

  §The totara is a pine with golden or bronze colored foliage, of great beauty. It grows to an enormous size.

Rest a thousand songsters, singing
　　Hymns of rapture ere they fly ;
Where are giant willows* growing,
　　From Napoleon's distant grave ;
Where are creeks for ever flowing,
　　Giving verdure as they lave ;
Where do sunclad wavelets wander
　　To Zealandia's fairest shore,
In embracing, growing fonder ?
　　'Tis in lovely Akaroa.

III.

Where do sunsets' rays of glory,
　　Gold and purple raiment, throw
O'er the hills† renowned in story
　　In the Maori long ago ;
Where does wild clematis,‡ flinging
　　Tendrils o'er the boughs below,
Cover sprays, where birds are singing,
　　With a cloak of purest snow ;
Where, in wild, sequestered valley,
　　Grows the wondrous nikau‖ palm,
Forming ever verdant alley,
　　Where there is eternal calm ;
Where are silver fern-trees§ spreading
　　Fairy fronds of beauty pure,
Aromatic fragrance shedding ?
　　'Tis in lovely Akaroa.

---

*The weeping willows growing in Akaroa are all said to have sprung from a slip brought by a Frenchman from Napoleon's tomb at St. Helena.　They are of enormous size.

†The hills around Akaroa were the scenes of many a renowned Maori conflict.

‡The wild clematis, with snowy blossoms fully a foot in circumference, is of marvellous beauty.

‖The nikau palm grows only in the most sequestered and sheltered valleys.

§The silver fern-tree's fronds are a brilliant green above, and pure silver underneath.

IV.

Where, when storms are raging madly,
   'Neath the bitter tempest's blast,
Does the sailor enter gladly,
   Finding peaceful seas at last;
Where does the titoki's* glory
   Blaze with scarlet many a glade,
Sheltered from nor'-wester's† fury
   By the pine tree's‡ tasselled shade;
Where are feet for ever pressing
   Wondrous ferns‖ of beauty rare,
Robed in Nature's choicest dressing,
   Ever fresh and passing fair;
Where, when from the world we sever,
   Seeking peace for evermore,
Should we choose to rest for ever?
   'Tis in lovely Akaroa.

SILAS WEGG.

---

*The titoki is the native ash. It bears masses of scarlet berries like gigantic raspberries.

†The nor'-westers are hot winds in Akaroa, and wither vegetation.

‡The native bush consisted originally principally of gigantic pines.

‖The ferns in Akaroa are of marvellous variety and beauty.

OUR JUBILEE.

The years roll on in this new land that gems the
   Southern Sea,
As many an aᵧed pioneer can prove right wearily ;
Men that shaped out the future for the thousands of
   their race,
Who needed sore in crowded homes a new abiding
   place.
They taught this stubborn earth to smile with
   Europe's plants and flowers ;
They made the primal rocks reveal a Danaé's golden
   showers ;
They bridged the flood, they drained the swamp,
   they tore the forest down,
And made the golden corn to smile where waved the
   tussock brown.
Nor they alone the victory won, for by their sides
   there stood
Full many an angel of the wild, a heroine of the wood,
Who urged them forth to high emprise, or where
   misfortune fell,
Would many a word of peace and hope and gentlest
   comfort tell ;
Who, like the rata, when the pine is tottering to its
   fall,
Still held them in strong loving bands and made
   them tower o'er all ;
And should not they who reap the toil of all those
   early days,
Give to the veterans their meed of due and hard
   earned praise ?
Remember in luxurious days the trials of the past,
And trumpet forth these heroes' deeds with no un-
   certain blast.
Tis more than fifty years ago that Waitemata heard
That this fair haven—Akaroa—had beautiful ap-
   peared

To sons of the fair land of joy, of chivalry and song,
Who meant to seize its favoured shores, and hold
them firm and strong.
Then all the Viking spirit rose in that small British
band :
What ! Should they lose this favoured isle, this
lovely southern land ?
Perish the thought ! Should England's might like
this be trampled down ?
A gem lost from her diadem, a jewel from her
crown !
So on her mission of emprise the Britomart was
sent ;
True Argonauts were those brave hearts who in the
vessel went,
For sure they searched not vainly, and the fruit their
wanderings bore
Was not a single golden fleece, but many a million
more !
We know the end—with high result the British dart
was sped,
And in the race for empire, our doughty champions
led.
They gained our shores ; and loud the cheers that
rang across our seas
As old St. George's glorious cross flew bravely in
the breeze.
A greater or a happier day Zealandia never saw,
Than this, which bound to English rule her loveliest
Southern shore ;
But there has been one victory since—as great in
thinkers' eyes :
It brought no riches in its train, no vast material
prize,
Yet was a triumph for our laws, a glory to our
land,
That ne'er can fade while Britain's sons hold
France's loving hand.

The men who came to claim the soil—whom we had
    deemed our foes—
Settled our shores, and speedily fresh rivalry arose—
The rivalry of industry, the striving each to prove
Supremacy in deeds of toil, of kindness, and of
    love ;
And after working side by side for many a weary
    day,
At last the further time came round when they were
    called to say :
Will ye be France or Britain's sons ? ye know us
    now full well.
O noble was the answer that from their brave lips
    fell—
" We know you, and we love you, and this is our
    reply :
Together we will fight or fall, together live or die."
And now that fifty years are past since that old
    faithful band
Raised the proud standard of our Queen upon this
    fertile strand,
We seek to brand it for all time—a landmark of
    our race,—
So that when, in the distant years, historians shall
    trace
The records of the early days, when first this land
    of flowers
Was rendered by a daring deed for all the ages ours.
They can point out the sacred spot where first our
    standard braved
The winds that hover o'er the shores our peaceful
    waters laved ;
Still tell how France and Britain here forgot the
    feuds of old,
And hand in hand, and heart to heart did lovingly
    enfold.

                           SILAS WEGG.

THE LEGEND OF ONAWE.

Land of the forest and the hill !
    Land of tall fern and tussock brown !
Where lake-like waters, calm and still,
    Reflect the crags that o'er them frown ;
Where mighty monsters of the deep—
    The Taniwhas* of ancient story—
Watched their grim infants' happy sleep
    Beneath the Southern planets' glory !
Land of tall pine, of graceful vines,
    Where tuis gurgle in the shade ;
Where, in white wreaths, clematis twines,
    And kaka screams in ferny glade.
How many a tale of passion past
    Thy rocks could tell, if speech were given,
Of heroes struggling to the last,
    Of dire revenge, of races driven
From this fair home—their last hopes riven !

Where the proud waves come swelling high
    Up Whangaroa's† Harbour fair,
A peak mounts startling to the sky,
    With base like some gigantic pear.
Sternly it meets the advancing tide,
    And bids the crested horses stay.
The conquered waters, baulked, divide,
    And form on either either side a bay ;
And there, in those wild days of yore,
    The Waka Maori‡ floated light,
And many a dusky maiden saw
    Her lover on some starry night,
And each read in the other's eyes
    The old, old story, that never dies.

---

*Before the advent of the whalers Akaroa Harbour was
the constant resort of the cow whales with their calves.
†Whangaroa is the real name of Akaroa.
‡Waka Maori : Maori canoe,

Lost is the time in ages dim,
  Since this stern peak first gained the name
From wise Tohunga's* visions grim,
  That placed it high in Maori fame.
Onawe ! Home of him who holds
  The mighty winds that restless sweep ;
Who bids them in their treacherous folds
  Engulph the wanderers o'er the deep,
Or curbs their restless course to calm,
  Or lets the gentle zephyr play
The wearied mariner to charm,
  And waft him on his watery way.

Home of the Spirit of the Wind !
  Where the dread Atua † held his sway,
When luckless mortal sought to find
  Him whom the winds alone obey,
A dreadful voice, in accents deep,
  Would call from out the rocky steep,
" What want you here ? Begone ! Begone !"
  And lucky he if, e'er the morn,
The winds had spared from vengeance dour
  One who had braved the Atua's power.

The ages passed, and from the North
  The restless pakeha races came ;
Their cannons belched loud thunders forth.
  The Taniwha's gigantic frame,
Pierced by their lances, gave its life ;
  And trees were felled, and a new light,
Foreboding change and peace from strife,
  Dawned on the ancient Maori night.
Then those stern gods, whose bloody reign
  Had lasted from the ages past,
Saw that the struggle must be vain,
  And that their power had gone at last,
For the blind faith that long had spread
  Its shelter o'er them was no more ;

---

*Tohunga : Maori priest or prophet. †Atua : Maori God.

And once that faith in creeds is dead,
  Their might is gone, their rule is o'er,

Yet lingered in his storied place,
  Onawe's spirit ; though despair ;
In windy tempests men might trace,
  That showed the Atuas of the air
Were restless in their ancient hold,
  Which ne'er again would faith enfold.
At last, upon a fatal day,
  A young Ngai Tahu* warrior came,
And fired a musket in his play !
  A shudder shook the mountain's frame ;
A mighty tempest swept the deep :
  The great waves rolled, the thunders pealed,
And dusky vapours sullen sweep
  And hide the heavens with livid shield !

And o'er the summit of the storm
  The Atua's voice came stern and high,
And shadow of a mighty form,
  Rose God-like towards the darkened sky.
" I go !" the giant spirit cried.
  " Never again will Atua's cry
Be borne on Whangaroa's tide
  To warn of stormy danger nigh.
But e'er I fly, Ngai Tahu hear :
  Thy faithless race has dared profane
My sacred shrine, once held so dear,
  With murderous offspring of the brain
Of that new race that swept away
  The records of the ages past.
Deluded Maori ! Thy brief day
  Is setting, and the shadows vast
Close o'er Ngai Tahu's hapless head,
  Till it is numbered with the dead !

---

*Ngai Tahu : The tribe that held the Peninsula at the time of its first being visited by Europeans.

Here, on Onawe's fated strand,
  The last poor remnant of thy race
Shall struggle for their fathers' land,
  And coming Pakehas will trace
The mighty earthworks raised in vain
  Against the conquering Northern train."

The tempest ceased, the spirit fled ;
  Once more the radiant sunbeams shed
Their glories over earth and sea ;
  And the fierce tribe that long had stood
Owners of land, and wave and wood,
  Knew well the Atua's prophecy
Was true, and that Ngai Tahu's race
  Should quickly fall from power and place,
And, conquered, fighting die !

True was the Atua's warning dread
  E'er fifty summer suns had shed
Their rays upon Onawe's head,
  The fierce Te Rauparaha* came,
And Ngatitoas'† warriors bold
  Stormed fierce Ngai Tahu's storied hold,
And left them—scarce a name !
  And where the Atua once had reigned,
The dreaded Northern warriors drained
  The life-blood of their foes.
But even now, when feuds are o'er,
  And peace reigns on the tranquil shore,
The Maori chieftain shows
  The mighty earthworks of the past—
Where brave Ngai Tahu made the last
  Great struggle for their land ;
And, fighting with their Northern foes,
  Found in grim death their last repose
On fair Onawe's strand !

                          —SILAS WEGG.

---

*Rauparaha : The Wellington chief that conquered
the Ngai Tahus.
  †Ngatitoas : The name of Rauparaha's tribe.

THE LEGEND OF GOUGH'S BAY.

Where thy dark surge, Okeruru,* rolls to its
    deafening ending,
Smiting the rolling sand and the base of the cliffs
    of obsidian—
There stood the fated few, the last of the pride of
    Ngai Tahu.†
News had been brought in the evening that mad
    Ngatiawas'‡ dread warriors,
Full of revenge and hate, had found the pass through
    Waimomo,
And waited the coming of eve to sweep them to
    utter oblivion.
Then spake Paihora, the chieftain, last of Arikis'‖
    relations,
Spoke to the trembling forty—all that were left of
    the Hapu—
" Take our remaining treasures ; take our pounamou
    meres§ ;
" Take the tikis,¶ that symbol the Atuas that once
    were protectors ;
" Take the teeth of the shark, the mats of flax and
    of feathers ;
" Take our choicest treasures, the wealth of our
    tottering hapu ;
" Place in the wakas** of Hiwi, the wakas that ply
    the wai Maori.††

---

*Okeruru is the Maori name of Gough's Bay.
†The Ngai Tahu were the dominant tribe on the
Peninsula.
‡The Ngatiawas were Northern Natives, who, under
Rauparaha, drove the Ngai Tahu, first to the remote
Bays, like Okeruru, and then almost annihilated them.
‖The Ariki was the supreme chief.
§Greenstone clubs.
¶Amulets, supposed to give peculiar luck to the
wearer.
**Canoes.   ††Fresh water.

" And you, oh, mothers of chieftains, Ohine, Rau-
    pau-te, Aroha !
" Take the treasures, and hide, from the spoilers of
    fell Ngatiawa.
" Say the sacred spells that will hide from the sight
    of Ngatoi ;
" Burn the sacred fire that will make the tapu so
    mighty,
" That Atuas of earth and of caverns, Atuas of air
    and of ocean—
" All of those that are left of the fallen Gods of
    Ngai Tahu—
" Shall watch with their terrible eyes the treasure
    bequeathed to their keeping."
When the Ariki had spoken, forth went the mothers
    of chieftains,
Gathered the treasures, and placed them, into the
    wakas of Hiwi ;
Fastened the two together with strong korari* most
    holy ;
Took their paddles and started, up from the sea to
    the valley,
Singing the sacred songs, the songs of the mightiest
    Tohungas.
Then Paihora gathered the remnant of weeping
    Ngai Tahu ;
Placed in the wai ti,† wakas, the wakas that sail on
    the ocean ;
Launched in the deadened surf, that moaned at the
    loss of the Hapu,
Gaining the open sea, in search of a haven of safety.
Vain the fugitives' hopes ! for the taniwhas‡ dread
    of Ngatoi,

---

*A kind of flax.
†Salt water.
‡Sea Monsters. Certain cliefs were supposed to have
the power of calling them to their assistance.

Taniwhas mighty, and dread, rangitieras* of monsters
    misshapen,
That loved Ngatiawa and hated, the children of
    fated Ngai Tahu,
Stopped the beat of their paddles, held their blades
    in the water.
Vain the strain of their muscles ! Vain their pride
    and their courage !
Ngatiawa is coming ! Ngatiawa has conquered !
Nothing left them but death, or slavery bitter and
    hopeless !
But the treasures were saved from the foe, for the
    mighty spells had been spoken
To hide for ever from men, till a fair haired child of
    Ngai Tahu
Should come in the far off times, and claim the
    wealth of her people.
Well the Atuas† have guarded thy hidden treasures,
    Ngai Tahu !
Mighty the tapu‡ that covers the place where the
    wakas are lying.
Oft has the pakeha searched in the stream, in the
    cave, in the forest ;
But safe as the holy grail from the eyes of the base
    and the guilty,
Lie the buried wakas of Hiwi, the treasure of fallen
    Ngai Tahu.

---

*Mighty ones—Chiefs.
†Gods.
‡Spells.

Printed in Great Britain
by Amazon